East Anglian Church Porches and their Medieval Context

East Anglian Church Porches and their Medieval Context

HELEN E. LUNNON

THE BOYDELL PRESS

© Helen E. Lunnon 2020

All Rights Reserved. Except as permitted under current legislation
no part of this work may be photocopied, stored in a retrieval system,
published, performed in public, adapted, broadcast,
transmitted, recorded or reproduced in any form or by any means,
without the prior permission of the copyright owner

The right of Helen E. Lunnon to be identified as
the author of this work has been asserted in accordance with
sections 77 and 78 of the Copyright, Designs and Patents Act 1988

First published 2020
Paperback edition 2024

The Boydell Press, Woodbridge

ISBN 978-1-78327-526-7 (Hardback)
ISBN 978-1-83765-217-4 (Paperback)

The Boydell Press is an imprint of Boydell & Brewer Ltd
PO Box 9, Woodbridge, Suffolk IP12 3DF, UK
and of Boydell & Brewer Inc.
668 Mt Hope Avenue, Rochester, NY 14620–2731, USA
website: www.boydellandbrewer.com

A catalogue record of this publication is available
from the British Library

FOR MUM AND DAD, WITH LOVE

Contents

Illustrations	ix
Acknowledgements	xiii
Introduction – The English Medieval Church Porch	1
1 The English *Porticus*	19
2 Functions of Church Porches	55
3 The East Anglian Church Porch – Architecture and Decoration	101
4 Documenting East Anglia's Church Porches, c.1370 to c.1540	181
5 The Patrons' Share	221
Conclusion	249
Appendix	257
Glossary of Architectural Terms	277
Bibliography	281
Index	293

Illustrations

(Images are the author's own unless otherwise indicated.)

Figures

1 Exterior view, south porch, Barnack	4
2 Exterior view, west porch, Snettisham	6
3 Exterior view, north porch, St Mary Redcliffe, Bristol. Reproduced with thanks to St Mary Redcliffe	7
4 Exterior view, south porch, Over	12
5 Exterior view, north porch, Salisbury Cathedral. Reproduced with thanks to Salisbury Cathedral	40
6 Interior view, north porch, Salisbury Cathedral. Reproduced with thanks to Salisbury Cathedral	41
7 Corbel sculpture, *ex situ*, north porch exterior, St Mary Redcliffe, Bristol. Reproduced with thanks to St Mary Redcliffe	46
8 The Ethelbert Gate, Norwich	48
9 The Court Gate, Bury St Edmunds	49
10 Exterior view, south porch, Long Melford	61
11 Confession panel, Seven Sacraments font, Marsham	70
12 Sculptural detail, north door, Spalding	73
13 Galilee porch, south transept, Lincoln Cathedral	79
14 Benches probably originating from the upper room, south porch, Hevingham. Reproduced by permission of Hevingham parochial church council	84
15 Exterior inscription, north porch, Forncett St Peter	90
16 Exterior view, south porch, West Walton	103
17 Exterior view, south porch, Great Massingham	104
18 Parish church of St Mary, North Creake	107

19	Exterior view, south porch, Gooderstone	109
20	Exterior view, south porch, Hunstanton	110
21	Exterior view, north porch, Boxford	113
22	Exterior view, south tower-porch, Little Ellingham	122
23	Exterior view, south tower-porch, Holme-next-the-Sea	123
24	Exterior view, south tower-porch, Wicklewood	124
25	Exterior view, south porch, North Walsham	127
26	Exterior view, south porch, Lynn St Nicholas	129
27	Arch detail, south porch, Cley-next-the-Sea	131
28	Exterior view, south porch, Fressingfield	133
29	Exterior view, south porch, Norwich St Giles	136
30	Exterior view, north porch, Norwich St Laurence. Reproduced with thanks to The Churches Conservation Trust	138
31	Vault canopy, north porch, Norwich St Laurence. Reproduced with thanks to The Churches Conservation Trust	139
32	Exterior view, north tower-porch, Norwich St Stephen	140
33	Vault canopy, north porch, Norwich St Peter Mancroft. Reproduced with thanks to the Vicar and Churchwardens of St Peter Mancroft church	142
34	Design templates, masons' loft, York Minster © Chapter of York: Reproduced by kind permission	143
35	Exterior view, south porch, Walpole St Peter	144
36	Exterior view, north porch, Wiveton	145
37	Exterior view, south porch, Great Cressingham	146
38	Exterior view, south porch, Hilborough	147
39	Exterior view, south porch, Norwich St Mary Coslany	148
40	Exterior view, south porch, Colby	150
41	Exterior view, south porch, South Walsham	151
42	Exterior view, south porch, East Tuddenham	152
43	Exterior view, north porch, Acle	153
44	Exterior view, south porch, Rickinghall Inferior	154
45	Exterior view, south porch, Rickinghall Superior	155
46	Exterior view, south porch, Norwich St Michael at Pleas	157
47	Exterior view, north porch, Mildenhall	159
48	Exterior view, south porch, Cley-next-the-Sea	161
49	Exterior view, south porch, Pulham St Mary	162

ILLUSTRATIONS

50	Exterior view, south porch, Salle	166
51	Exterior view, north porch, Salle	167
52	Exterior view, south porch, Hessett	172
53	Arch detail, south porch, Great Witchingham	173
54	Exterior view, south porch, Alderford	193
55	Exterior view, south porch, Swaffham	194
56	Exterior view, south porch, Foulden	195
57	Exterior view, north porch, Langham	198
58	Exterior view, south porch, Aslacton	200
59	Exterior view, south porch, Dickleburgh	201
60	Exterior view, south porch, Swaffham	202
61	Exterior view, south porch, Wighton	203
62	Exterior view, south porch, Loddon	204
63	Exterior view, south porch, Norwich St Peter Hungate	205
64	Exterior view, south porch, East Dereham	206
65	Exterior view, south porch, Needham	208
66	Exterior view, south porch, Shadingfield	208
67	Exterior view, north porch, Attleborough	211
68	Fragmentary sculpture depicting St Michael, south porch niche, Great Cressingham	215
69	Exterior view, south porch, Little Fransham	218
70	Exterior view, south porch, Saffron Walden	223
71	Coronation of the Virgin vault boss, south porch, Worstead	234
72	Spandrel detail showing kneeling donor figures, north porch, Acle	235
73	Low-relief sculpture depicting St Andrew, south porch, Barton Bendish	237
74	Coronation of the Virgin sculpture, south porch niche, South Walsham	238
75	Exterior flushwork inscription, south porch, Swannington	245

Maps

Principal church porches in Norfolk   xiv
Principal church porches in Suffolk   xv

Graphs

1 Number of bequests to church porches by decade   186
2 Financial bequests to church porches (in pence) by decade   186

The author and publisher are grateful to all the institutions and individuals listed for permission to reproduce the materials in which they hold copyright. Every effort has been made to trace the copyright holders; apologies are offered for any omission, and the publisher will be pleased to add any necessary acknowledgement in subsequent editions.

This project was supported by funding from the
Norfolk and Norwich Archaeological Society.

Acknowledgements

The research work that informs this book was undertaken during a decade spent as a postgraduate student, researcher and teacher in the (then called) School of World Art Studies at the University of East Anglia. Joining UEA was my very good fortune; the academic community sparked and then nurtured in me a fascination for how people construct and use the environments in which they live. The breadth and depth of scholarly knowledge and interests in the School undoubtedly shaped my research interests and strengthened my methodologies. I am grateful to all my colleagues and students who made me think in new and different ways. Alongside this formal institutional affiliation has been my involvement with the British Archaeological Association, a remarkable group of passionate and generous scholars through whom I have gained so much, intellectually and personally; my sincere thanks go to them all.

My study of medieval church porches has coincided with increased interest in the academic community for the English parish; but when I started there was little established literature on porches and no gigantic shoulders on which to stand. This book results from years of exploration, investigation and several research trips down blind alleys, but I derived much pleasure from the necessity of treading a less well-worn research path. I hope its publication will spur other students of architectural history to think deeply about, and look hard at, church porches, continuing to ask new questions and challenging established wisdom. My thanks go to Boydell Press, especially to Caroline Palmer, for generously supporting my endeavours.

In bringing this research to publication the debts I owe to friends, colleagues and supporters are many and weighty. Attempting to offer my thanks and give due credit to everyone who helped along the way would risk offending anyone mistakenly forgotten or carelessly overlooked. I must, however, express my gratitude to Sarah Cassell, Claire Daunton, Simon Dell, Agata Gomolka, John Goodall, Clare Haynes, Sandy Heslop, Pippa Lacey, Bea Lea, Peter Ledger, Rob Liddiard, John McNeill, John Mitchell, Anastasia Moskvina, Margit Thofner, Nick Trend and Carol Rawcliffe.

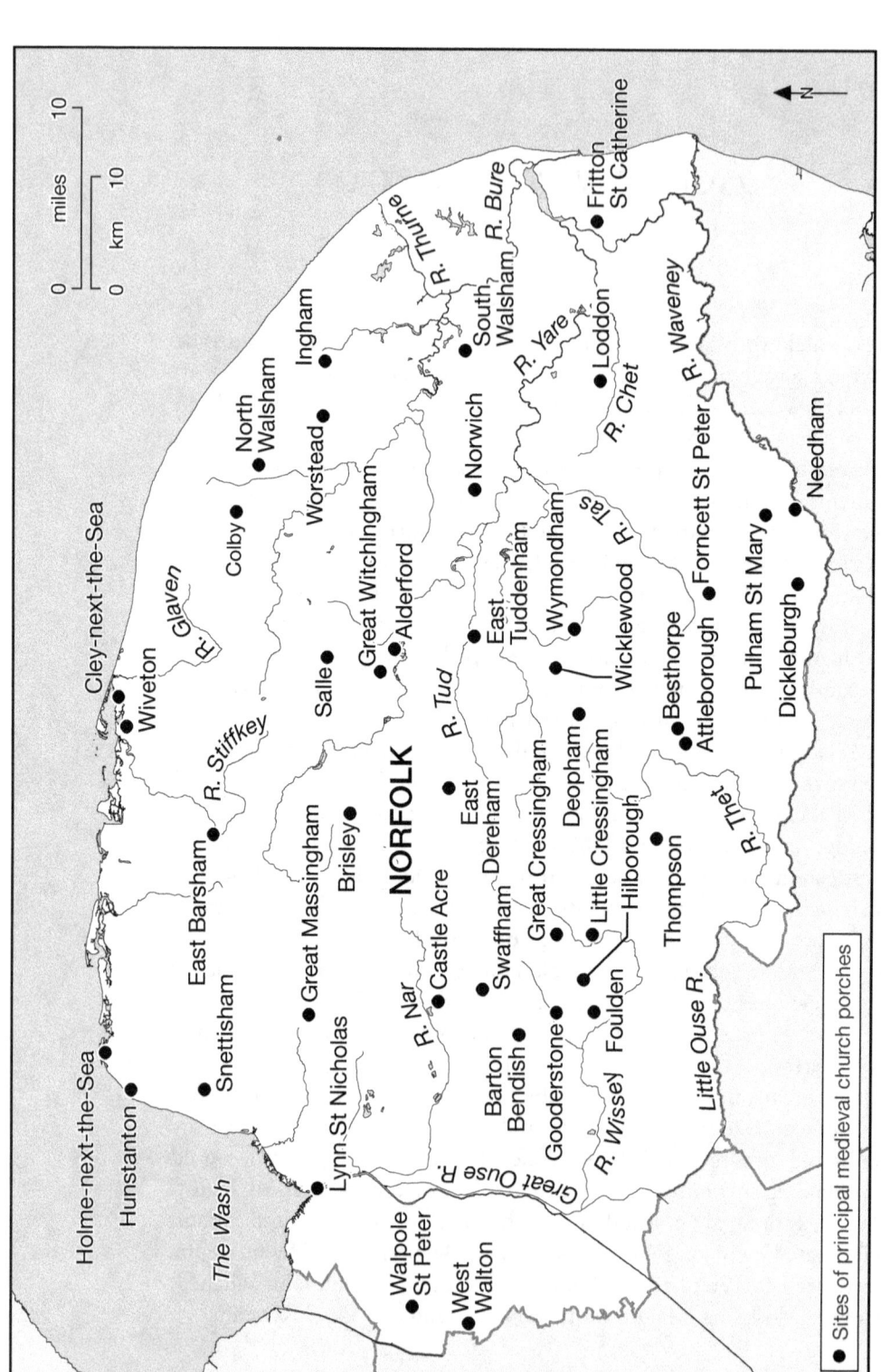

Principal church porches in Norfolk

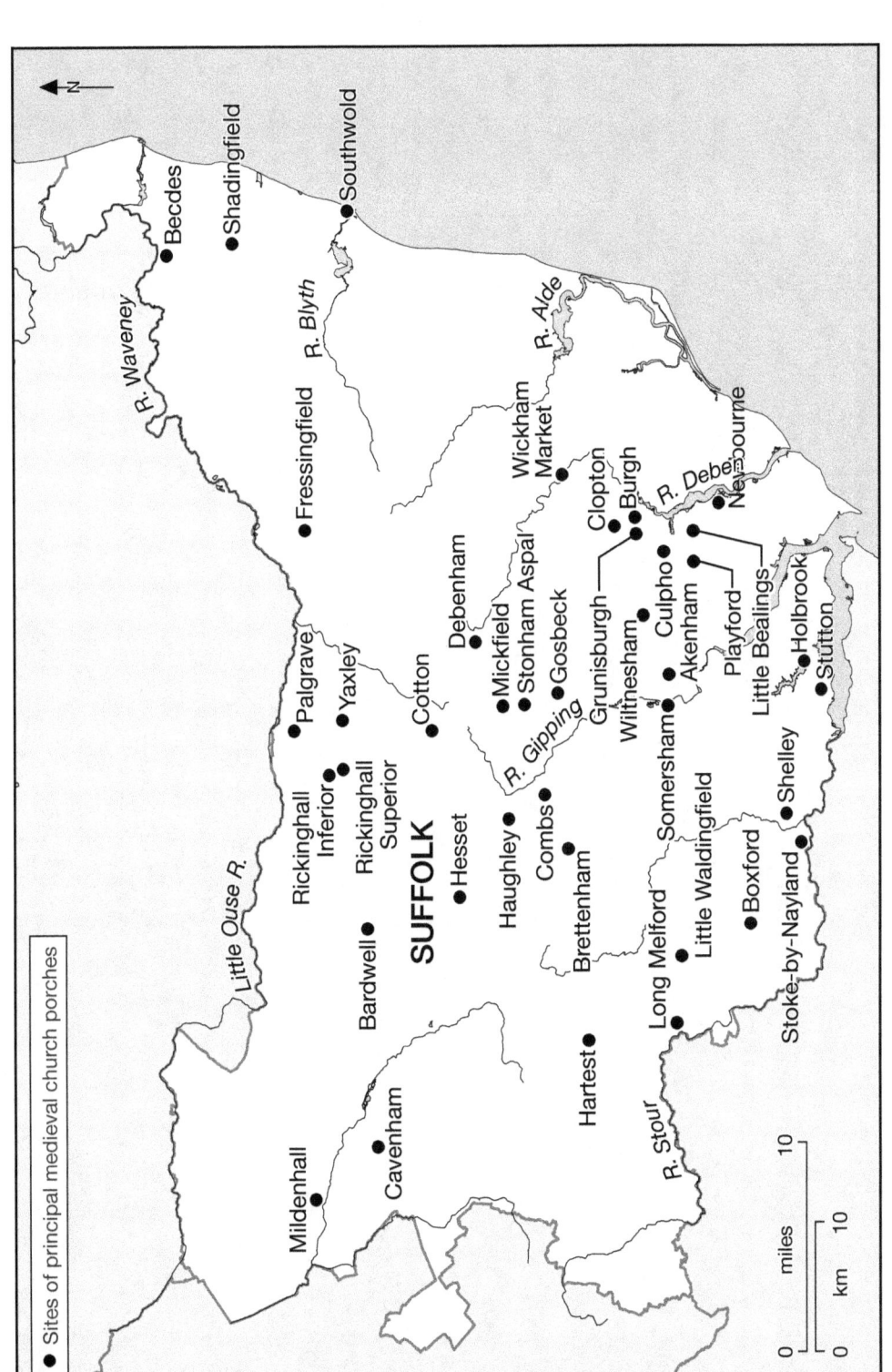

Principal church porches in Suffolk

Introduction
The English Medieval Church Porch

P ORCHES ARE ENIGMATIC buildings, difficult to define or contain. They present little formal coherence either as a building type or in how they relate to the larger structure of which they are part. They constitute a major visual element of most English medieval churches and no other buildings of medieval date are comparable to them architecturally, iconographically or functionally. In broad terms church porches are familiar and easily recognisable but the variety and excellence of their architectural form, aesthetic impact, and social and liturgical functioning are all remarkable. Often the most prominent feature of a church's exterior, a porch commands our attention. The visual and spatial prominence of these majestic showpiece façades clearly fascinated those who either designed or paid for them to be created. In writing this book my aim is to offer various ways to understand the sort of buildings porches were in England between the late thirteenth and mid sixteenth centuries. How were they thought of, and in what ways were they experienced? Where should we look for their architectural ancestors and close relations? What social and liturgical role did they play in medieval life? Who built them, when and to what model?

The 'modern era' of literature on church porches began in 1912 with J. C. Wall's publication of *Porches and Fonts*.[1] Intended for the general reader, its style and content very much of its own time, Wall's book continues to be the most widely referenced source for information about church

---

[1] J. C. Wall, *Porches and Fonts* (London, 1912). James Charles Wall, antiquary, ecclesiologist and fellow of the Royal Historical Society, contributed to the Victoria History of the Counties of England but his earliest individually published work was *The Tombs of the Kings of England* (1891). His other works concerned with parish churches are *An Old English Parish* (1907), *The Church Chests of Essex* (1913), co-authored with H. W. Lewer) and *Medieval Wall Paintings* (1914). His last publication was *Pilgrimage* (1925).

porches. Perhaps surprisingly, Wall's survey of porches and fonts did not stimulate a wider interest in porches, whereas fonts have received considerable scholarly and popular attention ever since.[2] Porches as a monographic topic have never been addressed. A century on and in the light of modern scholarship this book revisits many of the themes which Wall discussed, presenting a greater body of primary documentary evidence and drawing on knowledge attained through direct experience of the buildings. Ultimately the present book's purpose is to offer new ways to explore, engage with and understand the English medieval church porch.

Despite recent burgeoning academic and popular interest in the study of parish church architecture, porches have been little studied, whether by architectural, social or church historians. Exceptions do of course exist. Explorations of the stylistic and formal changes seen in English medieval architecture have attended to notable examples in singular isolation. Alternatively the generalised whole has been presented as nothing more than a convenient shelter for the rituals which took place before the church door in England's inclement climate.[3] No detailed modern study of church porches exists and this book is the first attempt to synthesise the building type by uniting their contextual, functional and architectural specificities. From the magnificence of the double-height hexagonal north porch at St Mary Redcliffe, Bristol, to the three-storey Renaissance palace preceding the south door at St John the Baptist, Cirencester, church porches display some of the most inventive and innovative architectural design of the English Middle Ages. This book aims to showcase their contribution to medieval architectural history and current knowledge of the Middle Ages more generally.

The Medieval English Church Porch as Architectural Object

Special treatment of entrances into buildings and points of transition between spaces is a theme familiar in the global history of man-made habitats. Demonstrations of collective confidence, bearers of apotropaic motifs and statements of faith and morality, entrance buildings act to define place

---

[2] Wall's *Porches and Fonts* was published at a time of considerable interest in the fabric and furnishings of England's parish churches, for example, Francis Bond, *Fonts and Font Covers* (London, 1908). An exemplary, and more recent, study which focuses on fonts is Ann E. Nichols, *Seeable Signs: The Iconography of the Seven Sacraments 1350–1544* (Woodbridge, 1994).

[3] Peter Draper, *The Formation of English Gothic* (New Haven and London, 2006), 205.

and people. The English medieval church porch is an exemplary model of the phenomenon because they were within reach of every patron or community and sufficiently mutable to meet their aesthetic and monetary economy. This book aims to establish their place in the long architectural history of entrance structures, challenging the reductionist view that they were little more than architectural preambles or convenient door coverings.

A principal objective is to investigate the wealth and variety of plausible definitions of the medieval church porch, but some basic parameters need setting out at the start. A major visual and functional attribute of most medieval churches, the porch as a type of forebuilding preceded and introduced a larger structure and complex of spaces. Having volumetric capacity porches physically contain, but also retain, a greater or lesser degree of physical and visual permeability. Although essentially cubic square-plan boxes, the balance of solid structure and open aperture was experimented with quite freely. Front façades were swallowed up by enormous arches and elaborate surface decoration, side walls disintegrated into colonnades or were subjugated by pairs of windows elongated from the dado to wall plate. All church porches are ceiled and roofed no matter how insubstantial their elevations become. Porches protrude beyond the dominant architectural plane of their adjoining building, interrupting the façade and stepping out to greet us. In this way they are quite unlike Romanesque portals which directly frame rather than anticipate the door. Fundamental to the identity of porches is the provision of a space into which humans can place themselves. Standing before an ornate multi-ordered frame of a church door such as that at Skelton, Yorkshire, one remains outside, looking at and physically separated from the building. The ornate framing of the door emphasises its presence and in doing so heightens our sense of exclusion. The primary function of all church porches is to 'introduce' the house of God. They are architectural introits, overtures or prologues, shaping our sense of the larger setting by similarity or difference, implying what we are to think and how we should behave before and as we enter.

Extant examples constructed before 1200 are the earliest known English experiments in porch design and belong to the great churches of monastic and secular foundations including Southwell, Tewkesbury and Selby. With the advantage of historical hindsight, it is easy to see how multi-ordered Romanesque doorways, with sculptural relief emerging from the surrounding wall plane, anticipated the fully formed church porch. But the change was certainly not inevitable and, with the possible exception of the south porch at Malmesbury Abbey, the sculptural characteristics familiar to Romanesque portal detailing were not maintained on early porch façades. At parish level porches are not known in England before the thirteenth century, with one of the first examples being the south porch at St John the Baptist, Barnack, in Cambridgeshire, constructed at the beginning of

1 Exterior view, south porch, Barnack

the century (fig. 1). As a phenomenon of the thirteenth century, parish church porches were invented in the milieu of European International Gothic style.

Architectural Allusion

Porches are not simply part of a church; they belong within the wider category of entrance architecture which defines and characterises the building it precedes. Their architectural format connoted social and cultural meanings familiar in other contexts. In writing on the Aerary Porch at St George's, Windsor, John Goodall rejected explanations of porches as 'a functional covering to the door' in favour of their symbolic nature 'as a miniaturised gatehouse, with the lordly connotations that implied'.[4] Allusions to gateways are apparent in the architecture of church porches, but fundamental differences exist. Porches are inherently accessible; their open-fronted form permits us to enter and be sheltered. Gatehouses are a means of managing access, setting the terms of engagement between people outside and places inside. The symbolically defended porch, crenellated and turreted as though a gatehouse, evokes the power of the church militant on earth, embracing the corporate spiritual fight of every believer. The transference of gatehouse signification is carried by architectural formality, but its effective translation relies on the cultural vibrations produced by porches also being retained.

Gatehouses are one of the many points of architectural reference made in the design of porches: castle entrances, city gates, vaulted passages, oriels, even tombs all feature in the associated architectural lexicon. Exchanges with such a wide range of architectural and micro-architectural objects gave porch designers a uniquely rich universe of modes with which to experiment when making a building. Church porches should never be seen as poor imitations of other architectural objects, and their scope for quite radical invention has to date been disguised by a lack of attention or by the tendency to explain porches as versions of other structures. The flexible and multivalent connotations embedded in medieval church porches is a line of enquiry which runs through this book and emphasises the progressive character of many examples.

Few of England's ubiquitous medieval church porches can be attributed to named commissioning patrons, and rarely are they the work of an identifiable mason. Only in exceptional circumstances can a porch be

---

[4] John A. A. Goodall, 'The Aerary Porch and its Influence on Late Medieval English Vaulting', in *St George's Chapel, Windsor, in the Fourteenth Century*, ed. Nigel Saul (Woodbridge, 2005), 166.

2 Exterior view, west porch, Snettisham

placed in a much wider web of architectural and patronal reference. One such example is the three-bay western porch or narthex at Snettisham in Norfolk (fig. 2). It was almost certainly built to designs drawn by John Ramsey (mason at Ely Cathedral) and provided the principal model for the porch of Prague Cathedral's south transept, designed by Peter Parler.[5] Parler's Prague is also indebted to the vibrant culture of Decorated architectural ambition in Bristol, particularly St Augustine's. Although unlikely to be the creation of the Bristol Cathedral master mason, St Mary Redcliffe's outer north porch is an exceptional evocation of the porch mode (fig. 3). It is one of only three hexagonal porches known in England and by far the most significant. The extent of the designer's inventive capacity is remarkable, perhaps unsurpassed; the building is an extreme case which challenges its audience to comprehend it. The external composition of niches arranged as a band extending the full breadth of the building is redolent of the gatehouse of St Augustine's Abbey, Canterbury, an observation

---

[5] Christopher Wilson, 'Why Did Peter Parler Come to England?', in *Architecture, Liturgy and Identity: liber amicorum Paul Crossley*, ed. Zoë Opačić and Achim Timmermann (Turnhout, 2011), 105.

3 Exterior view, north porch, St Mary Redcliffe, Bristol.
Reproduced with thanks to St Mary Redcliffe

which continues the familiarity between porches and gatehouses.⁶ Implicitly, St Mary Redcliffe's architectural allusions were also appropriate for gatehouses. Its planar articulation is augmented by decorative details largely derived from the Lady Chapels at Ely and Glastonbury (the latter built 150 years earlier). In the absence of an antecedent hexagonal porch it is apparent that the designer drew from other structures and architectural iconographies for inspirational source material, with shrine canopies and centrally planned baptistries being amongst the suggestions made in recent scholarship.⁷ Whilst observation of imitative details fits with our modern sense of copying, the repetition of carved details across a group of buildings does not necessarily reveal the significant iconographic (rather than stylistic) models for an overall conception. We must think beyond formal likeness if we are to recognise medieval understandings of shared or transferable iconographies.⁸ The theory of connotation extends beyond physical likeness to functional allusion and I suggest a conative process enabled the designer of St Mary Redcliffe to absorb from these other structures their semiotic type as much as their stylistic or formal conformation.

Threshold Rites and Ritual Passage

As outside places, existing beyond the main event, porches unsettle our sense of where we are. They dilute the delineation of outside and inside and compromise the boundary between the two. A defining feature of English medieval parish church porches from the beginning of their making through to the Reformation is the open entrance. Porches do not have doors; they never become fully enclosed. In porches built in the thirteenth and fourteenth centuries (like those at Barnack and Uffington) particular emphasis is placed on the openness of the entrance. Minimal walling surrounds the void and the enlarged aperture contrasts with the porch's solid side walls. This arrangement creates a darkened interior and the fall of natural light is cast directly onto the inner church door. The large entrance arch serves as a frame to the smaller church door, and this is a near ubiquitous trait of porches throughout the medieval period. Architectural manipulation of light and perspectival distance, both created by the difference

---

⁶ Christopher Wilson, 'St Mary Redcliffe, Bristol, Outer North Porch, North Side', in *Age of Chivalry: Art in Plantagenet England, 1200–1400*, ed. Jonathan Alexander and Paul Binski (London, 1987), 413, cat. no. 490.

⁷ Ibid. My thanks to Jon Cannon for sharing his thoughts on the relevance of centrally planned buildings to the hexagonal porch at Redcliffe.

⁸ Richard Krautheimer, 'Introduction to an "Iconography of Medieval Architecture"', *Journal of the Warburg and Courtauld Institutes* 5 no. 2 (1942), 1–33.

in size between the entrance arch and the church door, draws one towards the main event – entry into the temple. Porches thus heighten our sense of the anticipation, preparation and contemplation involved in entering. Churches without porches, such as Wacton in Suffolk – but examples are many, remind us of the alternative experience. The thirteenth-century porches at Polebrook in Northamptonshire, Algerkirk in Lincolnshire, and Blyth in Northumberland all have large gaping entrances as their principal architectural characteristic. At Polebrook, and Woodnewton and Nassington (Northamptonshire), the porch entrance arches are edged by Romanesque decorative motifs – they display how changes in the spatial and architectural form of entrance structures preceded the stylistic development of portal elaboration and detailing.

Porches exist beyond the bounds of the church's sacred envelope and defended threshold. Protection of the purified interior by the application of imagery is appropriately and clearly observed in the famous decorative ironwork at Stillingfleet in North Yorkshire, dated to c.1170. It depicts, amongst other things, Adam and Eve, and Noah's Ark, and conveys notions of both protection and redemption.[9] As will be discussed later on, this pairing of protection and redemption runs deeply through the character of English medieval church porches. A closed church door, iconographically decorated or not, emphasises the exclusion one feels within a porch and confirms its liminal character – the architectural form implies a habitable space, but one which remains segregated and at risk from malign forces. This is well demonstrated by the two-storey porch at Uffington, Oxfordshire, built c.1220–1250. The church retains eleven of its original twelve exterior consecration crosses, projecting stone roundels regularly positioned around the building. There was not a consecration cross on the porch, implicitly therefore it existed outside of the protected, sanctified church.

The ceremony of church consecration dramatically characterised the distinction between exclusion and inclusion and emphasised the importance of gaining access to the church interior: 'The bishop first goes round the church three times, and each time, when he comes to the door, he strikes it with his crosier and says: "*Attollite portas principes vestras* …" (Lift up your gates, O princes, and be lifted up, O eternal gates; and the king of glory shall enter in!) … The church is sprinkled inside and out with blessed water which comprises water, wine, salt and ash – ingredients harnessed for the reconciliation of Ash Wednesday penitents and preparation

---

[9] Jane Geddes, *Medieval Decorative Ironwork in England: English Ironwork from 1050–1550* (London, 1999), 66–7.

of baptismal candidates.'[10] Thus consecration of the church reverberates the rites of the Christian life-course, rites of passage, experienced in the church porch (see chapter two).

One of England's most celebrated early-fourteenth-century parish churches is St Andrew's, Heckington, Lincolnshire, built c.1307–1330, yet the porch has received little attention. By the date of its building an essential form for the now familiar church porch was established – large open archway, low wall plate and no side apertures. But there are important points at Heckington to be observed which mark its distinction from earlier examples. Internally the walls are not articulated by arcading and no vault covers the space. The interior is a modest space, intimate and approximate to human scale. The dramatic change is the exterior decoration of the porch: sinuous, tendril-like cusped scroll work, heraldic shields (the royal arms, plus those of St Edmund and Edward the Confessor) and high-relief figurative imagery (a pair of angels and two others which might be donor figures) are set against foliate (almost seaweed like) backgrounds. In contrast to the austere interior, the exterior is inhabited, brought alive visually through the use of sculpture and marked as belonging to Christ (although at least the upper part of the figure of Christ blessing which now occupies the gable image niche is a modern replacement). Church porches can aesthetically encapsulate the whole church, providing a way to understand the character of the associated belief system and the nature of its related behaviours. As Christopher Wilson has argued, the integration of imagery within the architecturally varied forms of church façades was an idiom particular to surface decoration in England.[11] The intimate association of image, architectural sculpture, and structure required viewers to visually explore the building in detail, a mode of engagement quite distinct from looking at a narrative frieze set upon the building as though a three-dimensional mural painting.

One's phenomenological experience of stepping into the porch at Heckington is affected by this imagery and its location. Whilst structurally the porch conforms to a pre-existing standard composition, its exterior treatment construes it as a shelter beneath the walls of God's kingdom on earth – not beyond them; and that point is important. Location actively formulates the nature of repeated events in individual and community life-cycles, including those which took place at the church entrance. In

---

[10] Timothy M. Thibodeau, trans., *The Rationale Divinorum Officiorum of William Durand of Mende, A New Translation of the Prologue and Book One* (New York, 2010).

[11] Christopher Wilson, 'Calling the Tune? The Involvement of King Henry III in the Design of the Abbey Church at Westminster', *Journal of the British Archaeological Association* 161 (2008), 70–1.

practical terms porches enabled one's earthly peers to participate in key events, and architecturally located sacramental experience on earth symbolically before Christ the door (John 10.9). The nature and social value of 'threshold rites' and Christian sacramental ritual are forms of 'territorial passage', a concept originated by anthropologist Arnold van Gennep.[12] A person's movement in space across a limen is, according to van Gennep, fundamental to human cultural constructions of rites of passage, experientially enforcing the social significance of the event. Transition between states of being could be both notional and actual. Actual transition (van Gennep's 'territorial passage') was made apparent by differentiated places framing a threshold. Whilst van Gennep's work was focused on cultures chronologically and geographically distant from medieval England, his foundational work retains a strong resonance. This discussion is picked up in more detail in chapter two. Porches such as that at Heckington, and this is an early example, imply that the significant limen of the church, the sacred threshold, was relocated during the fourteenth century from the church door to the porch entrance. The decorative and architectural detailing of porch façades indicate this change and accord with van Gennep's model of the universal habit of marking points of ritual transition.

Buildings for People

Architecture and people are inextricably connected, and this book is concerned with this symbiosis. We can think of church porches not only as buildings but as containing objects, social artefacts within and before which our bodies can be placed, our senses stimulated. English church porches were never passive or neutral objects and their facture explicates the involvement of people and dissolves distinctions between person, object and environment.

By the early fourteenth century the formal attributes and phenomenological effect of porch architecture were sent in a very different direction, as exemplified by porches such as that at Over in Cambridgeshire, built c.1320 (fig. 4). A large area of solid walling surmounts the entrance arch, the parapet is crenellated, shafted pinnacles stand as sentries on the roof, and sculpted ball-flower decoration is inhabited by animals, including dogs. The exterior is, however, emphatic in its lack of niches to house sacred imagery, its defence reliant on other apotropaic references. The walls of Over porch are pierced open, and evidence of glazing or shutters is absent. The structure's solidity is much reduced. Here visual penetration

---

[12] Arnold van Gennep, *The Rites of Passage*, trans. Monika B. Vizedom and Gabrielle L. Caffee (Chicago, 1960).

4 Exterior view, south porch, Over

of the building no longer relies on the entrance arch alone, light floods the space from all directions. The internal ground plan measures 12ft 2in square, the internal doorway measures 9ft x 5ft 9in, the exterior arch 10ft 5in x 6ft 2in (north door: 8ft 2in x 4ft). Yet these modest dimensions belie the cavernous interior. From floor to ceiling the space is approximately 25ft, far beyond human scale and twice as high as the building's plan is wide or deep. Volumetrically therefore the porch is a double cube stacked vertically. Part of the reason for this height might well be its relative external appearance as appropriate to the scale of the rest of the church. However, the phenomenological effect is to exacerbate the miniaturisation of the human standing before the door or seated on a low stone bench, heightening the dramatic sensation of entering the church.

Some of the very earliest church porches were built with integral, low-level stone benches running along the interior walls. Of equal importance to the architectural celebration of the church door is the provision made for the presence of people. The bench invites one to sit, rest awhile, linger, wait. In dramatic early (non-parochial) examples such as Southwell Minster and Malmesbury Abbey, long benches are set against side walls articulated by interlocking shafts and arches. These arcades form architectonic niches and hint at individualised seating being provided in a communal space. Porch benches are however very low, on average about 18 inches, and their horizontal surface is not divided into individual seats. The effect can be seen as one of humility, a feeling of being small (perhaps insignificant) within a cavernous space and before the ultimate judge. An Old Testament reference is being conjured with. On waking, Jacob quakes with fearfulness, an emotional and physical state generated by finding himself before the temple: *Pavensque, Quam terribilis est, inquit, locus iste! non est hic aliud nisi domus Dei, et porta caeli* (And trembling he said: How terrible is this place! this is no other but the house of God, and the gate of heaven. Genesis 28.17). In combination, stone benches and side apertures create layers of enclosure and exposure for the people inside. When sitting on the bench in a porch such as Great Massingham, Norfolk, or Little Chishill, Essex, a solid wall is at one's back and the body notionally tucks within the thickness of the masonry. The sill height of openings in the east and west walls of porches (through which sun, wind and rain might come) is commonly above seated head height, around 4ft above internal floor level. In summary, the bench encourages one to feel enclosed and shielded from the elements; the building both protects the body and maintains visual access for those outside. These points are returned to in chapter three.

How to Study a Church Porch

The concepts of decorum and appropriateness are apposite to the study of architecture, both in terms of how we understand artistic expression and what it tells us about the 'creators' of buildings. That architecture can be decorous or radical advises that buildings conform, to greater or lesser extent, to a sense of propriety. There are parameters within which they exist and boundaries they should respect, making them fit for purpose. The Oxford Divinity Schools, built c.1427–83, is a famous medieval case of how architecture, as opposed to mere buildings, was expected to suit its connotative function. Differences between the expansive and expensive fenestration of the ground floor and the meanness of the first-floor windows exemplify the design change enforced by a corporate patron which sought to avoid criticisms of excess.[13] Evidently, flamboyance and architectural opulence were not decorous for the function of this building (how it signified its people) and the 'errors' made at the start of the campaign on the ground floor were recognised and corrected as work progressed. It follows, I suggest, that analysis of the detailing and design of church porches will reveal the manner in which they were conceived, the aesthetic sensitivities of those commissioning them and, by association, what character of place they were considered to be. Porches exist because someone acted and caused others to do so too. Equally, architectural form and detail are not produced in a vacuum but in the world as it is known to a building's patron, designer and builders. The variation and prevalence of the medieval church porch in England is an excellent vehicle through which to explore these issues.

Medieval architectural history in England continues to be dominated by taxonomic classification established in the nineteenth century, based on the nomenclature formalised by Thomas Rickman and first published in 1817.[14] The principle of controlling or containing a subject, and thereby understanding it, through ordering and classification can easily be criticised in our post-modern world but measuring, recording and descriptively defining historic buildings remains a vital practice. Surveying a building, measuring, counting, translating into words, encourages engagement with its details in a way that looking alone does not. The recording of one's findings provides the groundwork from which to build an understanding of the range as well as specificity of built forms and their materials. Medieval precedent for an arithmetical approach to architectural study is in

---

[13] David Thomson, *Renaissance Architecture: Critics, Patrons, Luxury* (Manchester and New York, 1993), 6.

[14] Thomas Rickman, *An Attempt to Discriminate the Styles of Architecture in England: from the Conquest to the Reformation* (London, 1817).

William Worcestre's *Itineraries* (1478–80). Of the church at Wells, William noted: 'The north porch of St Andrew's church is 7 yards long and 5 yards wide.'[15] Measuring and recording plan dimensions were his basic method but he was also interested in moulded detailing. For St Stephen's, Bristol, he records architectural details using an impressive range of specialist language as well as noting the name of the mason:

> Of the ingenious workmanship of the [south] porch of the Church of St Stephen, the handiwork of Benedict [Crosse] the freemason. A [string] course outside; a casement, a bowtel, a fillet, a double ogee, a bowtel, a fillet, and ogee, a fillet, a casement with leaves, a fillet, a bowtell (*sic*), a fillet, an ogee, a fillet, a casement with trails of leaves, a fillet, a bowtel, a fillet, a casement, a fillet, a casement, a fillet; in the middle of the doorway a bowtel.[16]

William Worcestre's writings do not amount to an architectural treatise, but they do show how the eye and the mind of an Englishman in the late fifteenth century could attend to architectural details in a systematised manner dependent on his having a specialised vocabulary to employ. Similarly astute attention to the actuality of buildings remains central to the study of architecture as much as visual analysis continues as the foundation of art historical investigations of paintings and related works.

Architecture is more than the sum of its parts and as valuable as measurement and description can be, without analysis of the materials and composition as a whole architectural study can lack a sense of vitality, turning a building into a collection of stones rather than a fully sensory experience. Formal analysis alone is insufficient if we seek to understand historic architectural worlds, and matters are changing. Socially informed approaches to architectural study are increasingly commonplace. Churches continue to provide the bulk of study material for the historian of medieval architecture but the details of liturgy and performance have become a more dominant and widely respected aspect of the discipline of architectural history. How buildings were used is being addressed to a greater extent than ever before, inspired and informed by anthropological methods and theory. The burgeoning trend for spatial enquiry necessitates recognition of architecture's character beyond formal description.[17] The pertinence of such approaches to medieval buildings is well demonstrated by porches because of their

---

[15] John H. Harvey, ed., *Itineraries [of] William Worcestre Edited from the Unique MS. Corpus Christi College, Cambridge, 210* (Oxford, 1969), 293.

[16] Ibid., 299, 315.

[17] C. Pamela Graves, *The Form and Fabric of Belief: An Archaeology of the Lay Experience of Religion in Medieval Norfolk and Devon*, BAR British Series 311 (Oxford, 2001), 1–16.

central presence in transitional rituals. Mary Carruthers has explained how the notion of *ductus* (journeying or flow) can be used as a means of understanding the experience as well as the form of medieval art; application of the same idea to medieval architecture has been explored by Paul Crossley.[18] The detailed and subtle execution of entranceways of the great cathedrals – the transeptal entrances to Chartres Cathedral and the judgement portal at Lincoln Cathedral – were used by Crossley to indicate that medieval architectural composition could be understood as being based on the concept of *ductus*. Crossley's approach to Chartres Cathedral aimed 'to move from the cathedral as text to the cathedral as experience … shifting our gaze from author to audience'.[19] A challenge is made to enduring art historical obsessions with individual genius and the primacy given to the purity of conception and birth over the complex messiness of life. The method is well suited to the investigation of church porches as functional designed objects which mnemonically mark and respect ritualised human passage, following a route from external façade, through interior space, to entry into the church. This book is itself a form of *ductus*, a thorough investigation of the porch mode, offering insight into the manner in which architecture, decoration, historical significance and contemporary allusion coalesced and were made meaningful by human mind–body experience of the built environment.

The opening two chapters of this book are broad in scope. They present wide-ranging investigations of the English medieval church porch through texts, images and the performance of space. The subsequent architectural study is, however, restricted to East Anglia, a region rich in medieval buildings and their history. The purpose of the focused study is to look in detail at the full inventive range of porches which were built in a region with many consistencies. It has been my aim to survey plain, simple examples as well as the large, ornate ones and by doing so the trajectory of East Anglian porch form and design has become apparent, as discussed in chapter three. The primary documentation, mainly testamentary, and antiquarian studies of East Anglia's churches are considerable, and augment the profusion of extant buildings which largely retain their medieval form and ornament. The written accounts which document something of the circumstances in which porches were built and the associated patterns of benefaction and patronage in medieval East Anglia are the focus of chapters four and five. Alternative areas of England could have been selected and may have

---

[18] Mary Carruthers, 'The Concept of *Ductus*, or Journeying through a Work of Art', in *Rhetoric beyond Words*, ed. Mary Carruthers (Cambridge, 2010), 190–213; Paul Crossley, '*Ductus* and *Memoria*: Chartres Cathedral and the Workings of Rhetoric', ibid., 214–49.

[19] Crossley, '*Ductus* and *Memoria*', 215.

produced slightly different interpretations of the building type. For example, Northamptonshire or Lincolnshire, with the prevalence of available building stone, are wealthy in thirteenth- and fourteenth-century examples; Essex and Kent are rich in timber examples. The opportunity remains for other regional studies to be carried out, and they would certainly add detail and variety to the image offered by the present book.

Every porch defines its church and its people, and it is not difficult to find emotive adjectives to conjure their shared character – majestic, humble, ambitious, pious. This book is a detailed exploration of medieval church porches and offers ways to understand them with some clarity. Its chapters interrogate their architectural design and ornamentation, their ancestry and historical context, and the system of social morality built upon ubiquitous Christian belief. It is also a book about people, life and experience. As well as describing the form of porches and setting out their sacramental importance, the following pages attend to the familiarity of porches, their everyday presence in close-knit, interdependent communities. The book's focus is on the English Middle Ages, an extended period when churches were unquestionably special, sacred and mysterious. But at parish level churches were also local, familiar and personal. In East Anglia, at least from the mid thirteenth century, church porches were designed and used in relation to both spheres – extraordinary and ordinary, heavenly and terrestrial, and their study casts light on how engagement with the parish church enriched and sustained people's lives.

The English *Porticus*

BUILDINGS ARE ENCOUNTERED in a number of ways, principally (and most affectingly) by first-hand experience but also through their translation into words and pictures. Historically contextualising our understanding of them requires all three types of encounter, which shift and interact in constant dialogue. Conversations about porches revolve around the use, translation and transmission of a single Latin word: *porticus*. In Old English this becomes *portic*, referring to a 'porch, portico; enclosed place; place roofed in; arch recess in a church.'[1] In modern English a porch is either 'an exterior structure forming a covered approach to the entrance of a building' or, less commonly, 'an interior space serving as a vestibule or hallway'.[2] The interiority of the latter evokes something of the Anglo-Saxon *portic*. Words have their meaning through shared recognition of their cultural application, people who use them aim to be understood by their listener or reader; the agreement of both parties is implicit. Exploring the historic use of the vocabulary of buildings, combined with analysis of their structural form, provides a 'back-story' for the late medieval church porch. As we will see, although neither *porticus* nor porches maintained a single architectural form, the social conventions and meanings identifiable within them allow for a unified and coherent class of building. Taking this longer view of the English *porticus* reveals significances which were largely concealed by mid-sixteenth-century liturgical and sacramental changes.

The Anglo-Saxon *Porticus*

Bede, living at the Benedictine monastery at Jarrow in the late eighth and early ninth centuries, is not renowned as an architectural historian, but in recording the location of high status burials at SS Peter and Paul Canterbury, his Latin text includes a valuable account of the Anglo-Saxon *porticus*. The Northumbrian monk-chronicler's record reveals that the porch was an internal space providing for elite and precious corporeal

---

[1] Henry Sweet, *The Student's Dictionary of Anglo-Saxon* (Oxford, 1896), 137.
[2] Oxford English Dictionary: http://www.oed.com/view/Entry/147952

interments. According to Bede, in the year 604, 'the beloved of God, Father Augustine, died, and his body was deposited without, close by the church of the apostles, Peter and Paul ... by reason that the same was not yet finished, nor consecrated, but as soon as it was dedicated, the body was brought in, and decently buried in the north porch (*portico*) thereof.' The burial of St Augustine's body in the north *porticus* of the newly built abbey established a pattern and here 'also were interred the bodies of all the succeeding archbishops, except two only, Theodorus and Berthwald, whose bodies are within that church, because the aforesaid porch could contain no more'.[3] As a site favoured for archiepiscopal interments, the porch also attracted royal burials. Ethelbert, king of Kent, having been converted to the Christian faith and baptised by Augustine in 596, died in 616 and 'was buried in St Martin's porch within the church of the blessed apostles Peter and Paul, where also lies his queen, Bertha.'[4]

Bede defined *porticus* as a place of sanctity within but distinct from the body of the church and carrying its own discrete dedication. We are given the impression that the building's priority was to shelter elite graves, effectively constructing a place of intramural burial. Before this date bodies had been interred in external cemeteries with worthy persons being respectfully given a *memoria* or *martyrium* over their grave. However, a growing interest in being buried close to the holiest part of a church, a saint's relics or the Eucharistic altar, saw deviation from accepted practice. In the early seventh century the Church came under increasing pressure to change its stance and give consent for internal burials. The Church Council of Nantes held in 658 ruled that inhumation of corpses within the body of the church was not permitted but would be allowed in separated parts of the same building – either the *atrium* or the *porticus*.[5] Bede's description of Augustine's, Ethelbert's and Bertha's burials rather suggests that the Nantes decree did not instigate change in England, but rather secured and

---

[3] '*Defunctus est autem Deo dilectus pater Augustinus, et positum corpus eius supra meminimus, quia necdum fuerat perfecta nec dedicata. Mox uero ut dedicta est, intro inlatum et in portico illius aquilonali decenter sepultum est; in qua etiam sequentium archiepiscoporum omnium sunt corpora tumulata praetor duorum tantummodo, id est Theodori et Berctualdi, quorum in ipsa ecclesia posita sunt, eo quod praedicta porticus plura capere nequiuit*': Bertram Colgrave and R. A. B. Mynors, eds, *Bede's Ecclesiastical History of the English People* (Oxford, 1969), 142–4.

[4] '*Defunctus uero est rex Aedilberct die XXIIII mensis Februarii post xx et unum annos acceptae fidei, atque in porticu sancti Martini intro ecclesiam beatorum apostolorum Petri et Pauli sepultus, ubi et Berctae regina condita est.*' Ibid., 150.

[5] Eric Fernie, *The Architecture of the Anglo-Saxons* (London, 1983), 43. See also David Park, 'Medieval Burials and Monuments', in *The Temple Church in London: History, Architecture, Art,* ed. Robin Griffith-Jones and David Park (Woodbridge, 2010), 72.

authorised existing practice which favoured intramural interment for elite churchmen and royal patrons alike.

But what of their architectural form? The Anglo-Saxon *porticus* is known largely through archaeological evidence but key sites have produced varying interpretations. Rehearsing some of the debated points confirms the relationship between Anglo-Saxon *porticus* and late medieval porches as based partly on physical attributes. In 1958 Dudley, Jackson and Fletcher re-evaluated the distinction between *porticus* and porch.[6] They reported that archaeological excavations of the site of St Peter and St Paul's Canterbury (later St Augustine's Abbey) revealed that north and south *porticus* were lateral adjuncts (transeptal wings) and could only be accessed from inside the church. Having established their model at Canterbury, Dudley, Jackson and Fletcher moved on to confirm the distinction between Old English and post-Conquest Norman vocabulary. They asserted that the Anglo-Saxon *portic* was an internal lateral chapel for sepulchral and liturgical purposes, whereas the post-Conquest *porticus* took the form of projecting entrance porches.

In 1930 Sir Alfred (A. W.) Clapham, scholar of Romanesque and Secretary of the Royal Commission on Historical Monuments, had published on English architecture before the Conquest, and included brief consideration of late Anglo-Saxon porches. Clapham observed that many were of a scale larger than their primary purpose required (without stating what he considered this to be) and that, developmentally, they were successors to the earlier form of *porticus* in having the distinction of an exterior point of entry.[7] Using ground plans of Bradford on Avon, Wareham St Martin and Bishopstone to illustrate his point, Clapham argued that the entrance arches, which are misaligned to the church doors, were off-set to give space for an altar against the east wall 'thus making the structure serve the dual purpose of a porch and a chapel'.[8] Clapham's interpretation of the visual evidence was clearly skewed by what he knew of *porticus* chapels from Bede and similar writings. He effectively conflated the internal *porticus* and its conventions as a consecrated chapel (in the manner of the Canterbury *porticus*) and much later porches which covered the church door and were accessed from outside.

The argument hinged on whether or not the exterior entrance arches were understood as original features or secondary, apertures cut through previously solid walls. According to Dudley, Jackson and Fletcher, during

---

[6] E. Dudley, C. Jackson and Eric G. M. Fletcher, 'Porch and Porticus in Saxon Churches', *Journal of the British Archaeological Association* 19 (1956), 1–13.

[7] A. W. Clapham, *English Romanesque Architecture Before the Conquest* (Oxford, 1930), 120.

[8] Ibid., 122.

building works at Bradford on Avon c.1000, an off-centre doorway was cut into the northern *porticus*, giving external access but retaining the altar against the east wall. On the south side, they argued, the steep slope of the land could make ground-floor entry difficult if not impossible, and therefore a plausible reconstruction of the southern *porticus* is that it was only accessible from within the church. More recently Eric Fernie has argued that the south *porticus* is unlikely to have had an external opening on the basis of the lack of strip work on either face, but maintained that the north *porticus* is likely always to have had an external portal, based on the same reasoning.[9]

For Bishopstone, Dudley, Jackson and Fletcher drew their conclusions from architectural analysis. The stone blocks and style of construction used for the exterior arch and jambs differ from those used on the quoins of the original chamber. This distinction points to the possibility of the portal being of later date. Before the post-Conquest enlargement of the church and erection of the west tower, access to the church was through a door in the west wall of the nave; the southern lateral chamber is unlikely to have had an exterior arch. Building the west tower (without an external door) necessitated a change to how people could access the church interior. The solution was the provision of a doorway cut through the south wall of the southern *porticus*.[10] It therefore seems certain that the Anglo-Saxon *porticus* at Bishopstone were internal transept chapels, with alterations coming as part of a larger post-Conquest remodelling of the church.

By refuting Clapham's conclusions, Dudley, Jackson and Fletcher insisted on a fundamental distinction between the late Anglo-Saxon *porticus* and the post-Conquest 'porch', and this understanding of the two building types is common in accounts of medieval architectural history. However, I suggest that this is an oversimplification, relying on formal characterisation at the exclusion of understanding buildings through shared meanings and associations. Retention of the altar when a doorway was cut into the north *porticus* at Bradford on Avon, for example, blended the earlier internal *porticus* (equating to transeptal or aisle chapels) and porches which facilitate entry (*porticus ingressus*). Textual sources also convey how the cultural resonances of these buildings were carried forward despite architectural changes.

---

[9] Fernie, *Architecture of the Anglo-Saxons*, 148.

[10] H. M. Taylor and Joan Taylor, *Anglo-Saxon Architecture. Volume 1* (Cambridge, 1965), 71.

The Written Sources

The *Anglo-Saxon Chronicle* records the death of Bishop Aylric in 1072. Before the Norman invasion Aylric's episcopal career began briefly at York and continued at Durham. Despite having spent twelve years in retirement at Peterborough, King William I summoned him to officiate at Westminster. Here Aylric died and was buried 'within the minster, in the porch (*portice*) of St Nicholas'.[11] The chronicler's report of a senior ecclesiastic buried inside the church at Westminster, in a discrete location carrying its own dedication is immediately reminiscent of Bede's accounts of similar interments in seventh-century Canterbury. This continuity implies how burial practices in England ignored the rupture of Conquest.

Shifts in vocabulary, translations from Old English into Latin, also suggest continuity of understanding through time. The circumstances in which Sideman, bishop of Crediton (d.977), was buried were recounted in the *Anglo-Saxon Chronicle* and subsequently repeated in *The History of the Church of Abingdon*, written in Latin c.1164. The *Abingdon Chronicle* makes a straight translation of the Old English *portice* to the Latin *porticu*.[12] We cannot be certain that, by the second half of the twelfth century, *porticus* still had currency as a term for an aisle chapel or transept or if it was an archaic term used for deliberate effect. But, as most authors do, the Abingdon chronicler wrote so that his readers would understand the meaning of his words. We can therefore assume with some confidence that it would not seem alien or inappropriate for him to imply that a burial could be achieved *decenter* within a building called *porticus*.

The excavated remains of St Dunstan's building at Glastonbury Abbey, although fragmentary and uncertain, give a brief but important glimpse of the relationship between pre-Conquest architecture and a post-Conquest written description of it. The Wiltshire-based monk-historian William of Malmesbury (c.1095–1193), whose mother was English and father Norman, wrote an account of the *Life of St Dunstan*. The text contains the well-known description of the building campaign undertaken by Dunstan at Glastonbury: 'That man [Dunstan], having added a tower, prolonged this [church] a great extent; and that the width might be made square to the length, he added aisles or porticus (*alas vel porticus*) as they call them.'[13]

---

[11] '*He forðferde on Idus Octobris, he is bebyrged þær innan þam mynstre innon Sanctes Nicholaus portice.*' Cecily Clark, ed., *The Peterborough Chronicle 1070–1154* (Oxford, 1958), 4.

[12] '*in porticu sancti Pauli apostoli illic decenter humatur*', John Hudson, ed. and trans., *Historia Ecclesie Abbendonensis: The History of the Church of Abingdon Volume I* (Oxford, 2007), 137–9.

[13] William Stubbs, ed., *Memorials of Saint Dunstan, Archbishop of Canterbury*, Rolls Series no. 63 (London, 1874), 271. Neither Osbern's *Sancti Dunstani* or Eadmer's

For the north-south measurement to approximate the east-west measurement of the nave and tower combined, the structures described as *alas vel porticus* must be the rectangular protrusions abutting the tower, which extend beyond the pre-existing aisles flanking the nave.[14] William of Malmesbury's notable interjection of 'as they call them' intimates his familiarity with the Anglo-Saxon use of *portice* to denote flanking chambers accessible from within the church. There is, however, a derisive intonation in William's words. In classical Latin *ala* translates to wings which, based on Glastonbury's excavated ground plan, is a fitting term for the transepts. William subtly displays his ability to employ classical terminology and, as a counterpoint to his own learnedness, the sub-clause '*vel porticus, quas vocant adiecit*' disparages the English tongue. By using the present active form *vocant* William alludes to Anglo-Saxon people calling these buildings *porticus* and suggests that his less linguistically-skilled contemporaries continued to do likewise.

William's Romanising tendencies had august precedents. Bede's use of the word *porticus* had also alluded to the architecture of Rome. His description of the burial of St Augustine, the earliest Anglo-Saxon written source to include the Latin term *porticus*, is significant because Bede chose this word, not a more conventional term such as *capella*, when referring to a chapel. Despite the formal differences between them, the author apparently saw, and wished to make, a connection between the Roman architectural term and the spaces in which elite people, including St Augustine, King Ethelbert and Queen Bertha, were laid to rest. The conscious Roman reference made by Anglo-Saxon ecclesiastics, including Bede, and why such allusions were sought, has been most eloquently discussed by Éamonn Ó Carragáin.[15]

The Continental building type termed *porticus* and the Anglo-Saxon buildings of the same name have often been distinguished; the former being an external structure, a linking building or passageway, the latter

---

Vita Sancti Dunstani (both in the same volume) use this phrase. It is notable that *porticus* is not translated. William Worcestre had more confidence: '*Longitudo a fenestra que est proxima latitudinis brachiorum, que jncipit in parte occidental latitudini brachiorum quasi anglice a porche vsque principium navis ecclesie continent .7. virgas.*' Harvey, ed., *Itineraries [of] William Worcestre*, 296.

[14] For the layout of Glastonbury Abbey see Fernie, *Architecture of the Anglo-Saxons*, 95 fig. 48.

[15] Éamonn Ó Carragáin, 'The Term *Porticus* and *Imitatio Romae*', in *Text and Gloss: Insular Learning and Literature Presented to Joseph Donovan Pheifer*, ed. Helen Conrad O'Briain, Anne Marie D'Arcy and John Scattergood (Dublin, 1999), 13–34.

an internal space, usually a side chapel.[16] In similar manner to the work of Dudley, Jackson and Fletcher in the 1950s, continued focus on formal architectural difference has enforced a distinction between Continental and Anglo-Saxon usage. But the term used for these buildings is not the only thing they have in common. The first important piece of this particular puzzle is that in the early medieval period *porticus* was firmly established as a site of burial beyond England. In the *porticus* of Old St Peter's in Rome were 'the graves of almost all the popes of the sixth and seventh centuries'.[17] However, the entrance was not the only part of the basilica referred to as *porticus*. In Continental usage the word could mean an entrance or an aisle made distinct from the nave by a row of columns. Yet neither of these meanings brings to mind the Anglo-Saxon application of *porticus* to mean a transept or chapel. The resolution of the puzzle comes through a metonymic process, that is 'substituting for the name of a thing the name of an attribute of it or of something closely related'.[18]

The meaning of *porticus* expanded from a colonnaded walkway, such as the double aisles of Old St Peter's in Rome, to include enclosed internal chapels, which were focused on a grave or relics. The starting point for this shift in meaning was Paulinus' basilica at Nola, constructed in the fifth century, and planned with four funerary chapels within the aisles (*cubicula inter porticus quaterna*).[19] By means of metonymy *porticus* became the term for the enclosed chapel as well as the part of the basilica in which it was located. The important detail is this; the term *porticus* could be appropriately adopted for internal funerary chapels because established inhumation practices took place at the west entrance in a place also termed *porticus*. The mid-eighth-century text *Notitia Ecclesiarum Urbis Romae, Codice Topografico* shows that by this date 'the word *porticus* was used for chapels or altars, even when these do not actually stand within the rows of columns of the great double aisles'.[20]

How was the Roman linguistic model for the use of *porticus* applied in the Anglo-Saxon context? The influence of Rome on Augustine's buildings at Canterbury is strongly felt in the dedications. The cathedral of Christ at Canterbury alludes to the cathedral of the Saviour in Rome (later St John Lateran) and, in being dedicated to St Peter and St Paul, the monastic foundation at Canterbury referenced St Peter's on the Vatican and St Paul's

---

[16] This distinction was set out by David Parsons in his Jarrow lecture of 1987, as quoted by Ó Carragáin: ibid., 15–16.
[17] Ibid., 20.
[18] Ibid., 25 and n.47.
[19] Ibid., 24.
[20] Ibid., 25.

Outside the Walls of Rome.[21] According to Bede, the southern *porticus* in which St Augustine and many subsequent archbishops were buried was dedicated to St Gregory (Pope Gregory the Great, 590–604). The northern *porticus*, the place of burial of the earliest Christian rulers of Kent, was dedicated to St Martin of Tours (a fourth-century Roman cavalryman who converted to Christianity after a dream vision). As Ó Carragáin succinctly states, 'It is reasonable to see in these arrangements a systematization of the situation at St Peter's on the Vatican in the early-7th century. To call the two funerary chapels *porticus* was to be faithful to the metonymic development of the word.'[22] No longer is it necessary to differentiate between the Anglo-Saxon and the Continental *porticus*. Whether a western *porticus* anticipating the church entrance or a funerary chapel placed securely within and subsuming the colonnaded aisle, by the eighth century the fundamental significance of the word *porticus* was as a place of burial and liturgical celebration.

Other textual uses of *porticus* support the suggestion that the two-fold Roman application of the term found currency in Anglo-Saxon England, and continued after the Norman Conquest, negating Dudley, Jackson and Fletcher's attempts to differentiate *porticus* and porches. What *porticus* signified was much more than the form of building. In fact it is difficult to gain a sense of the architectural specificity of any building simply termed *porticus*. Instead, the word's diachronic durability relates to its significance as a place. Writing in the 1120s, William of Malmesbury recorded that Aethelred, ealdorman of Mercia, and his wife Aethelflaed, daughter of King Alfred, were buried at Gloucester '*in porticu australi*'. As founding patrons, Aethelred and Aethelflaed had built the new minster to receive the relics of St Oswald, translated there in 909 from Bardney in Lincolnshire.[23] By being buried in the southern *porticus* the ealdorman and his royal wife actively alluded to the inhumation of King Ethelbert and Queen Bertha at Canterbury, adopting their mantle as royal founders of English Christianity in their own actions at Gloucester. The personal, intergenerational referencing might also extend to the authors. Inclusion of the *porticus* burial at Gloucester once again hints at William's own veneration and imitation of Bede, as well as evoking the precedent of Ethelbert and Bertha in the siting of Aethelred and Aethelflaed's graves.

Goscelin, monk of St Bertin, came to Canterbury in the early 1060s, before the Norman invasion of England. His corpus of writings comprises the most significant collection of hagiographic accounts of Anglo-Saxon

---

[21] Ibid., 27–8.
[22] Ibid., 28.
[23] William of Malmesbury, *Gesta Regum Anglorum, The History of the English Kings*, ed. and trans. R. M. Thomson (Oxford, 1999), volume II, chapter 5.

saints. In about 1080 Goscelin penned an account of the life of St Edith of Wilton (961–84), including the building at Wilton Abbey. The structure was enlarged 'with a three-fold porticus on the scheme of a cross'.[24] The western arm, dedicated to the Holy Trinity, was the first resting place of St Edith's body. Her remains were later translated to the southern *porticus*, dedicated to St Gabriel. The original tomb of the church's patron saint and ultimately her shrine were sited in buildings known as *porticus*, places in which, presumably, St Edith *decenter sepultum est*.

The cross-shaped ground plan adopted at Wilton, the arms of which Goscelin termed *porticus*, was also the basic form of the abbey church at Ramsey. Begun under the patronage of Oswald of Worcester, bishop of York, in the spring of 969, Ramsey was built '[i]n the fashion of a cross: a *porticus* on the east, on the south, and on the north; a tower in the middle, which having been increased might be supported by the *porticus* butting against it; then in the west he [Oswald] annexed to the tower the church.'[25] In this instance the *porticus* must be distinct arms, corresponding more to wing-like transepts than to aisles extending along the flanks of the main vessel. The cruciform plan and the appropriation of the term *porticus* for the projections which radiated from a central vessel suggest a development in the meaning of the word. Unfortunately, the extent to which the chambers were open to the church through arches, or enclosed spaces with small entrance doors, is unknown.

Further indication of *porticus* being places of regular liturgical events is provided by the *Regularis Concordia* composed c.974 by Aethelwold, bishop of Winchester. There is just one mention of *porticus* in this document, and in Symons' English translation it became a 'chapel': 'After these they shall go to Matins of All Saints singing an antiphon in honour of the saint to whom the chapel to which they are bound is dedicated: there follow Lauds of the Dead.'[26] In this context there is no mention of burial but rather remembrance and commemoration of the dead, but the intentional conjunction of honouring the dead and *porticus* is evident; it emphasises that *porticus* were places of liturgical performance.

Whilst *Regularis Concordia* gives no indication of the type of space referred to as *porticus*, the buildings at Winchester (those with which

---

[24] '*Trina porticu incrucis scemate ampliauit*', Andre Wilmart, 'La Legende de Ste Edith in prose et vers par le moine Goscelin', *Analecta Bollandiana* 56 (1938), 86.

[25] Richard Gem, 'Tenth-Century Architecture in England', in *Settimane di Studio del Centro Italiano di Studi sull'alto Medioevo, 38. Il Secolo di Ferro: Mito e Realta del Secolo X.* 2 vols (Spoleto, 1991), vol. 2, 822–3.

[26] '*Post quas eundum est ad Matutinales Laudes De Omnibus Sanctis, decantando antiphonam ad uenerationem sancti cui porticus ad quam itur dedicata est; post quas Laudes Pro Defunctis.*' Thomas Symons, trans., *The Monastic Agreement of the Monks and Nuns of the English Nation* (London, 1953), 14–15.

the Rule was most closely associated) further our discussion, although it cannot be suggested that either the east or west ends of Winchester bore any formal relation to the *porticus* referred to in the Rule. The *Life of St Aethelwold*, written by his student Wulfstan, mentions King Eadred's benefaction in the mid tenth century and his intention, life permitting, 'to decorate the eastern *porticus* [*porticum*] of the same church at Winchester with gilded tiles' – a possible allusion to the gilded walls of Solomon's Temple.[27] The east end of the church as it would have been known by Eadred was a square vessel which survived from the church built by Cenwalh in the 640s.[28] In the event, the Old Minster at Winchester did not undergo major alteration until Aethelwold set about creating a building in keeping with the demands of the monastic reform movement in the late tenth century. In his *Narratio Metrica de S. Swithuno*, a hexametrical poem recounting the life and translation of St Swithin, Wulfstan explains how Aethelwold repaired the Old Minster with the provision of high walls and new roofs, strengthening its southern and northern parts with firm *porticus* and arches.[29] As was the case at Ramsey, the Winchester *porticus* supported a structure of greater height. The passage continues:

> And he added several buildings for sacred altars, which keep the entrance of the threshold doubtful, so that whoever walks these atria with unfamiliar tread, knows not from what place he passes, nor to which place he is carried by his feet, because in all directions openings are to be seen.[30]

Evidently the 'various arches' created access routes, for the eyes and the feet, between the different chambers, including the *porticus* which flanked the *atria*.

To secure our awareness of the English adoption of a Roman model for the *porticus* as a place of liturgical performance we can turn to a final example: the twelfth-century Ely chronicle, *Liber Eliensis*. The history of the abbey is told with people at its centre, and through their experiences we learn something of its buildings, including the *porticus*. Some years after the Danes had burnt the abbey in 870, a group of eight monks returned to the church and '[p]atching up the *porticus* of the church as best they could at a time of such calamity, they carried out due observance of the divine

---

[27] Wulfstan of Winchester, *Life of St Aethelwold*, ed. and trans. Michael Lapidge and Michael Winterbottom (Oxford, 1991), 18–19 and n.4

[28] See Fernie, *Architecture of the Anglo-Saxons*, 98 fig. 50.

[29] See Wulfstan of Winchester, *St Aethelwold*, 29 n.2.

[30] This translation is the author's own.

office'.[31] Here, once again, we see the ease with which a twelfth-century historian could use the word *porticus* to describe a lost ninth-century liturgical building. Such a text shows how the use of *porticus* for an internal liturgical space was frequently and confidently used well into the twelfth century, despite William of Malmesbury's attempted dismissal of the term.

Building in Solomon's Wake

The cultural connotations of the term *porticus* were maintained in England from the seventh to the twelfth century, encouraged by an intellectual climate in which history writing, chronicle and hagiography, was the primary route to understanding the past and present. The origins and antecedents of English church porches rely not only on Roman influences and continuation of Anglo-Saxon traditions, but also the influence of biblical history on European architecture from the late eleventh century. Medieval architecture was a mnemonic mode, forging associations between buildings and people beyond the constraints of human chronology.[32] Stephen Murray's study of the Sainte-Chapelle sets out the range of references apparent in this one remarkable structure, clearly demonstrating the medieval interest in combining forms and principles from contemporary and historical buildings, what he terms 'the synchronic power of architecture'.[33] Amongst the Sainte-Chapelle's mnemonic allusions was the work of the Old Testament King Solomon. The use of biblical prototypes was not seen as out-dated, out-moded or retrospective in any negative sense.[34] Medieval buildings contain mixed messages and contradictions in the language of their forms, conflations of classical, biblical and contemporary history. They 'should never be treated as a passive receptacle'.[35] The currency of ancient architectural prototypes was highly valued in medieval England, but, as will be seen, not at the expense of innovation and progressive design.

---

[31] Janet Fairweather, trans., *Liber Eliensis: A History of the Isle of Ely from the Seventh Century to the Twelfth* (Woodbridge, 2005), 75.

[32] Peter Fergusson, 'Modernization and Mnemonics at Christ Church, Canterbury: The Treasury Building', *Journal of the Society of Architectural Historians* 65.1 (2006), 50–67; Stephen Murray, 'The Architectural Envelope of the Sainte-Chapelle of Paris', in *Pierre, Lumiere, Couleur: Etudes de histoire de l'art du moyen age en l'honneur de Anne Prache: Cultures et Civilisations Médiévale, 20*, ed. Fabienne Joubert and Dany Sandron (Paris, 1999), 223–30.

[33] Murray, 'The Architectural Envelope', 229.

[34] For pertinent discussion of the relationship between invention and tradition see Paul Binski, *Gothic Wonder: Art, Artifice, and the Decorated Style, 1290–1350* (New Haven, 2014), 68–76.

[35] Murray, 'The Architectural Envelope', 230.

Builders and patrons of medieval porches could wish for no greater ancestor than King Solomon and the architecture he commissioned, as recounted in the First Book of Kings, the Second Book of Chronicles and the prophecies of Ezekiel the priest. *Porticus* were specified constituents of Solomon's Temple and his royal palace. Narratives of their construction campaigns in the three Old Testament books present how the buildings' forms were specified. They present the sense of an architectural blueprint and the translation of an idea into built reality, a process which (as discussed below) would subsequently inspire Richard of St Victor's exploration of Solomon's *porticus* in his *Commentary on Ezekiel*.

To King David God gave instruction for the Temple to be built; to Solomon God gave responsibility for its realisation.[36] In his first-hand account of the situation King David speaks directly to his people: 'Hear me, my brethren and my people: I had a thought to have built a house, in which the ark of the Lord, and the footstool of our God might rest: and I prepared all things for the building. And God said to me: Thou shalt not build a house to my name: because thou art a man of war, and hast shed blood.' Continuing, David confirms Solomon was God's chosen builder: 'And he said to me: Solomon thy son shall build my house, and my courts: for I have chosen him to be my son, and I will be a father to him. And I will establish his kingdom for ever, if he continue to keep my commandments, and my judgements, as at this day.' (1 Chronicles 28.2–7).[37] Solomon inherited from his warring father a kingdom at peace and his role was to consolidate the nation's security by governing well through adherence to God's will.[38]

'David gave to Solomon his son a description of the porch, and of the temple, and of the treasure, and of the upper floor, and of the inner chambers, and of the house of the mercy seat' (1 Chronicles 28.11). Whether Solomon received the description verbally or visually is not told, but the chronicler's words conjure experiential notions rather than physical forms (the treasury, upper floor, inner chambers) and *porticus* can here

---

[36] Gerard Brett stated that of Solomon's three legendary roles, of magician, wise man and builder, in medieval England 'the third one seems to have been the main one from the start'. Gerard Brett, 'King Solomon in the Middle Ages', in *The Collected Prestonian Lectures, volume 2, 1961–1974*, ed. Harry Carr (London, 1983).

[37] Biblical passages are taken from the Latin Vulgate or Douay Rheims editions, unless otherwise stated.

[38] For discussion of the interpretation of King Solomon in the Book of Chronicles and his role as God's chosen builder see Roddy L. Braun, 'Solomonic Apologetic in Chronicles', *Journal of Biblical Literature* 92.4 (1973), 503–16; and Roddy Braun, 'Solomon, the Chosen Temple Builder: The Significance of 1 Chronicles 22, 28, and 29 for the Theology of Chronicles', *Journal of Biblical Literature* 95.4 (1976), 581–90.

be taken as allegorical with implications beyond formal appearance. Solomon's priority was to build the Temple, which took seven years (1 Kings 6.38). The duration of the building campaign would become a topos for medieval architectural patrons; Eadmer's chronicling of Archbishop Lanfranc's seven-year campaign to rebuild Christchurch Canterbury in the late eleventh century being one such instance. Brief but revealing mention of the Temple porch unmistakably shows the *porticus* to be a forebuilding, described as 'before the temple' (*ante templum*, 1 Kings 6.3) or 'in the front' (*ante frontem*, 2 Chronicles 3.4). Old Testament texts also present a basic template for the porch and key repeatable design elements, sufficient to give a sense of what the building looked like and sufficient for later builders to weave into the fabric of their own structures. The Temple porch measured 20 cubits long, 10 cubits wide and 120 cubits high (1 Kings 6.3; 2 Chronicles 3.4). A standard cubit approximates to the length of a man's forearm, from elbow to the tip of his middle finger, around 18in. On this basis the Temple porch measured (in English feet) 30ft long, 15ft wide and 180ft high. Solomon's Temple porch was therefore a form of tower, rising from a 2:1 rectangular ground plan.

The Old Testament chronicler also noted specific design elements and materials. The interior of the Temple porch was gilded, 'overlaid ... within with pure gold' (*et deauravit eam intrinsecus auro mundissimo*: 2 Chronicles 3.4). The same finish was used on the building's main vessel, indicating a continuity of effect from one chamber to the next. The main details of the porch's form and decoration are intimately associated with Hiram of Tyre, who was summoned by Solomon to work on the Temple because of his reputation as 'an artificer in brass, and full of wisdom, and understanding, and skill' (1 Kings 7.14). Hiram provided materials but most importantly a work force of skilled labour able to realise Solomon's vision. The master craftman's own contributions were not the mundane stone blocks composing the bulk of the building; his skill was directed towards ornament, decoration and furnishings of lavish detail and proportions. In the porch, at the entrance to the Temple, two large pillars were erected, the heads, or chapiters, decorated with rows of chain-like wreaths and set with pomegranates; that on the right hand called Jachin and that on the left Booz (1 Kings 7.13–22; 2 Chronicles 3.15–17). The elaboration at the top of these pillars was made in the manner of lilies (*opus in modum lilii*) and completion of this detailing brought the work to an end.

Once work was complete on the Temple, Solomon turned to building his own residence, a palace complex containing the seat of his power and governance founded on his selection by God and his promotion as David's chosen son and successor. Architecture was a mode adopted by Solomon for the construction and maintenance of his irrefutable authority, and the royal complex he built included three porches:

> And he made a porch of pillars of fifty cubits in length, and thirty cubits in breadth: and another porch before the greater porch, and pillars, and chapiters upon the pillars. He made also the porch of the throne wherein is the seat of judgement; and covered it with cedar wood from the floor to the top. (1 Kings 7.6–7)

Precisely where the first mentioned porch was located is not specified beyond it being related to the main vessel (the house or *domum*) but its primacy is conveyed in the same passage. A second porch (*alteram porticum*) is described as '*in facie maioris porticus*' which, as translated in both the Wycliffite and the Douay-Rheims Bibles, clearly means 'before' or 'in front of' the greater porch.

The 'greater porch' was 50 cubits in length and 30 cubits in width (approximately 75ft x 45ft) and proportionally had a length/width ratio of 5:3. Like the porch of the Temple, this ground plan is rectangular but here the height is not stated. Architectural detail is scant but, importantly, the passage commences: 'And he made a porch of pillars' (*et porticum columnarum fecit*). Emphasis is on the pillars as giving the building form and solidity, they were structural rather than ornamental and implicitly the porch was built as an open arcade rather than with solid walls. This makes it unlikely that in height the 'greater porch' was tower-like, and therefore a fundamentally different sort of structure to the porch of the Temple. It is fitting that references to buildings attributed to King Solomon as *porticus* convey the same inconsistency of built form as do the texts discussed in the first half of this chapter. Clearly the multiple and fluid meanings of the term *porticus* have deep historical resonances.

The third porch, built of woven cedarwood (*est fecit et texit lignis cedrinis*), contained the seat of judgement (*solii in qua tribunal*) in a separate structure termed *domuncula* (1 Kings 7.7–8). The phrasing of the biblical passage leaves the architectural arrangement unclear but medieval visual representations of Solomon enthroned show that it was understood to be a seat raised above a flight of steps and placed beneath a vault or canopy. Medieval visual conceptions of the *domuncula* offer varying interpretations. Either the canopy and the *porticus* are conflated, or Solomon sits upon a raised throne with integral canopy, all of which is set within a porch. The latter form clearly construes the *porticus* as made of pillars, implying that the porch of the throne was formally comparable to the 'greater porch' of the preceding verse. As an example of the former, see British Library MS Sloane 361, f. 13, and of the latter British Library MS Royal 18 D X, f. 244.

Commentary on Ezekiel Chapter 40

Chapter 40 of Ezekiel's prophecies augments insight into the biblical application of the term *porticus* gathered from the history writing of Kings and Chronicles. Essentially framed as a dream narrative, Ezekiel's account conveys his prophetic experience of being guided by God to witness a city built in the land of Israel. God set Ezekiel on a very high mountain, with the city to the south. Revealed to him is the manifestation of God's promise to those who adhere to his law and Ezekiel's job was to relate all that he saw to the Israelites who, at this time, were captives. Their suffering resulted from their disobedience; the envisioned land would be reward for obedience. The city Ezekiel was shown was evidently that built by Solomon. At the start of his tour around the complex of buildings, the prophet encounters 'a man, whose appearance was like the appearance of brass, with a line of flax in his hand, and a measuring reed in his hand, and he stood in the gate' (Ezekiel 40.3) – the 'man' is the personification of the brass pillars cast by Hiram of Tyre to flank the Temple porch. This is the first of several instances in Ezekiel 40 where *porticus* is not used although one might expect it to be. Using the term *porta* (gate) rather than *porticus* (porch) emphasises that where the pillar/man stands is an entrance, a means of accessing the building. The word choice implies a structure which blurs the distinction between outside and inside space. The imprecision, or rather the multiplicity of meaning, renders the word *porticus* potentially misleading and to ensure clarity other terms could, as here, be substituted.

The bewildering confusion of buildings, entrances and chambers mentioned by Ezekiel leaves one doubting the form of the building described. At verse 48 of the same chapter, the narrative clarifies the priest-prophet's situation; the Latin Vulgate reads '*et introduxit me in vestibulum templi*'. English translations of this text, including the Wycliffite, King James and Douay-Rheims versions, consistently translate *vestibulum* as porch and in doing so the complexes built by Solomon, recounted in the book of Chronicles, resonate with those witnessed in vision by Ezekiel. This penultimate verse specifies that, in the context of Ezekiel's vision, *vestibulum* connoted the structure's meaning with buildings which elsewhere in the Bible are referred to as *porticus*. Recognising this difference does not simply highlight terminological inconsistencies. It suggests that observation of other instances where the term *vestibulum* is employed in Ezekiel 40 may provide insight into the type of buildings which in modern parlance, as the Douay-Rheims translation shows, might be termed 'porch'. Doing so reveals two elements which deserve attention: the first being windows and the second steps.

Windows were a feature of the porches as witnessed by Ezekiel: *et in vestibulis fenestrae per gyrum intrinsecus* (Ezekiel 40.16, and the same detail is repeated in verse 25). The passage establishes a biblical precedent for their inclusion in the design of medieval porches, and in the absence of detail specifying size, location or fitments, architectural designers had *carte blanche* to invent. The character of the steps leading to the porch is a little more complicated, and they differ numerically from porch to porch: that before the gates of the palace is preceded by seven steps, the porch of the Temple has eight steps leading to it. Within Ezekiel 40 is also a plethora of measurements and lengths relating to the buildings being viewed. How these measurements, and other elements of the Temple porch, should be interpreted was addressed in the twelfth century by Richard of St Victor.

Richard (d.1173), the Scottish-born prior of the Parisian Augustinian abbey of St Victor, adopted the mode of an illustrated commentary to investigate the viability of the structures that Ezekiel witnessed. Those illustrations, particularly the elevation drawings, tell much about the medieval re-imagining of the Temple complex and are available to us through multiple manuscript versions dateable to the second half of the twelfth century. According to Walter Cahn, whose seminal article investigates how Richard apparently made sense of Ezekiel's visions, '[u]nlike the plans, whose reticent geometry might well belong to any time, the elevations are immediately recognisable as medieval architecture'.[39] The Victorine mystic-scholar tackled the problem of the steps preceding the porch. His practical treatment of the eight steps is to place them within the porch rather than outside. This permits negotiation of a hillside without needing to level an area of ground to provide a floor of the porch.[40] As visually translated, the building is composed of three storeys on the façade side but only two on the inner side. Key features of the buildings are wall arches, pairs of windows segregated by a central column, internal divisions glimpsed as though through the windows, and internal and external crenellated walls. The image is devised for optical exploration of how the structure's volumes, spaces and formal attributes might be composed.

King Solomon's building campaigns contained several structures termed as *porticus*. However, the term lacked sufficient precision in certain instances and was substituted by *porta* or *vestibulum*, whichever was most appropriate to the context and could connote the building's significance

---

[39] Walter Cahn, 'Architectural Draftsmanship in Twelfth-Century Paris: The Illustrations of Richard of Saint-Victor's Commentary on Ezekiel's Temple Vision', *Gesta* 15.1-2 (1976), *Essays in Honor of Sumner McKnight Crosby*, 250.

[40] Cahn also notes examples of porches with internal flights of steps on mountainous sites in the Auvergne region of France: the church of Châtel-Montagne and the cathedral of Le Puy-en-Velay (ibid., 250, 254).

most effectively. The biblical texts provided a model to medieval commissioning patrons and designing architects in two ways: the first being the dimensions of the ground plan which could be translated as proportional ratios just as readily as they could provide actual measurements, and the second were formal features vital to the designed character of the buildings, including the prominence of pillars and the presence of windows. These elements, when built into the design of a church porch, could serve as architectural conductors of iconographic significance from biblical past to medieval present. The royal person of Solomon and his master craftsman Hiram of Tyre also offered a model for medieval architectural patrons and their masons. Processes of commissioning, designing and constructing a building in medieval Europe are rich seams of insight into how this sphere of medieval life could function. Thoughts on where Solomon's influence is perceptible in the fabric of English porches will be picked up again later in this book.

The Architecture of Words and the Language of Buildings

In its narrowest sense 'architectural iconography', as a study of the symbolism of churches and their fittings, counts as one of the oldest art historical disciplines. From Isidore of Seville in the seventh century and William Durandus in the thirteenth, to Joseph Sauer's monumental volume on the symbolism of churches published in 1924, medieval churches and their components have been encoded and decoded with a bewildering variety of analogies and references.[41]

Paul Crossley's words cut through to the inherent challenge faced by all medievalists, whether students of the period's history, politics, literature, music, art or architecture. The primary sources available to us are scant at best, and often entirely absent largely because modern minds ask and seek answers to questions which pre-Humanist intellects rarely considered of any interest or relevance. Yet buildings stimulate us to understand them and have done so for millennia (as Crossley's summary avers). Imaginative responses or inventive interpretations give meaning to architectural forms, but they need not be fixed, permanent or singular.[42] That is not to suggest

---

[41] Paul Crossley, 'Medieval Architecture and Meaning: The Limits of Iconography', *The Burlington Magazine* 130.1019 (1988), 116.

[42] Here I agree with William Whyte, who terms the perceptible shifts in meaning as 'transitions' and gives to the historian responsibility for tracing them 'as a way to uncover the meanings of architecture': William Whyte, 'How Do Buildings

that all interpretations or explanations of historical meaning are pertinent or of equal validity – art history is not an intellectual exercise in inventive liberty. Contextualising iconographic relevance and its interpretation in its historical moment is paramount, so too is attending to the palimpsest nature of diachronically accrued meaning.

The joint model of the Temple and King Solomon is well recognised as having influenced the art and architecture of medieval England, a notable example being the eleventh and twelfth century work at Canterbury Cathedral priory and conventual buildings. As Peter Fergusson has demonstrated, in form, materials and elaboration, the cathedral's Treasury and Prior Wibert's *Aula Nova* perform as architectural mnemonic devices, forging memory pathways between monastic Canterbury and biblical prototypes.[43] Fergusson is also intellectually courageous enough to ask the crucial question – how could a medieval patron (in this case Prior Wibert) be aware of the archetypes, such as the Temple of Solomon, that modern scholarship wishes to impose upon his buildings? European interest in Solomon's Temple was renewed following the conquest of Jerusalem by the first crusaders in 1099. Exploration of the Temple was both intellectual and practical, with crusaders repairing and rebuilding the surviving monuments they found and seeking scriptural understanding through lived reality. Twelfth-century European scholarship also embraced the opportunity to set theological exegesis on a new course derived from practically-obtained knowledge as a complement to moral and allegorical foundations. Intellectual elites, including Richard of St Victor, were at the forefront of these architectural investigations, but the Bible and interpretation of its contents touched every corner of medieval society. The Bible was the book most numerously reproduced in manuscript and incunabula through the Middle Ages and its content, aided by exegetical intercession, provided guidance on every challenge faced through earthly life. In architectural terms the biblical accounts of Solomon's Temple in Jerusalem were 'the source *par excellence*' and the 'accounts written by pilgrims visiting the *loca sancta* would have supplemented the scriptural accounts'.[44]

The immediate context for Prior Wibert's work at Canterbury was St Anselm's rebuilding of the eastern arm of his cathedral church, commencing in the last decade of the eleventh century. Fergusson's proposition is that Wibert's interest in Solomon and the Temple was both a continuation of the earlier work and honourable reference (a 'lithic genuflection') to the former archbishop. Solomonic influence has also been recognised in

---

Mean? Some Issues of Interpretation in the History of Architecture', *History and Theory* 45.2 (2006), 155.

[43] Fergusson, 'Modernization and Mnemonics', 59.

[44] Ibid., 50–67.

St Anselm's own architectural achievements at Canterbury, which fluently align and meld Old Testament templates with modes acquired directly from Anselm's knowledge and experience of Rome.[45] The way in which Solomon's Temple served English medieval architecture was as an archetype rather than as a tangible model; a skeleton needing to be fleshed out and, at least in the case of Christchurch Canterbury, the buildings of Rome, most notably the Lateran, provided much of that flesh.[46] Canterbury Cathedral priory exemplifies how the cultural utility of European medieval architecture was connoted visually, mnemonically and allegorically, generative of an artistic mode independent from representation, imitative likeness or iconographic imagery.

The 'cleanest' (least cluttered) means of linking one's own architecture to that of Solomon, however, was to integrate specific details drawn from the biblical accounts. Whilst the influence of the Old Testament king on patrons of architecture in the Christian West has long been recognised, one obvious line of enquiry – comparing medieval porches with those built by Solomon – has not been attempted before. Accepting that Solomon's Temple, palace and judgement seat held currency in the minds of those inventing the forms of English medieval architecture, it is to be expected that the influence of *porticus Salomonis* will be traceable in the English medieval *porticus*. However, the term's lack of inherent specificity poses difficulties. What buildings should we turn to if we wish to investigate the influence of Solomon's porches in medieval England? Continuing with the methodology adopted so far in this chapter, and allying with Crossley's sentiments, identifying a building which was termed *porticus* by contemporary writers permits investigation of designs and forms nominated as *porticus*; one such instance is the chapter house at Lincoln Cathedral, as conveyed in the writing of the poet Henry of Avranches (d.1262).

The earliest written source to directly associate a medieval English building with Solomon's porch, Henry's *Metrical Life of St Hugh* was written at the same time as, or very soon after, the construction of the Lincoln chapter house between 1220 and 1235. Of the poem's 1308 lines, 132 are an encomium to the new edifice.[47] Within his narrative Henry twists together

---

[45] T. A. Heslop, 'Contemplating Chimera in Medieval Imagination: St Anselm's Crypt at Canterbury', in *Raising the Eyebrow: John Onians and World Art Studies*, BAR International Series 996, ed. Lauren Golden (Oxford, 2001), 153–68.

[46] Fergusson's paper also presents the case for buildings in Rome serving as architectural models for the Treasury Building and suggests that 'business trips' of Canterbury personnel in the mid twelfth century would have given them first-hand knowledge of the papal court at the Lateran. Fergusson, 'Modernization and Mnemonics', 64.

[47] Paul Binski, *Becket's Crown: Art and Imagination in Gothic England, 1170–1300* (New Haven and London, 2004), 56.

two strands of architectural meaning. The process of construction is presented as an act of humility to exemplify Hugh's spiritual propriety whilst the resulting building is an expression of theoretical iconographies, for example, 'soaring walls and a vault reaching towards the stars'.[48] Henry of Avranches presents good evidence of the way in which medieval authors brought together significances from sources which to the modern mind may seem contradictory or at least inconsistent and thereby ill-considered. The passage that includes mention of a *porticus* demonstrates this point:

> Beside the cathedral stands the chapter house, which has a character that never a Roman roof possessed; the coin wealth of Croesus would scarcely make a start on the marvellous work of it. Its entrance way is like a square porch, while inside there extends a circular space, rivalling Solomon's Temple in its materials and skill.[49]

The textility of the biblical and classical references is notable, allusions to the *porticus* of Solomon's Temple and, in the combination of a square forebuilding preceding a circular inner hall, an intellectual nod to the Roman Pantheon.[50] The *Metrical Life* shows that Henry clearly took inspiration from the writings of Roman poet Ovid, particularly his *Metamorphoses*. This creative debt contextualises Henry's act of drawing connections between architectural models of classical Rome and the form of the new work at Lincoln.

For investigations into porches, however, the primary interest is in Henry's use of the term *porticus* when referring to the chapterhouse entrance. Doing this enhanced the allegorical association between this cathedral and Solomon's Temple, and the chapterhouse was not alone. A Solomonic architectural motif may already have existed at Lincoln when Henry was composing his poem. Beyond the eastern apse of the building, begun in 1192 and superseded by the Angel Choir, was a large hexagonal chapel. This eastern-most element has been explained as a version of the corona at Canterbury.[51] In essence a centrally planned octagonal structure,

---

[48] Ibid.
[49] '*Astant ecclesiae capitolia, qualia nunquam/ Romanus possedit apex; spectabile quorum/ Vix opus inciperet nummosa pecunia Croesi./ Scilicet introitus ipsorum sunt quasi quadra/ Porticus; interius spatium patet orbiculare,/ Materia tentans templum Salomonis et arte.*' Otto Lehmann-Brockhaus, *Lateinische Schriftquellen zur Kunst in England, Wales und Schottland vom Jahre 901 bis zum Jahre 1307, Band II.* (Munich, 1956), 30. The English translation above is taken from C. Garton, ed. and trans., *Metrical Life of St Hugh* (Lincoln, 1986), 61, except that I have replaced 'portico' with 'porch'.
[50] Binski, *Becket's Crown*, 57.
[51] Peter Kidson, 'Architectural History', in *A History of Lincoln Minster*, ed. Dorothy Owen (Cambridge, 1994), 27.

the Canterbury corona might have been one reference, but it does not justify Lincoln's hexagonal shape, which continues to require explanation. Lincoln's eastern apsidal chapel was an architectural hexagram and as such contained a geometric device closely associated with King Solomon. Implicitly Henry of Avranches' interests in conveying the chapter house's structural significance as alluding to King Solomon's architectural experiments were immediately present at the church about which he wrote.

Another, more contentious, textual indication that Solomon's Temple porch was employed as a model for English church porches is the north porch at Salisbury Cathedral – the *porta speciosa* or 'beautiful gate' (Acts 3.10).[52] The north entrance carrying this epithet dates to the mid fifteenth century and therefore tells that those who knew and experienced the porch many years after its construction saw this biblical allusion in the building. Investigation of the architecture provides some indication that the thirteenth-century designers were cognisant of the same reference. As noted below, the contemporary writer William Durandus also linguistically conflated gates and porches.

As already noted, it is the dimensions of Solomonic porches that are most readily comprehensible. Therefore, a good basis on which to enquire of the Solomonic influence on a medieval porch is the ground plan. The building of a new cathedral at Salisbury began c.1213–18, the ceremony of laying the foundation stone took place in 1220, and in 1226 the building was sufficiently complete for the tombs of Bishops Osmund, Roger and Jocelyn to be translated from the site at Old Sarum.[53] Construction work progressed westward down the nave and the north porch (fig. 5) was built as an integral part of this original scheme, its masonry neatly and continuously coursing with that of the adjacent nave walls. The nave at Salisbury was laid out according to a standardised grid system, made up of squares each measuring 19ft 6in. This proportional formality is found in the nave, but not in the eastern arm. The standard bay length of the nave is 19ft 6in, the width of the main vessel is 39ft and the overall internal width is 78ft. Therefore the aisles, being of equal width, are 19ft 6in.[54] Given the proximity between the north porch and the nave we might expect that the *porta speciosa* would follow in the nave's footprints and be either square or a 2:1 rectangle composed of two 19ft 6in squares. Whilst its width/length ratio is 2:1 it is not based on the nave's standard unit of measurement and

---

[52] Thomas Cocke and Peter Kidson, *Salisbury Cathedral: Perspectives on the Architectural History* (London, 1996), 4. Lehmann-Brockhaus does not provide a reference for the use of *porta speciosa* at Salisbury and this is evidence against the tag being used pre-1307.

[53] Cocke and Kidson, *Salisbury Cathedral*, 3.

[54] Ibid., 62.

5 Exterior view, north porch, Salisbury Cathedral.
Reproduced with thanks to Salisbury Cathedral

cannot be explained as two additional conjoined nave-bays. The porch measures 36ft 4in (north-south) by 18ft 2in (east-west). The evidence of the building's label (at least from 1443) of *porta speciosa* references Acts 3.1–11, and the ratio of width to breadth of 2:1 echoes the ground plan of the porch before the Temple (1 Kings 6.3). Together the nomenclatural and dimensional evidence suggests that the north porch at Salisbury was designed as an architectural allusion to the Temple porch in Jerusalem. Once the Salisbury porch is explored with this significance in mind, other architectural elements can also be explained.

6 Interior view, north porch, Salisbury Cathedral.
Reproduced with thanks to Salisbury Cathedral

Primary to the design of the Salisbury porch interior are three registers of stone shafts (fig. 6). At the lowest register, a regular parade of shafts with capitals and bases supports a continuous frieze of cusped arches. At the mid-point on each side, an additional shaft extends beyond the row of arches and links the lower register with the one above and ultimately with the ceiling vault. The upper register is also adorned with shafts, this time arranged as a gallery of two-bay units, each unit having a framing arch and tympanum pierced by a quatrefoil. Shafts are a defining characteristic of Salisbury Cathedral, perhaps even of architectural design of the period, but that does not diminish their potential to have connotative resonance. This visual plethora of shafts creates a sense of a building constructed of pillars, and the clustering of shafts at both entrances (the entrance into the porch and from the porch into the church) strengthens this notion. The model for a building constructed of pillars is not the porch of the Temple but the Great Porch of Solomon's own palace: '*et porticum columnarum fecit*' (1 Kings 7.6). The jambs of the entrance to the north porch at Salisbury display a dramatic alternation system, interchanging shafts of dark Purbeck marble with those of the light-coloured limestone, probably local Chilmark, of which the bulk of the church is understood to be built. At the entrance and within the porch, Purbeck marble is only used for shafts and, in being monolithic, these are distinguished from the Chilmark stone in form as well as effect.

Reading these shafts as references to Solomonic architecture is loaded with uncertainty, at least in part because it is a design motif prevalent throughout Salisbury Cathedral, not specific to the north porch. But the fifteenth-century soubriquet *porta speciosa* gives weight to the suggestion, so too the distinctive plan measurements. An important factor in the circumstances of building the new cathedral at Salisbury was rivalry, specifically rivalry with the building under construction at Wells, about 45 miles to the west. Historical circumstances had caused a long tradition of friction between the two communities. The relocation of Sarum cathedral to a virgin site inevitably stripped away the tangible bonds that living members of the community could share with their community's past, through the longevity of association with place and the building where they worshipped. Continuity of the see between sites was emphasised by the translation of the bishops' tombs from Old Sarum into the new cathedral.[55] In addition, I suggest, the desire to construct a new architectural lineage was also part of the rationale for the building's design. If the biblical account of Solomon's building projects did provide a model for the north porch, this new building on a virgin site was invented to take its place in a direct line of descent from Solomon's architectural activities in observance of God's will.[56]

Lincoln and Salisbury are particularly relevant to the theme traced through the whole of this chapter, the fungibility of the term *porticus* and

---

[55] Ibid., 94.
[56] Fergusson's discussion of the Solomonic underpinning of Prior Wibert's modernisation of Canterbury Cathedral priory notes that the use of expensive marbles in Wibert's Great Cloister was imitated at the Temple Church (c.1160), at Durham (c.1170), and in the choir and Trinity chapel at Canterbury after the 1174 fire. See Peter Fergusson, *Canterbury Cathedral Priory in the Age of Becket* (New Haven and London, 2011), 57. In this historical context the influence of Jerusalem on the building of Salisbury would appear not to have been restricted to the porch.

the forms of buildings it connotes. In the case of the entrance to the chapter house at Lincoln, investigation was of a structure unlikely today to be called a 'porch' but which a contemporary writer termed *porticus*. By contrast, the north entrance to Salisbury is today commonly referred to as the 'north porch' but in the fifteenth century was labelled the 'beautiful gate' (*porta speciosa* not *porticu speciosa*). There can be little doubt that the reference made is to Acts 3.10. The arguments I have presented for the north porch at Salisbury's *porta speciosa* being modelled on the textual accounts of Solomon's porch building is founded on its fifteenth-century epithet, the 2:1 width/length ratio and the prominent semi-precious faux-marble shafts. As a one-off example, Salisbury would not be sufficient evidence to argue plausibly for Solomonic allusions being widely adopted in the architecture of English medieval porches. However, the abundance of architectural evidence available in other examples collectively demonstrates that *porticus Salomonis* was a prevalent archetype for medieval porch builders. It is now time to investigate the most prominent examples.

In England only three medieval church porches are built on a hexagonal plan: St Mary Redcliffe, Bristol, St Mary's, Chipping Norton and St Lawrence's, Ludlow.[57] The six-sided ground plan is such a rarity in medieval buildings that, as a group, these porches are notable, although by far the most elaborate and architecturally ambitious is the famous example at Redcliffe.[58] Unconventional in shape, the north porch at Redcliffe is also curious for being an appendage to a pre-existing porch. Prosaic explanations have been offered, notably that sometime before c.1320 an additional porch was necessitated when the existing one became the site of a cult miracle-working image of the Virgin.[59] Pervasive popularity of Decorated style, its forms and characteristic enjoyment of the unexpected certainly suffuses the Redcliffe porch. It was strongly contemporary in character and a major contributor to early fourteenth-century architectural experiments with surface decoration and the staging of public sculpture in the context of grandiose entrance buildings.[60] The hexagonal plan does, of course, have its antecedents in England and elsewhere, including the canopy over

[57] Documentary evidence suggests that the Ludlow porch was built sometime before 1327/8, as in that year Matthew Hoptone was paid to repair it. See Michael Faraday, *Ludlow 1085–1660. A Social, Economic and Political History* (Chichester, 1991), 53, n.5 and n.6.

[58] Other hexagonal buildings include the church towers at Ozleworth (Gloucestershire) and Swindon (Wiltshire). See Fernie, *Architecture of the Anglo-Saxons*, 243, and the previously discussed eastern chapel at Lincoln.

[59] Wilson, 'St Mary Redcliffe', 413.

[60] Julian Luxford, 'Architecture and Environment: St Benet's Holm and the Fashioning of the English Monastic Gatehouse', *Architectural History* 57 (2014), 31–72. Luxford does not mention the Redcliffe porch in this paper but its design, perhaps

the shrine of St-Sernin at Toulouse (1258, destroyed) or the Eleanor Cross of Waltham.[61] Undoubtedly a subtle admixture of architectural reference is bound together in the Redcliffe porch, but the primary idealised models for its form were, I suggest, *porticus Salomonis*.

The striking hexagonal porch is the aesthetic façade and main entrance to Redcliffe church, but it does not give access into the main vessel. When the hexagon was constructed c.1320 the church already had a north porch. No matter how the building of a hexagon resonates, the decision not to demolish the existing porch must be taken as significant. The combination of both structures, old and new, did not create a double-depth porch; the formal dissimilarity between the two buildings precludes their integration and both porches remain independent spaces. The arrangement is legible as two porches, one set before the other. Redcliffe's northern entrance complex is a patent fourteenth-century realisation of the text '*et alteram porticum in facie maioris porticus*' (1 Kings 7.7) and its arrangement sheds light on how this passage was read. Redcliffe's north porches encourage the word *maioris* to be understood in the sense of bestowing honour and esteem, specifying not that the porch is of great size but rather of great distinction and venerability. This chimes well with the decision taken at Redcliffe not to destroy the c.1200 porch but to employ it as a significant part in a new architectural programme. The inner porch was august, respected, and served the needs of the anonymous designer well in his interpretation of the biblical passage.[62] In playing with the concept of two porches and their architectural relationship with the Temple porch, the designing mason at Redcliffe made a series of responses to the biblical model, perhaps the most obvious being the hexagonal plan of the outer porch.[63]

The hexagonal ground plan is an architectural adaption of the hexagram, the six stellar points of which coincide with the angles of a geometric hexagon. Also known as the 'shield of David', the hexagram's designation as the 'seal of Solomon' has a deep history, for example in sixth-century

---

its very existence, owes much to the fourteenth-century explosion of interest in entrance architecture, including monastic gatehouses.

[61] Wilson, 'St Mary Redcliffe', 413; Binski, *Gothic Wonder*, 70–1.

[62] According to the study of medieval moulding profiles by Richard Morris, Redcliffe porch has more likeness with Malmesbury Abbey and Wells Cathedral than with other Bristol buildings. See Richard K. Morris, 'Thomas Witney at Exeter, Winchester and Wells', in *Medieval Art and Architecture at Exeter Cathedral*, British Archaeological Conference Transactions for 1985, ed. Frances Kelly (Leeds, 1991), 57–84.

[63] It has been suggested that the outer porch was the earlier work of the designer of the choir of Bristol Cathedral: Wilson, 'St Mary Redcliffe', 413.

Byzantine talismanic amulets.[64] In texts, the association of the hexagram with the seal of Solomon is conveyed in *The Testament of Solomon*, a Greek magical work in which the seal is the powerful weapon Solomon wields over demonic forces. In the narrative Solomon speaks directly to the reader, it is his own testament of building the Temple. Having heard from a young boy that each night a demon came and stole his food, Solomon goes to the Temple and prays with all his soul that he might have power and authority over the demon. Whilst in prayer Solomon received 'a little ring, having a seal consisting of an engraved stone' from the archangel St Michael, with the words 'Take, O Solomon, king, son of David, the gift which the Lord God has sent thee, the highest Sabaoth. With it thou shalt lock up all the demons of the earth, male and female; and with their help thou shalt build up Jerusalem. [But] thou [must] wear this seal of God. And this engraving of the seal of the ring sent thee is a Pentalpha.'[65] The hexagram and pentagram have a long tradition of interchangeability, and the names seal of Solomon and shield of David were applied to both forms.[66] This Greek text was certainly known in England in the early fourteenth century, but the extent to which it was consulted is unclear. The surviving manuscripts imply that the text remained in Greek rather than being translated into the more accessible Latin. What it does suggest, however, is that a way of understanding the seal of Solomon was as a protective force by which its holder could conquer satanic influences.

The outer north porch at Redcliffe is a regular hexagon with each side measuring a little over 9ft between the centre of each corner-shaft. The depth of the outer porch is 16ft 6in – or one perch. The main unit of measurement used for the porch is 16ft 6in, perhaps a clever play with the cognate words perch and porch in keeping with the subtle approach taken to the building's design. When the hexagon is added to the depth of the inner porch and the transitional steps between the two, the full depth from the entrance arch through to the church door is approximately 30ft. The width of the outer porch measures 18ft 6in. Therefore the depth/width ratio of the entire porch complex is 5:3, the source for which, again, is 1 Kings 7.6. Whilst the Solomonic porch is clearly the influencing prototype for the unusual arrangement at Redcliffe, it throws up certain problems. To adhere to the Solomonic ratio of 5:3, both north porches at Redcliffe need to be considered as a single depth, whilst in the biblical account it is the inner porch alone which has this proportion, no indications of the dimensions

---

[64] Skolnik, Fred, ed. in chief, *Encyclopaedia Judaica. Second Edition*, vol. 13 (Detroit etc., 2007). 337.

[65] F. C. Conybeare, 'The Testament of Solomon', *The Jewish Quarterly Review* 11.1 (1898), 16.

[66] See *Encyclopaedia Judaica. Second Edition*, vol. 13, 337.

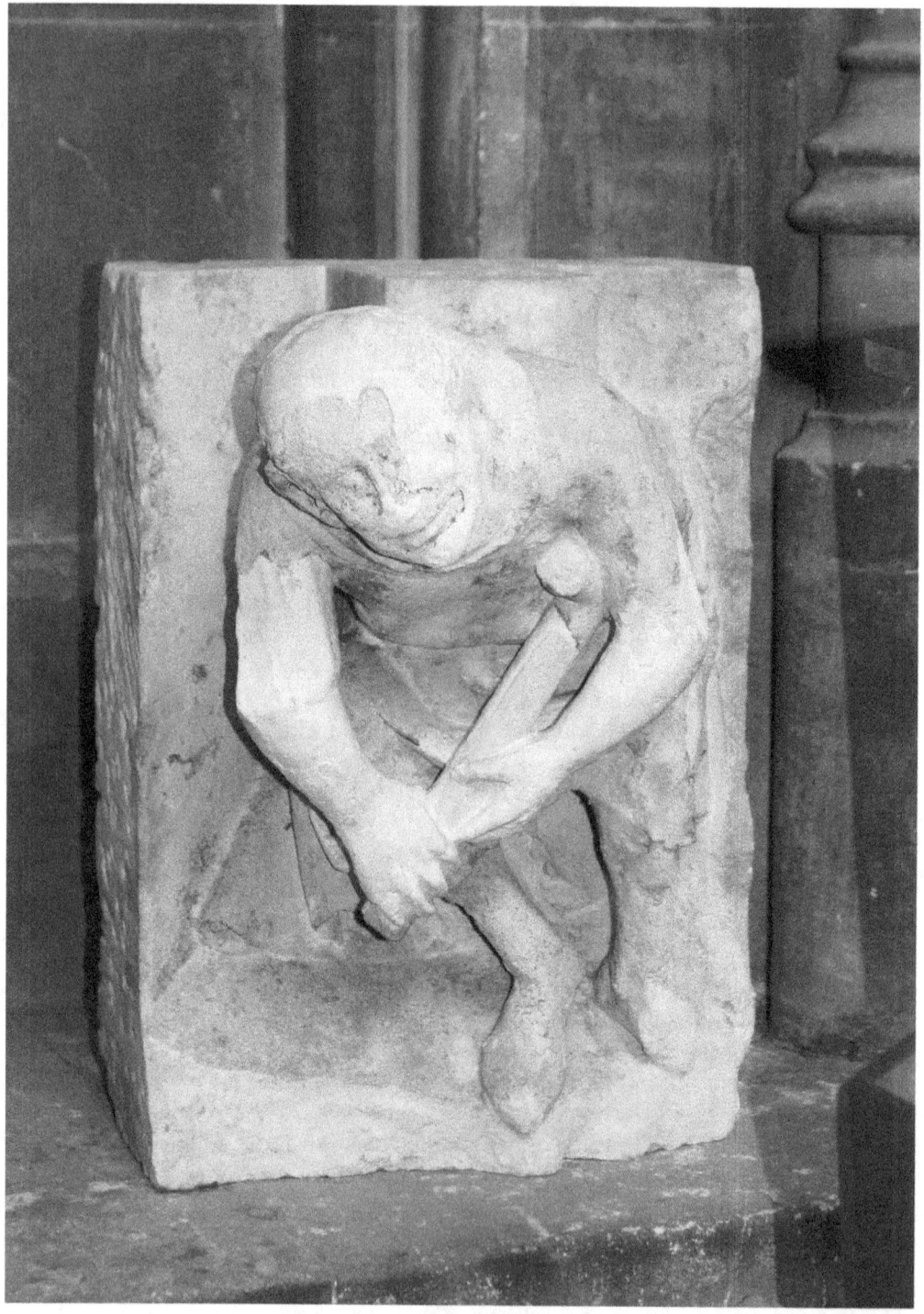

7 Corbel sculpture, *ex situ*, north porch exterior, St Mary Redcliffe, Bristol.
Reproduced with thanks to St Mary Redcliffe

of the outer porch are given. Seeing the form as inconsistent in its interpretation of the biblical prototype is to misunderstand the designer's aim. He did not seek to reconstruct the likeness of Solomon's buildings. In keeping with other architects of his time, the designer of Redcliffe brought together textual and architectural models, real and fictive, and reimagined them to form a new building. Similarly, in its details the Redcliffe porch stands as a panoply of allusions to Solomon's Temple. The extant corbel sculpture presents a range of indigent characters, including a beggar and a lame man with a crutch (fig. 7). These sculpted figures reference the biblical account of the miraculous healing of the lame man at the Beautiful Gate (Acts 3.1–9), and also the function of porches as places of almsgiving, which had biblical and contemporary significance (see chapter two).

The Ethelbert Gate, Norwich, and The Court Gate, Bury St Edmunds

The examples discussed so far in this chapter have demonstrated how words and architectural forms could be manipulated, transferred and reappropriated. In keeping with the north porch at Salisbury being perceived as a *porta*, this chapter draws to a close with consideration of two well-known East Anglian entrance structures which deserve interpretation as architectural versions of the verbal fluidity woven through the history of the English *porticus*. The relationship between porches and gatehouses is developed further in chapter three.

Porches and gates are cognate architectural forms. Both occupy points of spatial transition, marking and occupying thresholds, and therefore a degree of formal overlap might be expected. This is true despite their differences; practical function demanded that gatehouses be mechanisms of control, whilst porches are usually more intimately human in scale and engagement, and are never closed. The architectural openness of porches reflects their role in facilitating human access to the Divine, as described by William Durandus (1230–96): 'The atrium of the church signifies Christ, through whom the entrance to the celestial Jerusalem is opened, which is called a porch [*porticus*], and is thus named from the word gate [*porta*] that it might be opened wide [*aperta*].'[67] Durandus' words typify the medieval propensity to apply the nomenclature of gates (*porta*) and porches (*porticus*) interchangeably, an authorial technique to effect positive connections and associations rather than evidence of linguistic imprecision.[68] The

---

[67] Thibodeau, *The Rationale Divinorum Officiorum*, 17–18.
[68] Luxford, 'Architecture and Environment', 59–60.

8 The Ethelbert Gate, Norwich

9 The Court Gate, Bury St Edmunds

relevance of this relationship has already been mentioned in relation to Salisbury's north porch.

The Ethelbert Gate (fig. 8) and the Bury Court Gate (fig. 9) were both rebuilt after aggressive civil unrest directed against the monastery. Damage to the Ethelbert Gate was associated with rioting in August 1272 but, according to the cathedral's accounts, structural renewal was not carried out until around 1316 – a generation later.[69] At Bury the riot of 1327 caused similar architectural injury, and the Court Gate was sufficiently damaged to warrant its rebuilding, which was realised more than two decades after the riot. Just as King Solomon, not the warrior King David, was cast as God's chosen builder, at Norwich and Bury it was succeeding generations rather than those involved in violent strife who carried out the work. The hiatus between riot and rebuilding is unlikely to have been contrived to permit this biblical allusion; financial or other matters probably delayed reconstruction of the gates. However, the integration of design elements alluding to Solomon's porches at the new court entrance would have conjured a powerful *post hoc* elision between architectural ambition, wisdom, judgement, and firm rule.

At Norwich, the low-relief sculptural imagery of the gate's façade makes reference to Isaiah's prophesies of the fall of Babylon and recalls the local disputes which necessitated the gate's remodelling.[70] Pre-restoration depictions show now lost additional key elements. According to John Adey Repton's visual document, a seated figure of Christ displaying his wounds occupied the central niche directly above the apex of the west portal. A subtle alternating arrangement of canopied niches and narrow windows places the figure of Christ at the centre of four other alcoves. Lower in the façade, two further niches flank the iconographic spandrels. Christ, shown seated in judgement, was likely surrounded by tetramorphic figures of the four evangelists, in which case this part of the façade's composition referenced the Apocalypse and the ultimate victory. The layered significance of the imagery also typologically alludes to Solomon as judge: 'He made also the porch of the throne wherein is the seat of judgment; and covered it with cedar wood from the floor to the top' (1 Kings 7:7). Repton showed a significant component lost during restoration – a flushwork hexagram or sexfoil in the gable immediately above the central figure.[71] As already dis-

---

[69] E. C. Fernie and A. B. Whittingham, eds, *The Early Communar and Pitancer Rolls of Norwich Cathedral Priory with an Account of the Building of the Cloister* (Norwich, 1972), 33 and 90.

[70] Veronica Sekules, 'The Gothic Sculpture', in *Norwich Cathedral: Church, City and Diocese, 1096–1996*, ed. Ian Atherton, Eric Fernie, Christopher Harper-Bill and Hassell Smith (London, 1996), 199–202.

[71] S. Rowland Pierce, ed., *John Adey Repton. Norwich Cathedral at the End of the Eighteenth Century with Descriptive Notes by William Wilkins* (Farnborough, 1965), plate 12.

cussed, this motif was associated with the seal of Solomon. The suggestion that a Solomonic model was consciously adopted by the gate's designer is little more than speculation, but one bolstered by the building's measurements. To achieve correct Solomonic proportions, the Romanesque gate (renewed rather than replaced) was extended eastwards to form a double square (each 16ft in length and width) and thus achieve a plan ratio of 2:1 – a convenient plan for a two-bay quadripartite stone vault, but also powerfully resonant.

Elaboration of the façade of the Court Gate at Bury St Edmunds includes a pair of cusped hexagrams set into roundels carved into the frieze of the façade's upper storey – a motif imbued with notions of defence and power to subdue errant forces.[72] The Court Gate also shares a number of formal elements with the 'Solomonic' buildings already discussed, including measurements of the ground plan. Internally the building measures 25ft 10in in width and 51ft 8in in length. As a single structure the Court Gate was laid out on a ratio of 2:1. However, whilst externally the structure reads as a single volume, internally the space is divided. The outer compartment measures approximately 12ft x 18ft 10in and the inner compartment 35ft 4in x 25ft 10in. It can thus be construed as a 'porch before a porch', a building designed in Solomonic imitation, as already suggested in relation to the north porch at St Mary Redcliffe.

The translation of biblical text into the design of actual (that is architecturally viable) structures echoes the process that Richard of St Victor followed, with similar results emerging. The Court Gate did not need to (indeed could not easily) incorporate a flight of steps. However, the external elevation of the Gate displays certain similarities to Richard's illustrations, most notably a three-storey façade and crenellated parapet. Whilst I am not aware of any documentary evidence for the Court Gate at Bury being referred to as a *porticus*, certain elements of the building indicate that it sits within a group of buildings which make reference to Solomonic ancestry. Certainly it reveals, once again, that the word *porticus* was loaded with dramatic resonance rather than taken simply as a formal architectural type.

Recognising the idealised Old Testament model as the pattern for Norwich's Ethelbert Gate and the Court Gate at Bury St Edmunds stresses the centrality of content and significance to medieval architectural iconographies. It is anachronistic to apply modern attitudes towards copying

---

[72] 'As a talisman, it was common in many of the magical versions of the *mezuzah* which were widespread between the tenth and 14th centuries.' *Encyclopaedia Judaica. Second Edition*, vol. 13, 337. The placing of *mezuzah* on doorframes and at entrances suggests something of the innate relationship between the seal and protection of portals. This is clearly pertinent to the investigation of the absorption of Solomonic symbolism into the fabric of medieval porches.

or imitation to medieval builders or their buildings. Modern obsession with absolute exactness or faithfulness 'omits the elements which were important to the Middle Ages: the content and the significance of the building.'[73] For designers of porches the archetype was primarily conveyed through words rather than structures. Architectural invention was therefore not only desirable on the part of the designer but essential if a structurally sound and modally appropriate building was to be achieved. Resonant motifs (for example, pillars) and mathematical proportions (that is, 1:2 and 3:5) could be easily extracted from the biblical narrative but they provided the designer with little more than a starting point. It would be necessary to combine, meld and revise architectural content to form the rest of the building, ensuring its suitability to the site and everyday function, and allowing for considerations of architectural decorum, style and patronal preferences. The success of this admixture relied on the unity of imagination and applied invention, skilfully blended to produce specific architectural mnemonics which could vibrate with significances in the minds of informed beholders.[74]

Conclusion

Allusions to Solomonic models were powerful constituents in the architectural repertoire of medieval England. St Augustine of Hippo's work of Christian philosophy *Civitas Dei* (*The City of God*) encouraged all churches to be conceived in the image of Jerusalem and Solomon's Temple 'constituted the archetype for all patrons and builders'.[75] The means of reference differed considerably, as did the biblical passages selected as inspiration for the form of these buildings. Neither the textual usage of the term *porticus* nor the buildings it denoted were ever consistent. Whether they take the form of towers or corridors, internal enclosed spaces or open arcaded façades, *porticus* were connected with significant events, most notably the passage into God's kingdom on earth, whether in life for the celebration of divine office or after death through remembrance and intercession. The primary building type termed *porticus* also altered over time, changing from an internal transept chapel to an entrance building. Burials in *porticus* and

---

[73] Krautheimer, 'Introduction', 1–33.
[74] Writing of the symbolic multiplicity of the number eight, Johannes Scotus Erigena uses sonorous metaphor to express how the different connotations sound together within him, a sensory experience which Krautheimer interpreted as vibration. See Krautheimer, 'Introduction', 9–10, and taken up in Crossley, 'Medieval Architecture and Meaning', 121.
[75] Fergusson, *Canterbury Cathedral Priory*, 57.

the altars located therein have given a sense of the early nature of the place and indicate the events and behaviours appropriate to them. Investigating the textual tradition of *porticus* has set up a series of questions regarding the architecture, function and commissioning patronage of English church porches. These will be addressed through the rest of this book, and the question of Solomonic resonance will be revisited.

Functions of Church Porches   2

> Architecture is a very special functional art; it confines space so we can dwell in it, creates the framework around our lives.[1]

THE WELL-KNOWN, elegantly simple axiom that form follows function coined by Chicago architect, and pioneer of the American sky-scraper, Louis Sullivan (1856–1924) today holds little sway with architectural practitioners, theorists or historians. Essentially reductionist in ambition, the phrase disguises, perhaps denies, the complexity of interactions between people (without which there is no function) and buildings, prioritising the often relatively short design/planning process over the subsequent years, decades and centuries of social entanglement. Our homes demonstrate this to us every day. No matter the age, size or design of our house, its functional or architectural description would fail to encompass the enmeshed relationship between ourselves, our family and our domestic environment. That a kitchen has the function of a meal-preparation area is a truism; that a kitchen can also be a place to share those meals through the addition of a table and chairs, the place where the dog shakes on returning from her morning walk, where my husband makes my morning cuppa, where casual conversations with friends and neighbours are accommodated because the room is conveniently located and informally furnished. Personal, human interactions such as these (and the examples one could offer are legion) are essential to understanding how built environments are used, attending to their cultural and historical specificity. If we seek to understand better the complicity between building and user, it is necessary to ask questions of more interest and with greater potential than 'what's it for?'.

As mentioned in the Introduction, James Charles Wall set the foundation for the modern understanding of porches and, until publication of the present book, his 1912 volume *Porches and Fonts* remained the principal source on the subject. As a historian of the English church writing either side of 1900, J. C. Wall's concern with porches was what people did in them, at what date, and how this related to biblical or early church practice. Looking to identify historical consistencies and propound good liturgical

---

[1] Steen Eiler Rasmussen, *Experiencing Architecture* (Cambridge, MA, 1962), 10.

practice according to a medieval template, Wall's interests in porches were broad and inclusive, confidently stating the range of functions they served from the reign of King Solomon to the aftermath of the sixteenth-century English Reformation. Following an introductory discussion, Wall presents the 'Liturgical Purposes of the Porch': discipline, baptism, purification, marriage, burials, Palm Sunday, Holy Water and The New Fire.[2] This section of his work has been particularly influential on subsequent understandings of what porches were used for, and has been accepted as an unquestioned authority, despite its inclusion of many unreferenced statements.[3]

J. C. Wall's approach to function was to distinguish between the 'Liturgical Purposes of the Porch' and the 'Other Uses of the Porch', which served to separate sacred (liturgical) purpose from secular use. In a culture defined by belief in an omnipotent creator God as ultimate judge and an intellectual universe in which scientific understanding was rooted in theological discourse, it is unclear how Wall's binary segregation of sacred and secular could be sustained. His distinction is particularly unhelpful if purpose implies events of greater importance than mere uses. In the intervening years, whether discussed as functions, uses or purposes, there has been insufficient consideration of the impact building a porch had on the events traditionally associated with the church door, or the ways in which anticipated functions affected their form and design. Work by British anthropologist Mary Douglas has freed the definition of ritual from special occasions with explicit religious context to the repeated performance of everyday social practices, for example the 10 am coffee break taken in a shared workplace, and coded social behaviours such as a greeting handshake, hug or kiss.[4] The close structuring of communities in England during the Middle Ages pervaded all levels of society; the parish as a microcosm mirrored the national state in being ordered by tightly coded interactions, responsibilities and behaviours borne out in a human-made environment. The church building was central to the affirmation and continuation of shared rituals. The present study of church porches is highly receptive to such an expanded sense of ritual because of their ubiquity, visual prominence and participation in bodily transition from beyond the church to within, no matter what the occasion.

Take, as an example, daily engagement with painted images of St Christopher. Inside many, perhaps the majority, of parish churches a large-scale mural or stained-glass image of the saint was positioned to be visually

---

[2] Wall, *Porches and Fonts*, 12–26.
[3] For example, A. Needham, *How to Study an Old Church* (London, 1944), 22–4.
[4] For architectural application of Mary Douglas' anthropological theories of ritual, see Peter Blundell-Jones, *Architecture and Ritual – How Buildings Shape Society* (London and New York, 2016), 8–10.

accessible when viewed from the church door or just inside. Reciting a prayer whilst looking upon the image was considered efficacious for ensuring a safe day ahead. The repeated daily ritual of walking through the porch, glancing through the door at the image and reciting a text off-by-heart might become commonplace and barely register in the individual's conscious experience of their day. In fact, in the context of medieval Christian belief, the act was no less important than raising the likelihood of ongoing life over the possibility of imminent death. Throughout England a church porch was the habitat for this ritual performance, the framing of the event. It would be curious, perhaps laughable, to claim that the prime function of any church porch was for seeing the image of St Christopher, yet it is just one instance of many human-building interactions which constitute their meaning and texture the relationship between people and places.

Function and Liminality

In 2007 David Postles wrote that '[i]t is tempting to perceive the south porch above all as a liminal or transitional space, between the "profane" (secular world) and the (putative) "sacred" (holy). While such an interpretation of the function of the porch has its merits, it fails to take into account the fuzzy, messy, unselfconscious and ambiguous use of space, by groups and individuals.'[5] Postles' interests are in spatial theory and social practices, ritual and behaviours, and his main concern with porches has been around their ambiguity and transformations. Postles' suggestion that an interpretation of porches as liminal or transitional spaces conceals their behavioural ambiguity does not sit comfortably with the anthropological application of the terms 'liminality' and 'transition' which originated in the work of Victor Turner and Arnold van Gennep. The work of both authors brings into focus the question of the difference between a threshold (or limen) and a space.[6]

As will be explored in more detail later in this book, a porch is a building, a door is not. The two are inextricable but not interchangeable. Formal written instructions tell how the opening acts of sacramental rites (including baptism and marriage) were conducted at, or before, the

---

[5] Dave Postles, 'Micro-Spaces: Church Porches in Pre-Modern England', *Journal of Historical Geography* 33.4 (2007), 750–1.

[6] For example, Turner defined liminality as 'the mid point of transition in a status-sequence between two positions'. Victor Turner, *Dramas, Fields and Metaphors: Symbolic Action in Human Society* (Ithaca, NY, and London, 1974), 237. See also van Gennep, *Rites of Passage*.

church door – the location's significance evident in the term '*in facie ecclesiae*'. Rather like the example of gazing up at the image of St Christopher, attending only to the thing on which a person focuses excludes awareness of the situation they actually inhabit. In terms of standing before the church door, for whatever reason and for however long, the individual could be either outside (where there was no porch) or inside (deep within a porch), or some state in between. The formal difference between doors and porches related to the varied ways in which they affected human experience. Doors and porches can both be described as forms of boundary or threshold, marking the point at which two different environments meet, yet the former lack spatial volume (i.e., it is impossible to be inside a door) whilst the latter provide habitable space in which the entire human body can be contained. In his pivotal work *Rites of Passage*, ethnographer and anthropologist Arnold van Gennep argues that 'the threshold is only part of the door' and therefore rites associated with the threshold 'should be understood as direct and physical rites of entrance, of waiting, and of departure – that is, as rites of passage'.[7] Although now nearly sixty years old, van Gennep's observation is pertinent to the church porch in relation to the preparatory sections of baptism and marriage ceremonies (discussed later in this chapter), even the viewing of St Christopher's image. However, some functions of church porches did not involve a subsequent or even 'main' event to follow within the church. Resting on a porch bench or soliciting alms from passers-by did not require or involve passing through the church door or entering the body of the church. In many situations, porches were places of discrete significance.

The Function of Architecture

At the intersection of architecture and experience are people, those who construct layers of significance within the courses of stone or rubble. Engagement with, and thereby understanding of, a building is strongly influenced by the way the design and its materiality stimulate our senses. The resulting emotional responses shape the nature of the events deemed appropriate to happen in that place. The bodily basis of experience and perception, set forth by Maurice Merleau-Ponty and recently applied to constructed spaces by Christopher Tilley, is also central to my investigation of porch function.[8] Phenomenology offers a framework for exploration of

---

[7] van Gennep, *Rites of Passage*, 25.
[8] Christopher Tilley, *A Phenomenology of Landscape – Places, Paths and Monuments* (Oxford, 1994), 7–34; Christopher Tilley, *The Materiality of Stone: Explorations in Landscape Phenomenology* (Oxford, 2004), 1–32.

the way buildings functioned in English medieval society; a way to unify buildings and people rather than retaining them as discrete categories.

Buildings are not neutral spaces, they are imbued with power and meaning of historic and contemporary making. Whilst many uses of church porches have long been recognised, at least since J. C. Wall was writing in the early twentieth century, the function of porch architecture as an agent, shaping the significance of the events held therein, has been largely overlooked. It matters, as already noted, that the experiential difference between celebrating 'at the church door' or 'in the porch' is recognised, although much secondary literature conflates the two.[9] In his study of the English parish church, N. J. G. Pounds implies that, for performance of the marriage rite (which he contentiously states was not sacramental, despite its status being affirmed during the Fourth Lateran Council in 1215), the door was required, and it (rather than the ceremony and participants) deserved and benefitted from being covered by a porch. This excludes entirely the environment of the ritual itself. Such downplaying of the porch's importance is commonplace and regrettable. Built structures, in general and in their specificity, alter human experience and the act of covering is powerfully imbued with notions of both protective care and reverence. It is in this highly charged cultural context that porches need to be placed.

Having established some important methodological way markers, the rest of this chapter will investigate the nature and significance of how church porches functioned. It concludes by offering a definition of their meaning in English medieval society. As an antidote to Wall's problematic distinction of liturgical and other uses, the exploration of porch function offered here is prompted by Mary Douglas' encouragement that we attend to the ritual in the everyday, as well as the extraordinary or special. After all, the baptised child would come to attend Mass every week of their life from infancy to old age, in time they would make annual confession to their parish priest, partake in church ales and witness (perhaps contribute to) the inevitable periodic renewal of the church building. The following pages therefore present something of the consistency and complexity inherent in the entanglement between parishioners and their church porches. The 'functions' are presented to convey how repetition of multiple activities (which have coherence through their shared themes and participatory modes) and an identifiable built environment provided a place-specific framework for the detail of people's lives in medieval England.

---

[9] N. J. G. Pounds, *A History of The English Parish* (Cambridge, 2000), 387.

Re-enacting the Palm Sunday Procession

As a mature man in the 1580s or 1590s, Long Melford parishioner Roger Martin (c.1527–1615) penned a written account of going to church as a child before the English Reformation. In doing so, he left to history a vivid account of how sacramental and liturgical worship happened in the context of a large and wealthy Suffolk parish.[10] Martin's document closely describes the church, its layout, fitments and furnishings, altars, images and lights. Woven through the same narrative is Martin's memory of how the church was used, where people sat, how they processed and moved around the space. Processions seem to have particularly captured his imagination, times when he joined with other parishioners in collective semi-performative walks around the church and the village. It is easy to imagine how these pageants would excite a young boy and lodge in his mind. As well as a fascinating document in itself, Martin's brief description of the Palm Sunday procession at Long Melford demonstrates how parochial practice could diverge from the rubrics of the Sarum Rite. It is of greater historical insight because such performative detailing is absent from contemporary priests' manuals, such as that written by John Mirk. The latter absence may indicate practice continuing by oral transmission, whereas written instruction specified the correct words to be used by the celebrant. After all, the efficacy, or otherwise, of the sacraments when wrong words were used was a matter of considerable debate and concern.

Martin's memory of Palm Sunday recounts a vivid spectacle revolving around people, objects, movement and sound. Four yeomen carried the Blessed Sacrament under a 'fair canopy' accompanied by singing, the ringing of a little bell, and a young boy standing in a turret to signify a prophet singing '*Ecce rex tuus venit* etc.' to the assembled crowd kneeling in adoration below.[11] Ultimately the procession moved towards the church door as the congregation 'went singing together, into the church, and coming near the porch, a boy, or one of the clerks, did cast over among the boys flowers, and singing cakes, etc.'[12] This celebratory moment was Long Melford's mnemonic re-enactment of Christ's passing through the city gates of Jerusalem riding on an ass or colt, his path strewn with garments, tree boughs and palm branches.[13] From the incisive illumination of St Æthelwold's

---

[10] All information on Roger Martin's account is taken from David Dymond and Clive Paine, *The Spoil of Melford Church: The Reformation in a Suffolk Parish* (Ipswich, 1992), which includes a biographical history of Martin, and a history of his document, 'The State of Melford'.

[11] Dymond and Paine, *Spoil of Melford*, 5–6 and n.26.

[12] Ibid., 6.

[13] Matthew 21.1–11, Mark 11.1–11, Luke 19.28–44, John 12.12–19.

10 Exterior view, south porch, Long Melford

Benedictional (British Library, Add. MS 49598) to the lively naivety of the early-fifteenth-century illustrated manuscript of Boethius' *De consolatione philosophiae* (Cambridge, Trinity Hall MS 12, f. 14v), medieval illustrations of Christ's Triumphal Entry show a male figure almost falling from a tree as Christ passes beneath. In medieval Suffolk, adoration was expressed with flowers and cakes, cascading from height over the crowd entering their Jerusalem through the church porch.

In architectural terms the south porch at Long Melford frames the church door in elevated grandeur (fig. 10).[14] To conform to the width of a single bay and complement the vertical scale of the adjacent aisle the porch is tall and slender, enhancing the elegance of the church façade. Although of sufficient height to be double storey, the porch is an attenuated single-storey structure flanked by matching pairs of elongated two-light windows, which extend from around head height almost to the eaves. The entrance arch rises beyond two-thirds of the building's height; a triumphal arch set before the church door. Flowers and cakes strewn inside the porch, or close by, associated the building with parochial re-enactment of Christ's entry into Jerusalem. Long Melford's porch dictated the way in which Palm Sunday processions were performed in that parish. Suggesting the building was designed to 'function' as a station for the closing stage of the Palm Sunday procession would denigrate the richness of its contribution to the life-course of individuals such as Roger Martin and the parish corporate. Yet it fulfilled this role admirably and exemplifies architecture's primary task of framing people's mind–body interaction with the landscape.

Martin's written memory also gives insight into the scope for variation between instruction in the Sarum Rite and parochial practice. Designed for fulfilment of the liturgy on one of the largest ecclesiastical stages in medieval Europe, the secular cathedral of Salisbury, the Sarum Rite could not provide the equivalent of a measured drawing for liturgical performance across medieval England. Its format was more conducive to manipulation for parochial application than monastic liturgical practice but could rarely be maintained in pure form in the English parish. In the text of the Sarum Missal and Customary concerned with Palm Sunday, the faithful gathered in the church nave were exorcised of the devil and purified with the sprinkling of holy water before palm leaves were distributed to all. The faithful then processed from the church through the west door, moved around the south side of the exterior pausing for the singing of anthems at noted staging points, and ultimately re-entered the church by the same

---

[14] Long Melford's medieval west tower fell in 1701, a red brick replacement was built 1712–25 by Daniel Hills, and Gothic Revivalist architect George F. Bodley erected the present tower 1897–1903. See Dymond and Paine, *Spoil of Melford*, 159.

door, beneath the shrine of the relics held aloft for them to enter.[15] In any parish church without a west door, alternative arrangements had to be made and the north or south doors, as at Long Melford, played the role of the Jerusalem's gates.[16]

'Palm Sunday processions in most Norfolk parish churches before the last quarter of the 14th century would have had to have used a lateral door in the absence of a western entrance.'[17] Throughout England lateral porches were more widely numerous than western towers with axial doorways before the end of the fourteenth century, but also through the fifteenth century. Over the course of the late thirteenth and fourteenth centuries an increasing number of English parish churches had a porch to shelter at least one of its lateral doorways. Although the heightened importance of Palm Sunday and Corpus Christi processions from the late fourteenth century stimulated interest in the architecture and iconography of grand west towers, numerous churches feature elaborate porches as well. Apparently the new fashion for grand western entrances did not dispel the parochial tradition of having a porch, and implies once again that the Palm Sunday procession should be seen as one example of the ways in which porches offered multivalent practical facilities and significant meanings.

Fire and Water

The Easter vigil of striking the new fire and lighting the paschal candle would follow a week after the Palm Sunday procession. Wall suggested

---

[15] s.n., *The Sarum Missal in English* (London, 1868), 108–12. '*Hiis peractis, eat processio ad ostium occidentale, et ibi intret sub capsula reliquiarum ex transuerso ostii eleuata*'. Walter Howard Frere, ed., *The Use of Sarum: The Sarum Customs as set forth in the Consuetudinary and Customary* (Cambridge, 1898), 61. As the weight of material in the present study comes from the diocese of Norwich, the Sarum Rite provides the appropriate evidence for the role of church doors and porches in sacramental and liturgical events.

[16] A prominent related example (although not governed by the Use of Sarum) is provided by Durham Cathedral. The 'Rites of Durham' specify that the north door was the appropriate point of entry for a range of processions, including Corpus Christi, when the whole community symbolically overcame death and entered heaven. Lateral entry was necessitated at Durham by the setting of the church, but there is no suggestion that being unable to process through a door at the west end diminished the potency of the event. See John McKinnell, 'For the People/by the People. Public and Private Spaces in the Durham Sequence of the Sacrament', in *Ritual and Space in the Middle Ages*, ed. F. Andrews. Harlaxton Medieval Studies 21 (n.s.) (Donington, 2011), 213.

[17] Dominic Summers, 'Norfolk Church Towers of the Later Middle Ages', unpublished Ph.D. dissertation, University of East Anglia, Norwich, 2011, vol. I, 120.

that rekindling of the new fire took place outside the church, ordinarily in the porch.[18] Even accepting that parochial practice might be divergent, the suggestion is unlikely. The Sarum Rite instructs that this rebirthing ritual be conducted in the body of the church, which all communities could imitate with considerable accuracy. According to the Sarum Manual, the clergy gather in the choir at the ninth hour without a lighted candle, without a cross and without fire in the thurible. Acolytes, dressed in surplices, extinguish a three-tapered candle. The procession, accompanied by choristers singing, passes through the screen, which is blessed with the holy water, through the middle of the choir to the font to bless the new light. At a pillar in the south part of the church next to the font, the priest officially blesses the fire which is kindled there, that is, between two pillars.[19] Conventional practice situated the rekindling inside the church, towards the west end of the nave between the south door and the font – not in the porch. From utter darkness the church interior awoke with new light passed from one candle to the next.

Wall also stated that parishioners brought candles with them to the church so that they could return home with the rekindled light, giving the porch at Crostwick in Norfolk as an example of a fireplace for this purpose.[20] I have found no evidence of this at Crostwick, but the low-level external niches at South Acre and Castle Acre have more the appearance of light-holders than holy water stoups. As well as the possibility that the new fire might be placed in these locations, the provision of a lamp locker on the inside of the Hostry door at Norwich Cathedral, an idea put forward by Roberta Gilchrist as an explanation for the niche there, is equally fitting if rather more prosaic.[21] The many holes and niches in church porches are often explained as holy water stoups, but there is the possibility that at least some of them might have been light-holders, and thus the placing of a candle or fire at the entrance to a porch remains a possibility, but little more than that.

It is uncertain whether any porch 'basin' was provided for fire, but the presence of lustral water close to entrances into religious buildings has a certain, long and venerable history. In the Christian tradition the practice is seen in the atria fountains of Roman basilicas, and the forecourt of Solomon's Temple – two settings of considerable influence in the ancestry of

---

[18] Wall, *Porches and Fonts*, 26.

[19] '*et eat processio per medium chori et per ostium occidentale ad quondam columpnam ecclesie ex parte australi et ad nouum ignem benedicendum absque cruce et sine lumine in cereis et igne in thuribulo*'. Frere, *The Use of Sarum*, 146. The translated summary is my own.

[20] Wall, *Porches and Fonts*, 26.

[21] Roberta Gilchrist, *Norwich Cathedral Close: The Evolution of the English Cathedral Landscape* (Woodbridge, 2005), 134.

English church porches, as discussed in chapter one. Holy water, water transformed through verbal and performative ritual to be powerful beyond its life-giving and hygiene capacities, facilitated rebirth through spiritual cleansing and purification. As God explained to Ezekiel: 'And I will pour upon you clean water, and you shall be cleansed from all your filthiness, and I will cleanse you from all your idols' (Ezekiel 36.25).

Asperging, spiritual cleansing through physical contact with blessed water, was the most frequently repeated ritual demonstration of belief in the sinful human, the efficacy of repentance and promise of divine salvation.[22] From childhood parishioners learnt to cleanse themselves symbolically before the church door by dipping the fingers of their right hand into a dish of holy water and asperging their own bodies as they made the sign of the cross. Doing so sustained the purity of the parish church interior, defending it against the desecration of earthly dirt, although the physically cursory action could do little by way of practical hygiene. The efficacious holy water stoup of the late medieval parish church and associated ritualised behaviour demonstrated parishioners' commitment to a shared belief system which safeguarded the community as well as the individual. Cleansing and purification rituals are universally associated with thresholds as places of passage, cleansing the participant as they pass from darkness to light, from beyond to within.[23] A parishioner would experience repeated bodily engagement with lustral water through its use in the rites associated with transition between stages in a life-course performed within the architectural setting of a church porch. As detailed below, the water and the setting were two components which brought continuity, pattern and familiarity to a series of rituals which people would undergo themselves and bear witness to as parishioners.

Preparation for Baptism

In late medieval England infant baptism was firmly established and excommunication threatened those who failed to offer a child for baptism in the first few months of life. Ideally baptism would be performed on the day of the child's delivery, encouraged by fear of eternal damnation should an infant die unbaptised. Those presented for baptism were not adults and of necessity 'The Order for the Making of a Catechumen' (the part

---

[22] Spiritual cleansing was not restricted to the person, lustration was central to the anointing and dedication of altars and the church building. See Mgr. L. Duchesne, *Christian Worship, Its Origin and Evolution* (London, 1903), 410.

[23] Mary Douglas, *Collected Works II: Purity and Danger: An Analysis of Concepts of Pollution and Taboo* (London and New York, 1970), 162.

of the baptismal liturgy located at the church door and by association in the porch) became a much-reduced version of the early Christian rite.[24] That it continued despite infants being unable to fulfil the traditional role of one in preparation for full access to the Mass indicates its sustained importance. The rite begins, 'First, let the infant be brought to the doors of the church: and let the priest ask the midwife whether the infant is a male or female.'[25] The male infants are then set on the right of the priest and the females on the left and marked with the sign of the cross on the forehead and breast. The words of the first prayer conjure with integration between the priest's spoken words, the metaphor of the door of goodness, and the architectural setting in which belief and experience co-existed.

> Almighty and everlasting God, the Father of our Lord Jesus Christ, vouchsafe to look upon this thy servant (or this thine handmaid), ... N. whom thou hast vouchsafed to call to the first beginnings of faith: all blindness of heart drive from him (or her): break all the bonds of Satan with which he (or she) was bound. Open to him (or her), O Lord, the door of thy goodness, so that, wearing the sign of wisdom, he (or she) may be free from the defilements of all fleshly lusts: and rejoicing in the sweet odour of thy commandments may serve thee in thy Church, and may advance in goodness from day to day, so that he (or she) may be made worthy to attain to the grace of thy baptism having received thy medicine; through the same Christ our Lord. Amen.[26]

Recitation at the church door (the 'door of thy goodness') enables the setting to add a sense of reality, immediacy and authority to the words; lived experience and sacred promise dwelling in one place. The space before the church door was thus a place of preparation, from where the catechumen progressed to the font for the baptism. The making of a catechumen ritual focuses on the renunciation of sin, with sections of the prayers addressing Satan directly.

> Hearken, accursed Satan, adjured by the name of the eternal God and our Saviour his Son: with thy envy thou has been conquered: trembling and groaning depart: let there be nothing common to thee and to this servant of God N, who now ponders upon heavenly things, who is about to renounce thee and thy world, and is about to live in blessed immortality. Give honour therefore to the Holy Spirit as he draws near, who descending from the highest arch of heaven, having confounded

---

[24] Francis Procter and Walter Howard Frere, *A New History of the Book of Common Prayer* (London, 1901), 566–9.

[25] J. D. C. Fisher, *Christian Initiation: Baptism in the Medieval West: A Study of the Primitive Right of Initiation* (London, 1965), 158.

[26] Ibid., 159.

thy deceits, will make his breast cleansed in the divine fount and sanctified into a temple and dwelling-place for God, so that, inwardly set free from all the hurts of his past sins, this servant of God may ever give thanks to the everlasting God, and bless his holy name throughout all ages. Amen.[27]

As already mentioned, in medieval England, those being prepared for baptism were infants without the capacity to understand the words or their meaning. The intended audience was primarily the already baptised. Words and meaning beyond the comprehension of the new-born infant were powerful mnemonic devices intended for contemplation by the adult witnesses and godparents. The event thus served to remind and reinforce their fundamental shared Christian rights and responsibilities.

Themes central to the theological structure of the baptismal rite (contained in instructions issued by the Church) and referenced to historical practices with biblical authority were also relevant at parish level. Documented evidence from medieval inquisitions of proof of age reveals the immediate experience of a parish baptism. Compiled during witness-based hearings designed to establish a person's age (and therefore their rights) if disputed, the inquisition writs offer a unique window onto what happened on the day of a baptism. The ritual was rarely planned or scheduled; it was a hurriedly-arranged affair set into action by a mother's delivery of her child. From that moment others took over; the mother could not participate in any part of the baptism, being excluded from the church until her purification. At Halesworth, on 10 November 1427, a case came before Richard Elliswyk, the king's escheator for Norfolk and Suffolk. The purpose was to prove the age of Joan, wife of Robert Alyngton, and in so doing establish her right to inherit land following her brother's death whilst a minor. As was commonplace, witness statements affirming Joan's age centred on her baptism and how its date could be recalled by relation to other events:

> She was born at the manor of Halesworth on 24 June 1413 and is aged 14 and more. She was baptised in the church of St Mary there on the same day and the jurors were asked how they know that she is of age. William Merlond, 40, attended the baptism and carried salt, in a silver salt-cellar, and a towel to it. Nicholas Stampard, 36, carried a basin and ewer with water to the church so that William Hardy who baptised Joan, John Tolle, godfather, and Joan Elmy and Katherine Berneye, godmothers, could all wash their hands. Thomas Bret, 54, Robert Borell, 40, John Dobbes, 63, and William Randolf, 54, stood by the font while she was baptised, and held four lit torches. John Barbour, 42, William Elmy, 43, and Robert Payn, 46, were standing in the porch of the church and saw

---

[27] Ibid., 161–2.

Alice Hemme, midwife, carrying Joan to the church for baptism. William Fleccher, 60, Roger Barkere, 60, and Alexander Hovell, 38, were in the church on the Saturday that Joan was baptised, then went to the manor with the midwife who was carrying Joan. A great oak standing before the door of the hall suddenly fell, a branch hit the midwife, and she only just escaped with her life.[28]

This vivid account of a memorable day emphasises the sense of the community's involvement in an infant's baptism, the carrying of precious vessels containing salt and water for renunciation of the devil and ritual cleansing of the celebrant's and godparents' hands.

Purification of Women after Childbirth

Ritual cleansing was also an important performative element of the brief ceremony which purified a mother after childbirth. In accordance with Old Testament law, childbirth, just like monthly menstrual bleeding, was deemed to defile the human body and necessitated exclusion from the sacred church interior. If the mother had delivered a boy purification came 40 days after the birth or 80 days if the child was a girl (Leviticus 12:1–5). Standing in the church porch, the mother would be addressed by the priest reciting Psalm 123 and then an intercessory collect beseeching God to restore the woman to his faithful service in life and eternal rest beneath his merciful wings. The priest would asperge the woman with holy water saying, 'Purge me with hyssop', and then lead her by the right hand saying, 'Enter into the temple of God, that thou mayest have eternal life and live for ever and ever. Amen.'[29]

A new mother's status was debated by churchmen across centuries, however. In answering St Augustine's letter enquiring of the status of expectant and recently delivered mothers in relation to baptism and communion, Gregory the Great stated that the Old Testament proscription was to be 'understood as an allegory, for were a woman to enter church and return thanks in the very hours of her delivery, she would do nothing wrong'. The Penitential of Theodore of Tarsus is more restrictive in its warning. Any woman entering a church before purification after childbirth was to do penance. Honorius Augustodunesis [of Autun] writing in the twelfth century, citing Leviticus 15, also observes that after the birth of a child women

---

[28] TNA C 139/36/71, mm. 1–2, accessed via the website of the 'Mapping the Medieval Countryside' project online database, available at www.inquisitionspostmortem.ac.uk

[29] *The Sarum Missal in English*, 560.

were unclean and excluded from the heavenly temple. Because of this, Honorius explains, it was customary that women, joined by men, stand as penitents at the *foris* – a word which might be translated as porch area, atrium or door of the church.[30] The parochial application is uncertain but the resonance is clear.

Confession, Penance and Reconciliation

On Palm Sunday, Peter's denial of Christ was remembered through recitation, the singing of Christ's Passion as written in the gospels. After the denial Peter went out into the porch and the cock crew. No clearer evidence could be offered of the cultural and theological symbiosis of porch, bodily removal of the penitent and promise of reconciliation to come.[31]

Medieval confession was a tripartite sacrament, comprising the confession itself, penance and absolution, and reconciliation. The eighth-century cleric-scholar Alcuin of York wrote a brief moral treatise on the subject setting out the inevitability of confession:

> All sins are known to God: there is no concealing them; therefore, confess and do penance for your sins. Verily confession is a medicine to the soul; by it you will foil your adversary, the devil, and save your souls.

Alcuin's letter goes on to confirm the role of the priest, to whom confession should be made:

> But if ye will not confess to the priest neither will ye confess to God. The priest has the power of binding or loosing and of reconciling man with God; but how can his good offices avail those whose sins he knoweth not? Hence, have recourse to the specific of confession, and cleanse thyself with the medicine of penance that thou mayest be saved.[32]

Contemporary writings on confession and penance make almost no mention of where the sacrament was administered. According to the 1322 Compositions of the Archbishop of Canterbury, Walter Reynolds: 'Let the priest choose for himself a common place for hearing confessions, where he may be seen generally by all in the church.'[33] The priest could

---

[30] For all three references see Jane Tibbetts Schulenburg, *Forgetful of Their Sex: Female Sanctity and Society, ca. 500–1100* (Chicago, 1998), 479 n.15.
[31] *The Sarum Missal in English*, 117.
[32] Rolph Barlow Page, *The Letters of Alcuin* (New York, 1909), 35.
[33] Nicholas Rogers, 'The Location and Iconography of Confession in Late Medieval Europe', in *Ritual and Space in the Middle Ages*, ed. F. Andrews. Harlaxton Medieval Studies 21 (n.s.) (Donington, 2011), 299.

11 Confession panel, Seven Sacraments font, Marsham

choose almost anywhere, but plausibly within the body of the church. Visual explanations of the sacraments are more helpful in establishing the favoured locations, and in many pre-Reformation pontificals illustration rather than text was the primary means of establishing the choreography of confession.[34] Perhaps the most famous image of how the Christian sacraments happened is Rogier van der Weyden's *Seven Sacraments Altarpiece* of c.1440–45, now in the Koninkilijk Museum voor Schone Kunsten, Antwerp. The triptych shows the interior of a large church busy with ritualised activity. At the east end of the north nave aisle (in the middle distance of the dexter panel) a seated priest with their back against the screen and head covered, hears the confessions of a supplicant. A less well-known image is the confession panel of the c.1470 seven sacraments font at Marsham, Norfolk (fig. 11). The other six scenes, carved in low relief on the font, are set in architectonic frames beneath crocketed ogee arches. The confession scene is set within a church building, the fictive wall cut away to reveal the interior but with all figures clearly beneath a thatched roof. In the centre

---

[34] For examples see Walter Howard Frere, *Pontifical Services: Illustrated from Miniatures of the XVth and XVIth Centuries*, 2 volumes (London, 1901).

of the composition are a kneeling penitent and a seated priest, facing each other and watched over by an angel, larger in scale, standing behind them. To the right of the scene the devil creeps out of the open door but glances back to the penitent, priest and angel. Here the church door is vital to the event; the devil is expelled from the building as well as from the person. How might we read such an image to better understand the penitential role of the church porch? The interior presence of the priest and angel implies that all within the building is protected, discharge of the devil from the holy place makes plain that the world beyond the church enclosure is at risk. The limits or edges of these distinct zones are highly significant, and the status of the porch is a matter for debate.

Later medieval penance involved exclusion from the Mass as well as a public demonstration of contrition. According to Chaucer's *Parson's Tale*, penitence came in three species: solemn, common and private. The manner of solemn penance was 'to be put out of Holy Chirche in Lente for slaughtre of children and swich maner thing. Another is whan a man hath sinned openly, of which sinne the fame is openly spoken in the contree, and thanne Holy Chirche by jugement destreineth him for to do open penance.'[35] Contrastingly, common penance 'is that preestes enjoinen men communly in certein cas, as for to goon, paraventure, naked in pilgrimage or barefoot' and private penance 'is thilke that men doon alday for privee sinnes, of whiche we shrive us prively and receive privee penance'.[36]

Roman Pontificals from the twelfth century onwards antecede Chaucer's fourteenth-century account of *paenitententia solemnis* and the reservation of expulsion from the church for those confessing only the most heinous of sins.[37] The text of the Sarum Manual gives authority to porches as places of solace for the excluded. On Ash Wednesday (the first day of the Quadragesima or Lenten fast) the penitents' withdrawal from the body of the church is proscribed as by way of the south door.[38] 'When the penitents are ejected, the door of the church is shut.'[39] The sharply minimalist

---

[35] Geoffrey Chaucer, *The Canterbury Tales*, ed. Jill Mann (London, 2005), 696.
[36] Ibid.
[37] Martin R. Dudley, 'Sacramental Liturgies in the Middle Ages', in *The Liturgy of the Medieval Church*, ed. Thomas J. Heffernan and E. Ann Metter (Kalamazoo, 2001), 229.
[38] '*In capite ieiunii post cinerum suscepcionem, eat processio per medium chori ad ostium ecclesie australe, excellencioribus precedentibus, precedente uexillo cilicino. Deinde episcopus uel executor officii penitentes eiiciat singillatim per manus [officii] ministerio archidiaconi, si episcopus presens fuerit : [interim cantetur responsorium* Ecce aduenit *et responsorium* In sudore]. *Quibus eiectis redeat processio, ordine processionis seruato: [eiectis uero penitentibus, claudantur ianue. In redeundo cantetur responsorium* Emendemus: *nullus uersiculus nec oracio sequatur].*' Frere, *The Use of Sarum*, 138.
[39] *The Sarum Missal in English*, 56.

four words used in Bishop Grandisson's 1337 Ordinale for Exeter cathedral communicates the penitents' desolation: '*Eiectis penitentibus, claudatur ianua* [the penitents are ejected, the doors are closed]'.[40] Expelled from the body of the church on Ash Wednesday following confession, and awaiting reconciliation on Maundy Thursday, sinners could reside in the porch, a privilege granted also to the unbaptised and catechumen. On Maundy Thursday they would be reconciled and led back into church via the same route, prostrating themselves in the centre of the church before the deliverance of absolution by the officiating priest.[41]

Revivified interest in the church sacraments, including confession and associated fears of indictment for failure to follow orthodox Christian practice, coincides with the increase in the number of church porches built in England from the second quarter of the thirteenth century. At the Fourth Lateran Council in 1215, Pope Innocent III decreed that all Christian people were to confess to their own priest at least annually. Not doing so would result in them being excluded from the church in both life and death.[42] The papal decree reinvigorated and formalised existing custom, reimagined the condition of the penitent, and strengthened the place of reconciliation in the Christian contract. Ritual performance was essential to Pope Innocent's method of securing Church authority and a renewed interest in architecture's contribution to the human experience is evident in major building programmes across northern Europe. For example, the low-relief sculptural iconography of ecclesia/synagoga in the tympana of the south porch of Strasbourg Cathedral (completed c.1235) stages the penitential rituals and expulsion on Ash Wednesday and the performance of contrition and reconciliation on Holy Thursday.[43] A remarkable example of sculpture architecturally securing penitence in an English parish church porch is present at the north door of St Mary's, Spalding, Lincolnshire. Here enlarged cusp-roundels are figuratively carved and disturb the framing of the doorway (fig. 12). The dexter roundel depicts a figure holding a

[40] Dudley, 'Sacramental Liturgies', 229.
[41] '*In cena domini, nona cantata, eat processio ad ostium ecclesie, sicut in capite ieiunii, sintque presents in atrio ecclesie penitentes. Deinde, si episcopus adest, principalis archidiaconus, ex parte penitencium, extra ostium [quandam] leccionem legat in capa serica, que non legatur absente episcopo. Finita leccione [idem archidiaconus] incipiat antiphonam [*Venite*] bis continue; deinde diaconus ex parte penitencium dicat* Flectamus genua, *in alba; et diaconus ex parte episcope* Levate *in simili habitu; et ita fiat tribus uicibus : deinde penitentes singillatim per manus ecclesie restituat ministerio archidiaconorum. Quibus peractis procession more solito redeat.*' Frere, *The Use of Sarum*, 143–4.
[42] John T. McNeill and Helena M. Gamer, eds, *Medieval Handbooks of Penance* (New York, 1990), 413.
[43] Nina Rowe, *The Jew, the Cathedral and the Medieval City. Synagoga and Ecclesia in the Thirteenth Century* (Cambridge, 2011), 234.

12 Sculptural detail, north door, Spalding

scourge, the three thongs curved to suggest the object's movement through the air. Across from this, on the sinister side of the doorway, a penitent figure is depicted, head bowed and with hands together in a gesture of prayer. Positioned on the point of the cusping, these figures face inwards and downwards, physically in our presence and sight-line as we, the sinful, stand before the church door.

Marriage

To the people in whose habitat the parish porch was a prominent feature the repetition of activity across a range of rituals, not isolated or restricted to any one-off event, constructed an understanding of the building's purpose. Most medieval parishioners lived their entire life in one parish; the same church building situated the stations in their own life-course and those of their families and fellow parishioners. The event most widely recognised and frequently cited as having taken place in the medieval church porch was the opening section of the marriage rite. Seeking out literature about church porches often leads to reading books on medieval matrimony and finding a scant reference to its setting. However, looking through the lens of the porch (rather than through the rite itself) reveals the ceremony's similarity with that of baptism and confession and emphasises the continuity of meaning.

Although debate persisted over the status of matrimony and the extent of the Church's authority to sanction marriage, formalisation of the rite as a sacrament was confirmed at the 1215 Lateran Council. The social as well as religious value of all seven Christian sacraments in late medieval communities was deeply rooted and ubiquitous. It is plausible that most people would adhere to the correct (orthodox) mode of performing these rituals, following Church rule. Marriage would most often be a ceremony conducted by a priest at the parish church, witnessed by the community. In basic terms, the rite began at the church door and afterwards the party moved inside the church for a blessing or the celebration of Mass. Christopher Brooke asked the question of where medieval marriages happened, and surmised that before the church door was the common practice.[44] By locating the five marriages of his wife of Bath at the church door, Geoffrey Chaucer skilfully established a fictional truth. The Prologue's opening lines tell of the wife's multiple marriages and Chaucer devised his tale's authority and the character's believability by grounding this part of her back-story in terms familiar to the Tales' audience – that she was five-times married and each time at the church door:

> Experience, thogh noon auctoritèe/ Were in this world, is right ynogh for me/ To speke of wo that is in marriage;/ For, lordynges, sith I twelve year was of age,/ Thonked be God that is eterne on lyve,/ Housbondes

---

[44] 'Where did marriages take place? The question seems seldom to have been asked and has received only faint answers. Students of medieval literature acquainted with the Wife of Bath – who took five husbands to the church door to marry them – have readily replied: at the door of the church. There is copious evidence that this was the normal practice in the late Middle Ages.' Christopher N. L. Brooke, *The Medieval Idea of Marriage* (Oxford, 1989), 248.

at chirchedore I have had five –/ If I so ofte myghte had wedded be –/ And alle were worthy men in hir degrée.[45]

This passage from the *Wife of Bath* suggests that by the fourteenth century the Church had control of the marriage rite which, even though doctrinally a sacrament, could still be legitimate without either a priest or a church.[46] Chaucer's locating of marriage at the church door implies 'that one could use the phrase in the late-fourteenth century as part of the normal currency of social chit-chat'.[47] Setting the enactment of marriage at the church door in medieval England was not only a literary device. John Mirk, prior of the Shropshire Augustinian house of Lilleshall, wrote his clerical guidance manual *Instructions to Parish Priests* around the turn of the fifteenth century. Mirk used the same setting for marriage as Chaucer had, but elaborated a little on the location's necessary characteristics: 'Then let hem come and wytnes brynge/ to stoned by at here weddynge;/ so openlyche at the chyrche dore/ lete hem eyther wedde othere.'[48] Witnesses must be brought and the party be gathered 'openlyche', that is, in full sight, for all to see. As the passage continues the bride and groom are reminded of their duty to renounce deadly sin: 'Of lechery telle hem right þys/ that dedly synne for-sothe hyt ys;/ on what kynnes maner so hyt de wro[ugh]t,/ Dedly synne hyt ys forthe broght,/ Saue in here wedhode/ that ys feyre to-fore gode.'[49] In similar manner to the rite of baptism, the event which takes place at the church door is laden with threats of damnation for sinful action. The participants are required formally to reject sin and, in God's honour, to live well in the state of matrimony.

Church porches provided the setting for the marriage rite, not only for the bride, groom and priest, but for the witnesses and others assembled, including family members, children and fellow parishioners. The event was a collective experience and the porch the container of its repeated performance. In seeking to grasp the complexity of porch function it is useful to think of the building in two entwined ways: first, as an architectural device

---

[45] Geoffrey Chaucer, *The Preamble and Tale of the Wife of Bath*, ed. Richard J. Beck (London, 1964), 65 note 'at chirchedore': 'In medieval marriages the man stood at the woman's right hand at the church door while the priest published the banns and performed a ceremony similar to the modern marriage. This section of the service was in English, partly so that the witnesses might fully understand, partly to underline that the bride and groom were the chief actors. Then the bridal party went into the church itself, and the priest sang the nuptial mass in Latin; the roles were now reversed, for inside the church the priest must always take precedence.'
[46] Brooke, *Medieval Marriage*, 250.
[47] Ibid.
[48] Gillis Kristensson, ed. *John Mirk's Instructions for Parish Priests* (Lund, 1974), 79 lines 204–7.
[49] Ibid., lines 208–13.

which cohered a series of ritual events with shared characteristics; second as a shared ritual environment which accrued the historical imprint of a single rite being rehearsed by successive generations of parishioners. A few tantalising instances document the powerful association between marriage and the church porch in the parishioner's mind, implying that the functional association gave mnemonic meaning to the place. In 1492 Christopher Wace of Chipping Wycombe, Buckinghamshire, requested to be buried 'in the wedding porche'.[50] All Saints, High Wycombe (the modern name of Chipping Wycombe) was built c.1275, and included the south porch from this date (although subsequently renewed by nineteenth-century architect G. E. Street).[51] The appellation 'wedding porche' was documented over two hundred years later, a vestige of the building's significance and associations built up over years of experience and engagement. The evidence amounts to neither a formal designation nor an indication of a function which architectural form could blithely follow. A second, less secure example is the final testament, written in March 1500, of John Hasilbyche who desired burial in the churchyard of All Hallows, Northampton, against the wedding door.[52] Unfortunately we cannot be certain that All Hallows had a porch as the church was destroyed by fire in 1675 but John Hasilbyche's testament continues to convey how he understood the relevance of an architectural place based on his repeated engagement with it, attending the weddings of friends and family members, perhaps even his own marriage.

In what sort of environment was the marriage party situated when they met 'at the church door' and did the notional liminal threshold necessarily coincide with the timber valves which closed off the church interior? Contemporary visual descriptions of marriage ceremonies imply that the performance of matrimony could be conducted in front of the porch façade rather than at the door within. Evidently the external limen could be the significant threshold, the location commonly termed 'the church door'. British Library, MS Cotton Nero E ii, f. 217 clearly shows a marriage taking place outside the church building. The apparent double doorway indicates that it is happening not simply at the church door but in front of a porch. The arrangement certainly accommodated the witnesses which John Mirk's *Instructions* indicate were necessary participants at a marriage. Two other British Library manuscripts which include illustrations of marriage ceremonies set in architectural surrounds are MS Harley 4380, f. 6 and MS Harley 4418, f. 36. In Harley 4380 the couple (Philippe d'Artois

---

[50] Reference given in Postles, 'Micro-Spaces', 756.
[51] Nikolaus Pevsner and Elizabeth Williamson, *The Buildings of England: Buckinghamshire*, 2nd edn (London, 1994), 385.
[52] Dorothy Edwards et al., eds, *Early Northampton Wills*, Northamptonshire Record Society, 42 ([Northampton], 2005), 225.

and Marie, daughter of the Duc de Berry) are met by a priest in front of a porch-like entrance building – the couple are outside, the priest is within the porch. By contrast at the marriage of Melusine and Raymond, as depicted in Harley 4418, the wedding party – a priest, several witnesses, and the couple – all stand within a small building which, in having two opposing entrances, one leading outside, the other into another room, is evidently a porch. These manuscript illustrations, although not English, are visual evidence indicating that by the fifteenth century the opening scenes of the Christian sacrament of marriage could be staged either within or beyond a porch. Medieval marriages did not occur in church porches by default, simply because the building was there. Porches cannot be dismissed as merely a cover for the church door, nor conflated with it.

To conclude this brief investigation of the location of medieval marriage a prosaic point is relevant. From the mid thirteenth century the system of mass communication introduced by the preaching friars brought with it an increase in sermons on marriage. These were usually delivered when the Marriage at Cana was the subject of the Gospel reading.[53] Preaching on this theme emphasised the importance of a marriage taking place *in facie ecclesiae*. Parish church porches increased in prevalence from the second half of the thirteenth century and developed coevally with the enhanced status of matrimony and the other sacraments, notably baptism and confession. Although dispute continues over what could constitute a legitimate marriage in medieval England, couples and families who valued social acceptance, conservatism and tradition, as well as seeking God's blessing, would plausibly have sought matrimony at the church door. Where a porch existed, the architecture introduced a level of sophistication and refinement to the ceremony. I know of no extant source which indicates that any porch was built specifically to serve as a setting for marriage, but those commissioning a building are likely to have been aware of the association. Consent and witness are central to the legitimacy of marriage. It is tempting to suggest (although impossible to prove) that the large open entrances of thirteenth- and early fourteenth-century porches were partly a response to the requirement for the ritual of matrimony to be visually accessible to all gathered in participation. It would then follow that, by contrast, the ornate façades and smaller entrance arches of fifteenth-century porches worked as backdrops to extra-mural wedding celebrations. These architectural distinctions are discussed in detail in later chapters.

---

[53] David d'Avray, *Medieval Marriage Sermons, Mass Communication in a Culture without Print* (Oxford, 2000), 1–2.

Dispute and Judgement

You shall appoint judges and officers in all your gates, which the Lord your God gives you, according to your tribes, and they shall judge the people with just judgement. (Deuteronomy 16:18)

Do not grumble against one another, brethren, lest you be condemned. Behold, the Judge is standing at the door! (James 5.9).

As the above biblical passages show, in the Christian tradition thresholds and judgement were closely connected. To what extent did church porches facilitate the administration of just judgement in the medieval parish? Set at the edge of the sanctified church body, porches rested beneath the church's eaves, in God's presence on earth but primarily accessible from the world beyond. Early on in this chapter I commented that a hard border between sacred and secular domains and experiences is anachronistic when applied to the medieval period. A clear indication of this is the appropriation of the church porch as a gate of judgement, a practice which extended far beyond the English parish.

In detailing the Anglo-Saxon past of Christchurch Canterbury, the Benedictine monk-historian Eadmer told not only of the building but of its functional significances. Describing the cathedral as it had existed before Archbishop Lanfranc's rebuilding in the 1070s, Eadmer recounted that: 'At the side [of the south tower] was the principal door of the church which as of old by the English so even now is called "suthdure" and is often mentioned by this name in the law books of the ancient kings. For all disputes from the whole kingdom which cannot legally be resolved within the hundreds or the counties, or even in the king's court, must be settled here as if in the high king's court.'[54] Eadmer was writing in the context of Archbishop Anselm's confrontations with King William Rufus and the Investiture Controversy which spread to many European power bases, including King Henry I's dispute with Pope Paschal II. Eadmer's words are coloured with subtly applied comment on the hierarchy of church and state – God the high king and heaven his court, present on earth at Canterbury.

---

[54] '… et in latere principale ostium ecclesiae quod antiquitus ab Anglis et nunc usque "suthdure" dicitur. Quod ostium in antiquorum legibus regum suo nomine saepe exprimitur, in quibus etiam omnes querelas totius regni quae in hundredis vel comitatibus, uno vel pluribus, vel certe in curia regis non possent legaliter definiri, finem inibi, sicut in curia regis summi, sortiri debere decernitur.' cited in Otto Lehmann-Brockhaus, *Lateinische Schriftquellen zur Kunst in England, Wales und Schottland vom Jahre 901 bis zum Jahre 1307, Band I*. (Munich, 1956), 177. The translation above is taken from H. M. Taylor, 'The Anglo-Saxon Cathedral Church at Canterbury', *Archaeological Journal* 126 (1969), 106.

2. FUNCTIONS

The practice of judicial affairs being conducted at points of entry in great churches became well established; a famous example of later date is the 'Galilee' porch on the western side of Lincoln's south transept (fig. 13). Lincoln chapter's ownership of land, property and advowsons of parish churches bestowed on it jurisdiction over its tenants and clergy. This responsibility was formalised in 1219 when the king permitted the chapter 'to hear pleas of the Crown and other assizes and to receive and return royal writs concerning the prebends of Welton, and the manors of

13 Galilee porch, south transept, Lincoln Cathedral

Asgarby and Friesthorpe "at the door of the church", ... doubtless in the Galilee Porch at the south end of the south-west transept'.[55] The room above this porch also had a judicial function as a leet court, reinforcing the responsibilities of the Lincoln Chapter as manorial lord. In 1263 the jurisdictional liberty of this court was established and tenants and servants of the cathedral gained freedom from town jurisdiction.[56]

A very similar set of circumstances occurred at the cathedral of St Etienne in Bourges in the first half of the thirteenth century. In 1232, the trial of Petrus de Rocceto took place '"*in ipso introit ecclesie Bituricensis, scilicet in porta illa que est ex parte domus archiepiscopalis*", that is to say along the southern flank of the Cathedral where the archiepiscopal palace and the officiality were located'.[57] Branner identifies the place where the trial occurred as the south lateral portal which was not only deeper than the archbishop's portal but, being covered by a porch, commodious enough to enable the necessary personnel to gather.[58]

Evidence for the transmission of judicial function from the portals of great churches into the parish is tantalising and often elusive. However, a rare documented case of a parish church porch being a place of legal debate and judgement is known from late-thirteenth-century Yorkshire. In 1294, in the parish of Warter in the East Riding, a quarrel erupted regarding the extraction of oblations. To resolve the case Archbishop John le Romeyn instructed that an inquisition be conducted 'in the porch of the said church' with the plaintiffs 'being present and standing before a great number of the parishioners of the said church'.[59] There may well be other such instances in the surviving written record of low-level parish disagreements being brought to the pre-Reformation church porch for resolution – and did post-Reformation legal performance in church porches continue medieval practice?[60] The long tradition of judgement being administered at gates

---

[55] Dorothy Owen, 'Historical Summary', in *A History of Lincoln Minster*, ed. Dorothy Owen (Cambridge, 1994), 147.

[56] Ibid.

[57] Robert Branner, *The Cathedral of Bourges and Its Place in Gothic Architecture* (Cambridge, MA, and London, 1989), 58.

[58] Ibid.

[59] '*in porticu dicte ecclesie, presentibus dictis querelantibus et astante multitudine parochianorum*', see Andrew W. Taubman, 'Clergy and Commoners: Interactions between Medieval Clergy and Laity in a Regional Context', unpublished Ph.D. thesis (University of York, 2009), 166 and 180 n.61. My sincere thanks go to Claire Daunton for this reference.

[60] For post-Reformation discussion of the quasi-legal identity of church porches, see Steve Hindle, 'Destitution, Liminality and Belonging: the Church Porch and the Politics of Settlement in English Rural Communities, c.1590–1660', in *The Self-Contained Village? A Social History of Rural Communities, 1250–1900*, ed. Christopher Dyer (Hatfield, 2007), 46–71.

and its continuation in the great churches of medieval Europe make it conceivable that an appropriate form of the same practice would occur at the parish porch. Civil disputes did not need to involve formal legal action. Churches were appropriately impartial places where rival factions could meet and attempts be made to settle the disagreement before it dissolved into violence.[61] As Peter Fergusson has discussed in relation to Canterbury, the architecture of the entry complexes of the great churches is replete with motifs communicating notions of judgement from the specific to the awesome.[62] It has also been affirmed that upper chambers of castle and monastic gatehouses in England have a long tradition of serving judicial and administrative purposes, for example the twelfth-century gate-tower at Bury St Edmunds housed the court of the sacrist.[63] As already noted, the interchange of architectural ideas between church porches and other types of entrance building bolsters the suggestion that porches were places of judgement and perhaps even punishment; associations potentially appropriated from King Solomon and the throne of judgement set within the porch, as discussed in chapter one.

Upper Chambers

As in the case of the leet court at Lincoln and the sacrist's court at Bury St Edmunds, medieval judicial activity was often associated with the upper spaces of entrance buildings. It is plausible that the upper chambers of parish church porches were put to similar use, but primary evidence for this and the many other suggested functions of these rooms is scant. Even the popular terms 'parvise' and 'parvise room' might only have been applied to these upper spaces since the eighteenth century. In the mid eighteenth century, the Norfolk antiquary Francis Blomefield wrote: 'In 1300, I find Mention of a Publick School for Children to learn to read and sing, kept

---

[61] See Josephine Waters Bennett, 'The Medieval Loveday', *Speculum* 33.3 (1958), 361.

[62] Braswell also made the connection between expulsion of penitents and the role of visual narrative sequences in enforcing the sacramental message: 'many a sinner would not have made his annual confession had he not been motivated by the fear of eternal damnation. Gruesome portrayals of hell on the west portal of many a cathedral reminded him of what lay in store for the unrepentant. Furthermore, if he did not confess, he was not eligible to receive the sacrament of the Eucharist. Thereupon, he was excommunicated and shunned by the faithful. Upon death, he was denied a Christian burial, which precluded future resurrection.' Mary Flowers Braswell, *The Medieval Sinner: Characterization and Confession in the Literature of the English Middle Ages* (London, 1982), 27.

[63] John Goodall, 'The English Gatehouse', *Architectural History* 55 (2012), 6–7.

in the Parvis of this Church [sc. St Martin's, Norwich].'[64] It is, however, more plausible that this use of the word is of Blomefield's time rather than contemporary with the document to which he alludes.

As a type of forebuilding akin to city and monastic gates church porches were appropriated for legal activity and plausibly also for schooling. Historically a parvise was an open court in front of a church, such as that referred to by Chaucer as the place where lawyers met their clients at St Paul's.[65] Despite Chaucer's use of the word 'parvise' to refer to an open court, Matthew Paris' tale of a pauper-priest holding schools and selling books 'in the parvise' has been commonly taken to mean the chamber above a porch.[66] Paris did not, of course, describe the place or the building, but there is at least equal reason to read his 'parvise' as an open court as it is to think in terms of an upper chamber. Historical distance makes it almost impossible to be certain of Paris' meaning and examples which favour either definition are available. In early Christian practice the parvise was an open area at the edge of the sacred church where the catechumen's preparation for baptism occurred; the uninitiated given instruction beyond the confines of the church.[67] However, the sixteenth-century poet and antiquary John Leland referred to a favoured domestic apartment or studying chamber as being 'called paradise'. This usage leans towards the sort of hidden-away, confined room that would be found above a porch.[68]

In medieval England elementary education was provided in a range of locations and buildings, including in chambers above city gates. For example, in Bristol, Newgate was used in this way from the 1420s and Frome Gate from the 1530s.[69] The close functional relationship between church porches and city gates in medieval England fuels speculation around the parish church porch being the likely setting for parochial education. However, in most cases this use of the church porch is likely to have been adopted long after the medieval period. At Mildenhall (Suffolk), for example, the upper chamber was converted into a school room in the ninteenth century, but

---

[64] Francis Blomefield and Charles Parkin, *An Essay Towards a Topographical History of the County of Norfolk*, 11 vols (London, 1805–1810) (Blomefield, *Topographical History*), vol. 2, 748.

[65] This remains the definition and etymology given in the Oxford English Dictionary (http://www.oed.com/view/Entry/138366). In 1929, George Frost queried its meaning and supported the suggestion that it drew on an academic model of Oxford colleges to connect the Man of Law's parvise with education of students. George L. Frost, 'Chaucer's Man of Law at the Parvis', *Modern Language Notes* 44.8 (1929), 496–97 n.2.

[66] Wall, *Porches and Fonts*, 37.

[67] Wall, *Porches and Fonts*, 10 and 36.

[68] Lucy Toulmin Smith, ed. *The Itinerary of John Leland in or about the Years 1535–1543: Parts I–III* (London, 1907), 53.

[69] Wall, *Porch and Fonts*, 137 and 140 fig.33.

the mid-sixteenth-century school occupied a separate building abutting the 'church wall'.[70] The porch at Great Massingham was also used as a school room. According to his will of 1676, Charles Calthorpe gave £20 to 'make fit the schoolhouse over the porch by repairing and glazing the same and setting up suitable seats'.[71] Calthorpe is often credited as the founder of the school, but the wording of his will suggests renovation of an existing establishment rather than a new foundation. John Sell Cotman's 1819 depiction of the porch shows an inserted timber floor, a window at first-floor level in the west wall and a stair turret in the south-west angle of the porch and aisle. The porch is also shown with a panelled parapet, which today only survives on the aisle. Is it possible that the mid-fifteenth-century renovation of the church included building a stair turret to facilitate access to the upper room? and if so, was this stair for school children?

The detail of social activity is sometimes seen by the historian through negative documentation – castigation for wrongdoing or legislation against common practice. Evidence of children being given education in the Norfolk town of Lynn in the fourteenth century paints a picture very different to the modern Sunday school. In 1373 Henry Despenser, bishop of Norwich, issued episcopal rules for the clergy of Lynn with the aim of correcting behaviour and improving practice; the education and discipline of children in church was one area considered in need of reform. 'We also forbid any priest or anyone else to hold schools or admit children (*pueros*) for instruction in the same church or chapel lest when the children are crying while being whipped, divine services are interrupted and the people's devotion is more easily distracted.'[72] It is not known if the children's cries would still be heard from the upper chamber of a porch, but taken at face value the example argues against church buildings being places of schooling.

There is however some evidence suggesting that the upper room at Hevingham, Norfolk, was used for teaching. The benches now used as choir stalls are thought to have been removed from the upper chamber of the porch.[73] The form of these 'stalls' is not in keeping with choir seating of the fifteenth century, nor of nave pews (fig. 14). They are a different sort of seating to what is commonly found in parish church naves and choirs and, as their dimensions fit snuggly in the room over the porch, it is plausible that they were benches for pupils taught in that space.

[70] '[1555] ... Item payd to Tyd, the mason, for mendyng of the church wall next the end of the scole house 2s', Judith Middleton-Stewart, ed., *Records of the Churchwardens of Mildenhall* (Woodbridge, 2011), 135.
[71] Cited in the Great Massingham Church Guide, 2010.
[72] John Shinners and William J. Dohar, eds, *Pastors and the Care of Souls in Medieval England* (Notre Dame, IN, 1998), 106.
[73] Nikolaus Pevsner, *The Buildings of England: North-East Norfolk and Norwich* (Harmondsworth, 1962), 163.

14 Benches probably originating from the upper room, south porch, Hevingham. Reproduced by permission of Hevingham parochial church council

Although direct evidence is limited there is no reasonable argument against the upper chambers of some porches having been used for education and instruction in the medieval period. The circumstances of every parish were unique and generalising about the use of communal spaces is problematic. In fact, the uses to which upper chambers over porches could be put were as diverse as parishioners' imaginations and requirements. Such diversity of function underlines the point that parishioners were open-minded in their opinion of what a porch could be used for once built. Sometimes, however, the fabric evidence is suggestive. The room above the porch at St Nicholas' chapel in Lynn, Norfolk, appears to have been always intended as a place of regular use and some sophistication. The integral stone handrail in the vice shows that a good standard of provision was made, a point emphasised by the rail ending at the upper room door rather than continuing to the roof. Similarly, Pevsner suggested that the unusual three-storey porch at Ingham in Norfolk may have afforded accommodation for a priest and sacrist.[74] Ingham, like its three-storey

---

[74] 'The south porch is higher than the aisle. It is in fact three storeys in height, a great rarity. ... The upper floors may have been the living quarters of the parish priest, who was at the same time the sacrist of the priory. He may however have lived

counterpart at Edington in Wiltshire, was a secular college as well as the parish church and it is perhaps more than coincidence that these rare examples of three-storey church porches are associated with colleges. It has already been noted that the gate-tower at Bury St Edmunds was the location of the Abbey sacrist's court, and it is plausible that the official duties of a sacrist (rather than accommodation) might explain the arrangements at Ingham and Edington.[75]

Particular uses for the chambers above certain church porches are knowable on a case-by-case basis, but broader conclusions are difficult to draw. Refurbishment and renovation, the loss of ceilings/floors and original fittings, have left relatively few upper spaces with fabric evidence to indicate how they were to be used. However, architectural and documentary evidence does survive for one particular function of upper rooms, and that is when they were built to serve as chapels. Parishioners' wills from Northill, Bedfordshire, offer a case in point. A chantry was established in the chapel above the porch in accordance with the 1489 will of William Fitz. The messuage and its appurtenances Fitz bequeathed were 'for the maintenance or support of a suitable chaplain to celebrate there' not for the building or maintenance of the fabric. Implicitly the chapel probably already existed.[76] At the centre of the porch vault are the arms of Sir John Trailley: or, a cross between four martlets, gules. Trailley (d.1399/1400) was a knight of the shire who spent much of the late fourteenth century in Gascony and was mayor of Bordeaux in 1390. The only known remnant of a will was probably written in 1390 as he is styled 'mayor of Bordeaux'. On the basis of the heraldic evidence the porch was clearly John Trailley's benefaction, probably realised by his executors in the early years of the fifteenth century.[77] The popularity of the chapel, dedicated to St Anne, in the upper room of the porch continued well into the sixteenth century. William Percell, writing his will in 1518, gave 20d 'to St Annys chapel over

---

to the N[orth], where domestic accommodation evidently existed between the church and the priory.' Ibid., 177.

[75] 'In some cases an upper chamber over a church porch or vestry is popularly known as a "priest's chamber", but it seems difficult to find substantiation for this.' W. A. Pantin, 'Chantry Priests' Houses and other Medieval Lodgings', *Medieval Archaeology* 1 (1957), 257.

[76] William Fitz's will is TNA PROB11/8/343. See also Margaret McGregor, *Bedfordshire Wills Proved in the Prerogative Court of Canterbury 1383–1548* (Bedford, 1979), 28. Reference to William Fitz's foundation is also given in William Page, *The Victoria History of the County of Bedford*. Volume 3 (London, 1972), 242–51.

[77] N. Harris Nicholas, *The Controversy between Richard Scrope and Sir Robert Grosvenor in the Court of Chivalry* (London, 1832), 223–5. Also see J. E. Brown and F. A. Page-Turner, eds, *Chantry Certificates for Bedfordshire with Institutions of Chantry Priests in Bedfordshire* (Bedford, 1908).

the church door'.⁷⁸ In 1521 William Fitz's endowment was augmented by Cicily Beton's bequest of land to fund a priest to sing for her soul in the chapel of St Anne at Northill.⁷⁹ Finally, in 1530 Thomas Tomms left 'to St Anne in the chapel of Northivell [Northill] church a brown cow' and his will goes on to specify that 'a priest is to celebrate for as long as 10 marks lasts, for the most part in the chapel of St Anne'.⁸⁰ This upper chamber was no silent, dead space, distanced from the living. It would have resounded with the ritual recitation of intercessory chantry prayers, the priest and friends and family of the departed ascending and descending the narrow stairway, crossing paths with fellow parishioners as they did so. Such a porch chapel was an actively present constituent of the parish church, multiplying the celebration of divine office and facilitating memorialisation of ancestors; a place sufficiently important for parishioners to recall it when making their last testaments.

At Mildenhall in Suffolk the chamber above the north porch was also a chapel, in this case dedicated to the Blessed Virgin and approached through a doorway flanked by spandrels showing the Annunciation. The chapel's location and dedication are documented in the wills of John Gardener (1519) and Alice Bateman (1527).⁸¹ It is highly probable that this was the chapel of the gild of the Virgin, the most popular of eight gilds in the town.⁸² Despite the challenges posed by a gild chapel being located above a porch for the choreography of processions, similar arrangements are known. For example, the gild of St Mary at Thirsk, Yorkshire, was located in the porch.

Whether as a chantry, as at Northill, or for a gild, as at Mildenhall, chambers above porches served as chapels, extending the liturgical environment towards the west end of the church and into the building's upper register. Porch chapels brought sanctity into the western arm of the church. In doing so they add complexity to the church's sacred spatial patterning, traditionally focused on the chancel and high altar. Physical evidence for the same function is found in the chamber above the north porch at

---

⁷⁸ Patricia L. Bell, ed., *Bedfordshire Wills 1484–1533* (Bedford, 1997), 31. The reference being to the room above the church door, rather than above the porch, implies that the porch was considered as an extended door and thus once inside the porch one was effectively within the church.
⁷⁹ Ibid., 29.
⁸⁰ Ibid., 177.
⁸¹ Middleton-Stewart, ed., *Records of the Churchwardens of Mildenhall*, xxviii.
⁸² Ibid., xlvi–xlvii. Although the high altar is dedicated to St Mary the gild would have had a separate space in which to celebrate. The east end of the north aisle was the chapel of St John (serving the gild of St John the Baptist) and the corresponding south aisle chapel was dedicated to St Margaret; therefore neither of these prominent locations served Mildenhall's Marian gild.

St Peter and St Paul, Salle in Norfolk (see fig. 51). The church was subject to a major building campaign in the early fifteenth century and the fabric indicates that the porch was laid out with the aisle which, based on heraldic evidence on the west tower, was built c.1405–20.[83] The upper room was designed and built as a chapel dedicated to the Coronation of the Virgin, as indicated by the extant piscina and aumbry, and the subject matter of the imagery on the flamboyant tierceron star vault. On the central boss the Virgin, her palms together before her chest, sits to Christ's right, his hand raised in blessing. However, the specific nature of this chapel and altar, whether chantry, gild or otherwise, is unknown.

Chapels raised over points of transition and entry were familiar to a much larger architectural tradition, one which offers some insight into the significance of the arrangement. Royal castle architecture built in England in the second half of the twelfth century features just such an arrangement, notably at Scarborough (1159–69), Orford (1165–73) and Dover (1181–86). At all three sites a chapel occupied the first-floor chamber of the forebuilding.[84] The altar of the upper chapel at Henry II's Dover castle was dedicated to St Thomas Becket (murdered 1170, canonised 1173) – an example of cultic reverence being shown to the archiepiscopal martyr at the entrance to the largest tower in the Angevin world.[85] Church porches are firmly part of the wider history of entrance structures, in meaning as well as architectural form; a shared kinship which forged associations across the medieval built environment. These vaulted porch passageways with chapels over brought people into proximity with an altar. Crossing the liminal threshold correlated with passing beneath the holy sanctuary of the chapel above.[86]

The importance of physical, bodily proximity was central to medieval notions of experience. Pilgrims clambering through the Confessor's tomb at Westminster so they could be corporeally as close as possible to the saint's holy remains; the seeking and acquisition of relics or contact relics and wearing them upon the body beneath clothing – these were performative expressions of belief in the efficacy of material remains. The importance

---

[83] Paul Cattermole and Simon Cotton, 'Medieval Parish Church Building in Norfolk', *Norfolk Archaeology* 40 (1983), 263.

[84] John Goodall, *The English Castle* (New Haven and London, 2011), for Scarborough and Orford see 130, for Dover 141–4. For Orford see also T. A. Heslop, 'Orford Castle, Nostalgia and Sophisticated Living', *Architectural History* 34 (1991), 42

[85] Goodall, *English Castle*, 144.

[86] For discussion of the importance of proximity to altars in relation to chancel passageways see Katherine M. Boivin, 'The Chancel Passageways of Norwich', in *Norwich: Medieval and Early Modern Art, Architecture and Archaeology: Transactions of the British Archaeological Association Annual Conference 2012*, ed. T. A. Heslop and H. E. Lunnon (Leeds, 2015), 307–23.

placed on spatial proximity was not restricted to sacred relics, it came to permeate medieval society. Burial practices, for example, saw men and women seeking interment close to altars within the architectural spaces created by their patronage. This practice adapted the way in which altars had historically coalesced around the translated bodies of holy men and women or, for foundations lacking the body of their patron saint, treasures of bones, blood, hair or flesh efficaciously contained within the altar mensa slab. In the high and late Middle Ages those patronising the making of a church or chapel desired burial 'as close as convention permitted to the most sacred part of the church'.[87] Arrangements of people and objects were intentional and designed, creating networks of association and giving meaning to places and activities. The provision of an altar over the church door did no less than announce the fundamental significance of the whole building – a container for the sacred and facilitator of Christian salvation.

For most double-storey church porches, however, the activities which took place in upper chambers are undiscoverable, the fabric revealing nothing of the room's purpose and documentary evidence lacking. But the buildings do tell us something, quite mundane but important. Spaces above a porch, normally of sufficient height for a person to stand in comfortably and readily accessible by means of a stone vice, were designed for people. They are not cramped, dark, remote storage holes, but places where people spent time. The importance of an extra room, convenient but separated from the body of the church, is particularly evident where an upper chamber was added to a single-storey porch. The south porches at Acle, Catfield and Hemsby, all in Norfolk, were single storey when first built and subsequently heightened. The change of fabric and earlier roofline on the external elevations clearly show the extent of the new work – a space ready for integration into the life of the parish whatever the need of its people.[88]

Burial

Although J. C. Wall considered burial in a porch to be something of a privilege, more recent interpretations have viewed porch burials less positively. They have been seen as a way for a testator to ensure their body's resting

---

[87] Michael Michael, 'The Privilege of "Proximity": Towards a Re-definition of the Function of Armorials', *Journal of Medieval History* 23.1 (1997), 61.

[88] For a recent and detailed consideration of upper spaces in religious buildings see T. Huitson, *Stairway to Heaven: The Functions of Medieval Upper Spaces* (Oxford, 2014).

place was inside the building[89] or simply as evidence of preferences to be buried in the newest part of the church.[90] These inferences are at least an oversimplification of a complex arrangement, and perhaps even inaccurate as a reflection of burial choices and as an explanation of why porches were built.

In 1375 Dionysia de Ty of Barsham offered her soul to God, the blessed Mary and All Saints, specifying that her body should be buried outside the church door ('*sine fores ecclesiae sanctis trinitate*') and that a porch was to be built over her tomb ('*ubi volo unum porche fier[i] su[m]ptib[us] meis sup[ra] sepult[uram] mea[m]*').[91] Her will includes many donations to the fabric of other churches and gifts of money and goods to family members and other associates. All told, she left monetary bequests of over £80, a considerable sum for a late-fourteenth-century will. However, she left no money for the porch or any instruction as to what form it was to take. It is likely that Dionysia had made the necessary arrangements during life and therefore such details did not need including in the will. Suggesting she did not warrant burial in the church and therefore constructed an internal burial location for her own grave is implausible; the implication is that she did not wish her body to be buried inside the main vessel of the church. After death the laying of her body at the church door and the erection of an accompanying porch composed a very particular memorial. The memory-impression constructed in the minds of other parishioners would include at least an element of humility and almost certainly enshrine her role as benefactress of their community.

Dionysia de Ty's will is the earliest of several such Norfolk documents which together challenge the assumption that being buried in a porch was a poor substitute for interment in a superior location. Like Dionysia, Robert Ediman of Brisley had close personal links to the parish church and chose burial within the porch. He was rector of Brisley from 1395 and in his will of 1435 instructed his executors to bury his body in the north porch,

---

[89] 'John Wareyn of Nayland, baker, 29 Nov. 1441 In extremis; to be buried in the north porch of the church of St James of Nayland; to the emending of the church, that is, to the emending (*ad emendac*) of an antiphoner and the making of a new porch (*vestibuli*) ... This bequest has the appearance of one buying his burial-place inside the church by helping to pay for the porch that was going to be built over him.' Peter Northeast, ed., *Wills of the Archdeaconry of Sudbury 1439–1474: Wills from the Register 'Baldwyne' Part I: 1439–1461* (Woodbridge, 2001), 41.

[90] Simon Cotton, *NARG News* 49 (s.l. Norfolk Archaeological Rescue Group, 1987), 13.

[91] NRO NCC Heydon 94, 95. It is likely that this will relates to Holy Trinity, Barsham, Suffolk, with which the family had historic associations. However the dedication of East Barsham, Norfolk, is alluded to in Dionysia leaving her soul to All Saints.

which was to be covered with lead at Ediman's expense. Implicitly the porch was nearly complete, unlike the west tower to the building of which he bequeathed a third of the fruits of the rectory.[92] As rector and funder of the fabric, Ediman warranted burial within the body of the church, even in the chancel, but his expressed wish was to be interred in the porch. In these two East Anglian examples we see evidence of porches originating as places of burial and their architecture serving as tomb canopies.

Architectural detailing of church porches can also reveal their relationship with death and burial, although information about the individual might be lost. One such case is Forncett St Peter in Norfolk. In the late fourteenth and early fifteenth century this church was developed in a fashion common across East Anglia. The late eleventh-century round tower was retained, but the chancel and nave were renewed wholesale, with the addition of a clerestory, north and south aisles, and north porch. No matter the reason for entering the church, whether ceremonial or more mundane, one did so through the porch set at the west end of the north aisle. Cut in low relief the crossed keys and swords of the parish's apostolic

15 Exterior inscription, north porch, Forncett St Peter

[92] NRO NCC Surflete 182.

patrons SS Peter and Paul protectively flank the outer archway. Above is a horizontal ashlar frieze, the upper border of which rises to encompass a crowned IHC trigram presented in flint and limestone flushwork (fig. 15). The frieze inscription reads: 'St Peter and Paul Patronys of this Place Pray to I.H.S. [sic] in Heven yt I may see his face.' The reference is to God's promise to Moses in anticipation of him leading his people out of Egypt: 'And again he said: Thou canst not see my face: for man shall not see me and live' (Exodus 33.20).

Porches and burial have long-established associations. As descendants of Anglo-Saxon *portic*, late medieval porches are versions of a building type which for centuries served as burial chambers, as discussed in chapter one. Porches were places of frequent activity and the heightened presence of the living added to their appeal as places for burial. Accepting that a gravemarker would accompany a burial in a porch, at least for a period of time, perhaps a generation, the deceased, corporally present below parishioners' feet, would be remembered and prayers said for their soul's swift passage through purgatory. The high number of passers-by could be anticipated to equate to the quantity of prayers.

Burials at thresholds were penitential in nature, and humility as much as prominence was a primary impetus for interment in porches. In 1163 the remains of Geoffrey de Mandeville, first earl of Essex (d.1144), were moved into the porch of the new Temple Church in London following his absolution from excommunication for three years after his death, during which time his body hung on a tree.[93] The Temple porch provided the appropriate penitential location for Mandeville's burial but, as David Park has also explained, according to Templar customs, burial within the church would not have been possible.[94] A conflation of penitence and prestige (Mandeville was probably the founder of the new Temple Church) defines the character of tomb porches in relation to the status of the deceased.[95] Evidently, *porticus* offered appropriate places for the burial of dignitaries who sought humility as well as remembrance and the same practice occurred at monastic sites, notably in the western galilee-porches of Cistercian houses. For example, in the early thirteenth century, Matilda, countess of Warwick, was interred in the galilee at Fountains Abbey, and in the west porch at Rievaulx Abbey on one of the eight extant tombs is inscribed the name

---

[93] Park, 'Medieval Monuments', 69.
[94] Ibid., 74.
[95] Christopher Wilson, 'Gothic Architecture Transplanted: the Nave of the Temple Church in London', in *The Temple Church in London: History, Architecture, Art*, ed. Robin Griffith-Jones and David Park (Woodbridge, 2010), 19–44.

of Isabel de Roos, who died in 1264.[96] Burial before the church door placed the deceased prostrate at Christ's feet, he being analogous with the door to salvation ('I am the door. By me, if any man enters in, he shall be saved: and he shall go in and go out, and shall find pastures.' John 10.9). Ideas of penitence and humility are therefore fundamental but, as will be discussed in chapter three, the architecture of the accompanying porch also implies a subtle negotiation between pious humility and respectful decency.

Whether or not originally built to shelter a grave, the popularity of porches as chosen burial sites has to date been largely neglected. Studies of medieval burial practices give little attention to them and the relevance of burial to porch design has been misunderstood. The discrete nature of the church porch as a place for burial is witnessed in the placement of ledger slabs. Porch burials rarely cross the boundary either between churchyard and porch, or porch and church; instead they are placed immediately before the door, similar in manner to burials before chancel screen doors but differentiated by the functional character of the building.[97] The liminal state of the deceased is congruent with the ritualised character of the porch through repeated performance of baptisms, marriages and penitential waiting. Penitential burials inhabit the same space as the living when they actively renounce the devil. In Christian theology the eternal soul separated from the temporary body at the moment of death, and as the corpse corrupted the soul rested in limbo awaiting the Day of Judgement and pronouncement on its ultimate fate. The living function of the church porch, imbued with notions of penitence and forgiveness, provided an architectural mnemonic of the symbiosis between experience and belief.

To bring this discussion of tomb porches to a close, it remains to consider their practicality for the trappings of memorialisation. In fifteenth-century Norwich, Thomas Clerk, a parishioner of St Andrew's, and Robert Bois, a parishioner of St Peter Mancroft, each specified that a marble slab was to be laid over their grave within the porch.[98] A little more detail is given by

---

[96] For Fountains Abbey see M. Cassidy-Welch, *Monastic Spaces and their Meanings – Thirteenth-Century English Cistercian Monasteries* (Turnhout, 2003), and for Rievaulx Abbey see Peter Fergusson, Glynn Coppack and Stuart Harrison, *Rievaulx Abbey* (London, 2006).

[97] Christopher Daniell suggests that porch burials are an example of interments which cross boundaries: 'The two key areas were the thresholds between the outside and inside of the church (which, if there was a porch, was a larger area than simply the doorway); and the rood-screen, and especially its door, between the more secular nave and the holier chancel.' Christopher Daniell, *Death and Burial in Medieval England 1066–1550* (London, 1997), 100.

[98] Thomas Clerk, citizen and alderman of St Andrew's, Norwich, instructed that: 'my body to be berede in the churche porche of saynt Andrewe in Norwyche by Anabill late my mother in the sowthside next the wyndow of our ladyes chapell and I wyll ther by layde a stone of marbill upon us bothe wythe a scripture of our

John Hobard, priest of the Trinity Guild in Bassingbourn, Cambridgeshire. His will was written on 1 June 1518 and he desired burial by his mother in the 'sowthe porche of the chirche ther of the blessid apostellis Petur and Paule; for the buriall and grownd ther breking and pavyment reysing and ageyne repayring, I bequeathe iii s. Item for a marble stone with owr namys gravid theruppon to be layd upon owr gravys, for all maner costes to it fynished, I will xl s.'[99] In the late medieval English parish the predilection for floor slabs and elaborate brasses fitted well with the practical necessity of people moving through the porch, where a coped grave covering or standing monument would cause considerable inconvenience.

The often large ledger stones with inset brass memorials which cover porch graves sets them apart from the proliferation of largely anonymous churchyard burials. The roof of the porch protected the ledger slab, ensuring the long-term visual legibility of inscription and effigy. Looking upon the memorial, touching it with one's eyes, engaged the living with the dead. Monumental inscriptions were not simply 'representations of disembodied utterances' but visually tangible material objects.[100] The words, their meaning and intercessory agency were activated by the viewer's sight and their efficacy renewed through each recitation. An effigial image could do much the same. Whether text or image, devices used on medieval graves circumvented the need for the living onlooker to have known the deceased, or to conjure a self-willed remembrance of them. The monumental stone could trigger in the mind of any person able to look upon it a memory of the deceased and stimulate prayer for the safety of their soul. In addition the grave would be regularly asperged by living parishioners pausing as they cleansed themselves with water from the holy water stoup, droplets falling upon the tomb. Such a ritual created powerful phenomenological bonds between the living and the dead.

The orientation of grave-markers in porches and alignment of the body must, in many instances have been at odds. Tomb slabs in general are aligned along the north-south axis of the porch, the 'head' being immediately before the church door. Examples are legion but in East Anglia include the large tomb slab in the south porch at Snetterton and the rather smaller one in the porch at East Lexham. If the body beneath lay in the same direction as its overlying monument it would run counter to the

---

names'. NRO NCC Palgrave 39. Robert Bois's will reads: 'I wyll that my executors to provide for me a grave stone of marbill and to bild a porche over the dore wher at I shall lye buried.' NRO NCC Alblaster 148.

[99] Printed in David Dymond, ed., *The Churchwardens' Book of Bassingbourn 1496–c.1540* (Cambridge, 2004), 174–5.

[100] Antony Eastwood, ed., *Viewing Inscriptions in the Late Antique and Medieval World* (Cambridge, 2015), 2.

ubiquitous Christian tradition of aligning graves east-west. But, as Philip Rahtz points out, 'we should in some cases … distinguish the body orientation from that of the grave or container'.[101] English medieval parish church porches support his case very well.

Walter Burgess of Horsham in Sussex took matters a little further than most, founding a chantry in the north porch at Horsham. The space almost immediately proved inconvenient and inappropriate for the recitation of masses for the dead and in 1307 Burgess paid for a chapel to be built to the east of the porch and dedicated to the Holy Trinity. Connection between the two spaces was maintained as a door in the east wall of the porch gave access to the chapel.[102] Although the porch proved unsuitable for the daily workings of a chantry chapel, Burgess's initial action and subsequent maintenance of the spatial relationship between porch and chapel demonstrates how firmly grounded was the porch's association with burial and memorialisation.

Giving and Receiving Alms

Biblical text was the fundamental literature for the Christianity of medieval Europe, from papacy to parish. Through visual gloss and textural annotation, aural recitation and theological exegesis it stimulated performance of Christian belief through worldly analogies of biblical history; the Palm Sunday processions discussed early on in this chapter being one such example. The New Testament also provided a model for medieval porches being places where those in need sought aid and succour. In the five porches situated around the healing Pool of Bethsaida 'lay a great multitude of sick, of blind, of lame, of withered: waiting for the moving of the water' (John 5.2–3) A man who had spent thirty-eight years in one of the Pool's porches, unable to reach the water because of his infirmity, was instructed by Christ: 'Arise, take up thy bed and walk' (John 5.8). A similar event saw a man who sought alms in a porch miraculously healed. On this occasion the man, lame from birth, had lain daily at the Beautiful Gate seeking alms, was healed in the name of Christ by apostles Peter and John (Acts 3.3–11). The resonance of care and alms conveyed in these biblical texts was commuted to porches in medieval Europe. The appellation of the porch at Salisbury was discussed in chapter one. A vivid literary confirmation is a fifteenth-century poem inscribed in the south porch of Bourges Cathedral. It is worth citing the text in its entirety:

---

[101] Philip Rahtz, 'Grave Orientation', *Archaeological Journal* 135 (1978), 1.
[102] G. H. Cook, *The English Medieval Church* (London, 1954), 112.

Those who cry and are poor/ In spirit will always be happy/ For they shall laugh/ In the end Heaven will hold/ The poor to endure/ And many of the rich shall perish.

Those who beg and of whom no evil/ Can be said, and who ask for the/ Love of God and cry for alms will be happy/ If they pray for those who give/ And for him who had made this place.

The poor who have patience/ And live according to their conscience/ In keeping with love and harmony/ If they endure their indigence/ And hold that it is enough/ Then they shall have mercy.

Therefore, poor people, endure/ And suffer all evils/ Patiently and willingly/ For by so doing you will gain/ Beatitude and eternal paradise.

And everyone give, for God's sake/ Generously to the poor, for at the/ Judgement Our Lord will pay us back/ Giving alms usually will not impoverish a living man/ Who gives with an open heart.

Give, you who pass this place/ Alms for sinners/ To free them from Purgatory/ By means of the good and alms/ That each man does and gives to them/ They will receive the glory of Heaven.

The final stanza summarises the whole; resting beneath these words, supplicants waited, and the poem spoke for them.[103]

Almsgiving in the parish was closely associated with funerals and anniversaries. Late medieval testators' instructions were heavily laden with gifts to the poor in their community, practical realisations of the corporeal works of mercy. As often stipulated in the wording of a last testament, gifts of alms were made in the expectation that prayers would be said for the deceased's soul and the souls of family members and associates. Alms were often distributed at the funeral but testamentary instructions were also left that the act be repeated at the celebration of anniversary masses. Based on material from Bristol, Clive Burgess discusses the form taken by the anniversary and cites evidence for the prominent role of almsgiving in these rituals.[104] Benefactors expected their beneficiaries to attend their anniversary services and the alms (in the form of bread, ale or money) may

---

[103] The poem is cited in Michel Mollat, *The Poor in the Middle Ages: An Essay in Social History*, trans. Arthur Goldhammer (New Haven and London, 1986), 262–3.

[104] 'More money was devoted to it [i.e. almsgiving] that to any other, presumably as a result of the belief that spiritual benefit would increase with the amounts given ... [A]lms not unusually disposed of something in the region of half the total allocated to support a service.' Clive Burgess, 'A Service for the Dead: the Form and Function of the Anniversary in Late Medieval Bristol', *Transactions of the Bristol and Gloucestershire Archaeological Society* 105 (1987), 189.

have been given in return for attendance.[105] The giving of alms at Requiem services would logically come at the end of the event – in crude terms 'payment' would be made after the work had been done. Paupers attending the service, having been encouraged by the 'belman' announcing the event in the town, would leave through the church porch collecting purses or loaves, perhaps set out along the often-present stone benches, as they went.

Protective thresholds continue to entice the needy and destitute, and in medieval England monasteries, castles, bridges and civic gateways all attracted those seeking charity.[106] The nomenclature of the Penniless Porch, the c.1450 gateway to Wells cathedral green, carries with it the building's history – an ornately vaulted baldachin giving shelter to the destitute and providing a focus for the giving of alms by the city's wealthier citizens who sought to perform corporal acts of mercy. The chance of receiving benefice at the church door, as much as the guarantee of a penny in return for attending a funeral mass, would have brought those seeking succour to the entrance of an English parish church just as a lame man had sought alms and solace at the Beautiful Gate. Church porches thus facilitated the medieval sacred-social contract which was founded on the eight corporal works of mercy and gave moral guidance to individuals and communities across medieval England.

Conclusion

'The concept of space – a physical location to which complex cultural and religious meanings are ascribed – is always created and re-created by people using it. It is never static, and its interpretations are often ambiguous.'[107] Although this determination of the plasticity of space offered by Emilia Jamroziak relates to Cistercian monastic houses it can be applied to parish church porches equally well. Yet whilst the principal denotive function of a porch might be augmented or superseded by conative functions, a multiplicity of uses and meanings co-existed. A strong thread connected many of the ways in which porches functioned through human interaction with them, specifically notions of judgement inherent within the performance

---

[105] Ibid., 190.

[106] '[C]harity in the Middle Ages was distributed through ecclesiastical institutions in the form of alms to the poor. ... Gifts were usually in kind (bread, clothing, fuel), were normally distributed at the gate of the monastery or the door of the church.' William J. Courtney, 'Token Coinage and the Administration of Poor Relief during the Late Middle Ages', *The Journal of Interdisciplinary History* 3.2 (1972), 285.

[107] Emilia Jamroziak, 'Spaces of Lay-Religious Interaction in Cistercian Houses of Northern Europe', *Parergon* 27.2 (2010), 38.

of events which occurred at the church door and experienced in the presence of God, the ultimate judge standing forthright at the door.

Incessant expectations of honesty which the analogous church door bestowed upon activities realised there can be demonstrated by a final, controversial, use to which church porches were sometimes put – trade and the transacting of business. Consequential of the New Testament gospel accounts of Christ's expulsion of traders from the temple, conducting business affairs within the confines of a church was ideologically deemed to be miscreant behaviour. The reality of medieval life, however, has left evidence of a more pragmatic approach. Acceptance, perhaps even encouragement, of trade and business within church precincts appears to have been as common as attempts to uphold official values and restrict what a church was used for.[108] Where it proved beneficial, porches could readily be considered separate from the body of the church and thus beyond the boundary within which the conduct of business was forbidden. For example, as recorded at Riccall (Yorkshire) in 1519, on feast days pedlars sold goods at the church porch.[109] If the Yorkshire parish of Riccall positively assigned traders to the porch when events brought large numbers of people to the church, evidence of trading in church porches being outlawed indicates that some authorities saw it as an undesirable practice. Perhaps the fate of Ananias and Saphira, as recounted in Acts 5.1–11, served as a deterrent to anyone dishonestly transacting in a church porch. One such example is the documented prohibition of cloth sales from the porch of St Michael's, Coventry, in 1455.[110] As with so many of the possible uses to which porches were put, universally relevant generalities are difficult to conclude although individual cases can be known.

The resonance common to the sacramental and ritual activities which involved the church porch was renunciation of evil and celebration of God's victory, verbally and performatively driving the devil from the person, the community and the place simultaneously. The architectural function of the church porch might therefore be framed as constructing an environment or habitat in which the earthly could practice and demonstrate their commitment to the reality of salvation. In the medieval parish this central tenet of the Christian faith was more than an intellectual theological certainty, it was lived experience in a world fraught with hardship, danger

---

[108] See J. G. Davies, *The Secular Use of Church Buildings* (London, 1968).
[109] David Dymond, 'God's Disputed Acre', *Journal of Ecclesiastical History* 50.3 (1999), 474.
[110] Linda Monckton, 'St Michael's, the Architectural History of a Medieval Urban Parish Church', in *Coventry: Medieval Art, Architecture and Archaeology in the City and its Vicinity, British Archaeological Association Transactions XXXIII*, ed. Linda Monckton and Richard K. Morris (Leeds, 2011), 162 n.27.

and uncertainty. In such circumstances no meaningful distinction could be drawn between the body, the mind and the architectural environment to suggest what porches were used for. As this chapter has explored, the function of church porches in medieval England was multivalent, multi-layered and occasionally even ambiguous; the buildings an architectural constituent of a highly ritualised society.

It should be recognised that English medieval church porches proliferated from the early thirteenth century onwards, and the probable catalyst for this new architectural mode was a set of circumstances which historically coalesce around the same date. Two historical events which influenced this architectural development of the English parish church, and the relevance of the church porch, were the General Interdict of 1208 and the papal canons resulting from the Fourth Lateran Council of 1215. In combination they perhaps created a climate in which porches acquired greater relevance and desirability. Neither event can be considered as the cause and porches the effect, but the perceptible shift in the parishioner's engagement with the church building in the first and second decades of the thirteenth century broadly coincided with a new building type.

Underscoring and clarifying much existing custom, Pope Innocent III's sacramental decrees pronounced at the Lateran Council in 1215 were subsequently dispersed and adopted throughout Christian Europe by a network of bishops, clerics and papal legates. Failure to confess annually to one's parish priest risked personal excommunication, exclusion from the Mass and denial of Christian burial. In summary, Canon 21 required 'Everyone who has attained the age of reason is bound to confess his sins at least once a year to his own parish pastor with his permission to another, and to receive the Eucharist at least at Easter. A priest who reveals a sin confided to him in confession is to be deposed and relegated to a monastery for the remainder of his life.'[111]

Architectural precedent can be found in twelfth-century Rome, where the remodelling of churches and basilicas was instrumental in strengthening the papacy's moves to reform Christian practices and coincided with an intense flourishing of cultural and intellectual interests across Western Europe. From the early twelfth century the façades of Rome's churches gained the addition of projecting forebuildings, a form of columned porch extending the full width of the west front. Although distinct from English porches in both location and form, Roman architectural and liturgical developments of the twelfth and early thirteenth centuries offer a source of inspiration for similar changes in the designed habitats of Christian ritual in England.

[111] Medieval Sourcebook, *The Canons of the Fourth Lateran Council, 1215*: https://sourcebooks.fordham.edu/basis/lateran4.asp

2. FUNCTIONS

The ways in which people interacted with their church buildings, their very existence as the place for achievement of sacramental rites available to every Christian when necessary, was challenged in England in the early years of the thirteenth century. The almighty conflict between King John and Pope Innocent III over the appointment of Stephen Langton to the archiepiscopal seat at Canterbury, a case which would adjudge whether Church or state had ultimate power over investiture, saw John's lands in England and Wales and all they contained placed under general interdict on Sunday 23 March 1208. The impact of the Interdict on English liturgical performance and the risks posed to Christian souls through cessation of sacramental provision is not to be underestimated. As Stephen Church has confidently demonstrated in a study of the books requested by the king from Reading Abbey, the royal court's intellectual efforts were immediately put into resolving the minute detail of what the Interdict really meant in practical, everyday terms.[112] Negotiation and clever fudging of arrangements over borders and boundaries was necessary. In basic terms the Interdict meant ecclesiastical censure, no offices except baptism and confession by the dying were to be performed, access to churches was barred, the doors locked.

Renewed emphasis on correct and regular adherence to sacramental performance and the very real risk of being denied participation in the Eucharist coincided with the advent of porches becoming familiar constituents of the English medieval parish church. It is also worth noting that by the end of the thirteenth century parishioners formally held responsibility for upkeep of the nave, essentially everything west of the chancel arch. Some responsibility for building and maintaining part of their parish church, overseen, organised and exacted by the 'guardians of the church' (*gardiani ecclesiae*), those who would later come to be termed churchwardens, was first clearly defined in canon law in the twelfth century. In England, it was stated unequivocally in the synodal statutes of Exeter of 1287. Financial levies paid by individual parishioners were amalgamated and collectively underpinned corporate concerns with the form, decoration and architectural appropriateness of the church fabric, working to enhance the building which was the earthly focus of a good Christian life.

Relatively few examples existed by this date, and the status of the church porch was still uncertain. However, as it lacked doors or window glass access to it could not be denied easily. As we have seen, the church door was of powerful significance in parish rituals and the associated

---

[112] Stephen Church, 'King John's Books, Master Richard Marsh and the Interdict Proclaimed in 1208 on England and Wales', in *Writing History in the Anglo-Norman World: Manuscripts, Makers and Readers, c.1066–c.1250*, ed. Laura Cleaver and Andrea Worm (York, 2018), 149–65.

forebuilding was appropriately sanctified for Christian burial and cleansed from the lustral water stoup. In parishes where the church already had a form of porch, perhaps the impact of the Interdict was lessened. These parishes had a consecrated building in close proximity to the church where reduced versions of the sacraments, including confession, purification and confirmation, could be performed '*in facie ecclesiae*'. In such circumstances, a church porch presented a pragmatic solution to ensuring human salvation. In the national memory the Interdict was not simply a matter of high office, courtly politics or detailed intellectual discourse. In every parish its consequences would be felt, and responses sought. A central response to this, and to Pope Innocent's commitment to the seven sacraments, was realised in architectural form, and from the early thirteenth century England enthusiastically embraced the protective agency of church porches.

The East Anglian Church Porch
Architecture and Decoration

3

THIS CHAPTER DISCUSSES architectural themes and variations by identifying the form and content of East Anglian church porches built between c.1240 and c.1540. Key adjustments made to the design and conception of porches through to c.1540 were changes of greater significance than the adoption of current style. Observable shifts in the architectural form of church porches imply often subtle, sometimes more blatant, reappraisals of what porches could do and how they did it. As the previous chapter has demonstrated these buildings were intimately associated with the medieval life-course, neither neutral nor passive. This chapter continues our exploration of relationships between people and architectural spaces, attending to the formal details of buildings as a category of object and investigating how meaning was embedded in their design. To counteract any bias or predilection for the special or remarkable, the discussion is limited to East Anglia and the wealth of extant porches great and small built during the medieval period. The survey benefits from capturing the full scope of church porches as realised in this wealthy and populous region. Bounded to north and east by the North Sea, to the west by Cambridgeshire and the Isle of Ely (the kingdom of Mercia) and to the south by Essex (kingdom of the East Saxons), East Anglia is a geographical area of approximately 3650 square miles (9454 sq km) defined as much by its history as its physiography. Current political and governmental definitions include Cambridgeshire but for the purposes of this book East Anglia is understood to comprise the modern-day counties of Norfolk and Suffolk, thus approximating the Anglo-Saxon kingdom of the East Angles and the medieval ecclesiastical diocese of Norwich.

Church Porches in East Anglia, c.1240–c.1400

The earliest extant lateral porches in East Anglia are those at West Walton, built c.1240, and Great Massingham, built c.1280. Although it has been suggested that the two heavy cruck timbers which form the porch façade at Somersham, in Suffolk, date from the late thirteenth century, on comparison with Frating and Aldham (both in Essex) Somersham is more plausibly one of many fourteenth-century timber porches in Suffolk.[1] The paucity of thirteenth-century porches in East Anglia contrasts with their relative prevalence in counties to the north and west, especially Cambridgeshire, Northamptonshire and Lincolnshire. By way of comparison, Northamptonshire has at least thirty-four porches built before c.1350 and eight of those pre-date 1300.[2] Porches were built coevally with English parish churches from the late twelfth century and in some regions were an established building type well before the extant material evidence shows their popularity in East Anglia. West Walton and Great Massingham are both located in northwest Norfolk, a short journey from the Lincolnshire border, but present two very different architectural resolutions to the challenge of designing a church porch.

The Thirteenth Century – West Walton and Great Massingham

As we have it today, the porch at West Walton measures 13ft 8in (north-south) by 12ft 6in (east-west) with a floor area of 152 sq ft (fig. 16). It is a diminished version of the original building. When first built the porch was approximately twice as deep, from entrance arch to church door. When the south nave aisle was widened in the early fourteenth century the porch was not demolished but curtailed. Despite this change there is no indication that this porch ever had side openings. Externally the side walls are articulated by a string course running approximately at mid-height and a moulded plinth. A large entrance arch (14ft 5in x 8ft 10in) dominates the front elevation and the generously wide multi-ordered arch meets the polygonal buttresses, with no wall plane in between the two elements. The two-tier buttresses, the portal jambs and arch are all densely articulated with arcaded shafting of decorative rather than structural necessity creating a detailed layering of the building's surface. In height the arch also consumes the façade gable and the porch's aesthetic comprises a monumental

---

[1] J. C. Wall offers various instances of 'Romanesque porches' but several of these are unreliable. For example, the porch at Castle Rising (Norfolk) is taken by Wall to be Romanesque (Wall, *Porches and Fonts*, 106), but is actually a nineteenth-century building in which no attempt was made to adhere to the design of the early-fourteenth-century structure it replaced. For Frating and Aldham, see Cecil A. Hewett, *Church Carpentry: A Study Based on Essex Examples* (London and Chichester 1982), 28–9.

[2] My thanks go to Paul Barnwell for this information.

16 Exterior view, south porch, West Walton

void framed by architecturally-sculptural masonry. Internally detached shafts rising from narrow stone benches visually divide the solid walls into a series of framed bays – notional 'niches' functioning as individual seats. The form adds to the sense of spatial enclosure. It is also an architectural invitation to sit down, for the body to pause supported by the building, an arrangement imitative of seating provision in monastic or collegiate chapter houses. The provision of canopied seating makes the space more than a walkway by which to approach the church door. The impression of openness established by the porch's exterior does not anticipate the enclosed interior even though the motif of arcaded shafting is carried through. The design of West Walton porch also manipulates perceptions of scale. From the exaggerated supra-human dimensions of the entrance arch to the humbling intimacy of the interior environment, external conditions (sun-light, wind and temperature, bird-song, voices and the everyday noises of the parish) remain sensorially perceptive.

17 Exterior view, south porch, Great Massingham

By contrast the porch at Great Massingham is predominantly open architecture, with considerably more aperture than walling on all three sides (fig. 17). As at West Walton, a monumental arch (15ft 10in x 7ft 2in) dominates the façade, with a minimal weight of masonry surrounding it. Although only single storey, the building's height far exceeds human scale, emphasised by a strong sense of verticality and the apex of the roof breaking through the adjacent aisle parapet. The body of the porch is entirely different from the solid side walls at West Walton. The flanks at Massingham comprise six apertures made of ashlar shafts and plate-tracery archheads arranged to form a columnar arcade. Split flint masonry frames the elevation and is the only solid part. The continuous hood-mould, which serves all six arches, and the string course, which runs immediately above, both create a strong horizontal continuity rather than a structure divided into vertical bays. Internally, the effect is rather different. The openings commence approximately four feet above present floor level, and so there is a considerable depth of solid walling in the lower part of the building. The shaft bases are lower inside the porch than outside and divide the wall into compartments. Integral stone benches run the length of the elevation and one is protected by the masonry from exposure exposed to drafts coming through the apertures. The impression of openness created by the arcaded exterior is diminished but not removed on the inside of the porch.

Although West Walton is primarily an enclosed space and Great Massingham essentially an open one, both porches are constructed of series of columns, possibly an intentional allusion to the 'porch of pillars' built by King Solomon, as discussed in chapter one. A 'porch of pillars' was a strong design motif in the thirteenth century and interiors lined with columns or shafts quickly transferred from greater churches, including Salisbury, Southwell, Malmesbury and the Lincoln galilee, to the parish porch. The Solomonic connotation of the main formal elements was successfully transmitted between designing architects and commissioning patrons during the thirteenth century.

In thirteenth-century East Anglia a reasonably consistent design brief for church porches was widely shared but interpreted and realised in quite different ways. The generic brief might be summarised as follows: a façade dominated by an arch which impresses by its size and elaboration, an internal space of some sophistication where time could be spent in reasonable comfort, and through which processions could pass uninhibited from the churchyard to the church door. According to extant examples, one response to these demands was open architecture, the other enclosed. The relationship between solidity and permeability is a motif strongly present in the western porch at Ely and the transept porch at Lincoln. Both structures feature a proliferation of arcaded arches, bringing a sense of order and repetitious rhythm to each building. The arcades are composed of freestanding, en délit shafts brought away from the wall plane, introducing the effect of shadow and giving visual depth to structurally solid walls. Although no direct architectural debt is traceable between the two porches of these great churches and the earliest parish church porches in East Anglia, they are elite patterns which emphasise the likeness rather than the disparities between the porches at West Walton and Great Massingham.[3]

Available evidence suggests that porches only started to become a desirable part of East Anglian parish churches from the mid thirteenth century but even then they were only rarely adopted. The architectural form and geographical location of West Walton and Massingham, combined with the relative prevalence of porches elsewhere, suggest the building type was imported into Norfolk from the north and west. Yet neither of these porches was apparently immediately influential in East Anglia (as far as extant structures tell). The large open entrance was retained but otherwise, from around 1300, a very different model was prevalent.

Church Porches in the Early Fourteenth Century

Church porches built in East Anglia in the first quarter of the fourteenth century are architecturally severe, uncompromising in their simplicity and aesthetically unlike either West Walton or Great Massingham. Lying a little over 20 miles northeast of Great Massingham, the parish church of St Mary at North Creake is a substantial and imposing structure, built c.1301 (fig. 18). In the first half of the fifteenth century the nave was heightened and refenestrated, an aisle added on the north side and a west tower built, but the unaisled south façade survives from the original campaign.[4] The fabric evidence shows that the porch was constructed in the c.1301 phase of works. It is a straightforward unbuttressed box, measuring 12ft 10in (north-south) by 10ft (east-west) with ashlar quoins and entrance arch. Small quatrefoil openings pierce each side wall and the original roof pitch was considerably steeper than that which is present today. The front elevation is finished with consistently dark grey split flints, whereas the fabric of the side walls is much less uniform. The porch displays none of the florid elaboration of the contemporary sedilia and Easter sepulchre in the church. The entrance has a simple chamfer, the side openings are small, shaped holes or apertures rather than windows, and almost no element

---

[3] For further discussion of these architectural iconographies of these two Norfolk porches see Helen Lunnon, 'Inventio Porticus – Imagining Solomon's Porches in Late Medieval England', *British Art Studies* 6 (2017): http://dx.doi.org/10.17658/issn.2058-5462/issue-06/hlunnon

[4] Pevsner, *North-East Norfolk and Norwich*, 270.

18 Parish church of St Mary, North Creake

(except the entrance hood-mould) protrudes from the plane of the walling. The architectural sophistication and design detailing seen at West Walton and Great Massingham, and the associated sense of grand entrance, are absent. North Creake and its extant regional contemporaries, such as Honingham and Hockwold, indicate that around 1300 simple, minimally adorned structures had become acceptable as parish church porches in East Anglia.

These porches, although not expensive buildings, present consistent elements repeated between buildings, suggesting an awareness on the part of the designers of the type of structure a porch should be. The relationship between solid walling and open apertures had become regularised, the standardised form of small box-like building with an entrance arch set into solid walling, small side aperture and little, if any, exterior decoration. The north porch at St Mary Polstead is an example of this early-fourteenth-century architectural simplicity and reductive approach to building a church porch. No longer were church porches in East Anglia the reserve of sophisticated patrons and the highly skilled master masons they commissioned. By the early years of the fourteenth century the church porch had become a familiar constituent of the East Anglian parish church, and masons successfully responded to the varying financial means of their patrons by designing buildings more conservative than those of their predecessors.

Even architecturally ambitious examples imply that a degree of reserve was deemed appropriate for church porches built in early-fourteenth-century East Anglia. The south porch at Besthorpe exemplifies the point. The church of All Saints was built in a single campaign during the first quarter of the fourteenth century and is essentially unaltered. The high quality of the building's design and the skilful achievement of its details indicate a closely considered, thought-through programme of works. Although the name of the designer, mason and major benefactor are unknown, the building is itself evidence of the extent to which the church was cohesively planned, designed and executed. By 1303 the prior and convent of Wymondham held the rectory of Besthorpe and the right to appoint the vicar there. It is probable that the eastern arm of the church was built under the influence of the priory and, given the coherence between the main vessel and the chancel, it seems that this influence was exercised over the whole project.[5] The porch is of the same high build quality as seen throughout the church and they share many elements, including the ashlar-faced buttresses and unlabelled hood-moulds. The steepness of the roof pitch and the curvature of the entrance arch define the porch as a miniaturised complement to the south transept located one bay further east. The porch was clearly designed in the same mode as the rest of the church.

Besthorpe porch lacks architectural incident and decoration, internally and externally. The large open entrance is the main design element but is characterised by its austerity. Even the buttresses merely extend the width of the façade without adding any elaboration. The low springing point of the arch maximises its height, resulting in near-parity with the height of the jambs. In its proportions it is not dissimilar to Great Massingham and West Walton but, as at North Creake, Besthorpe's severity is in stark contrast to the clusters of multi-ordered shafts, capitals, arches and pinnacles of East Anglia's earliest surviving porches, built in the thirteenth century.

None of the East Anglian porches considered so far in this chapter have external imagery. Inside Besthorpe porch, above the church door, is a small image niche, mutilated by the removal of its moulded details when the roof timbers were replaced. This niche, which would have contained an apotropaic figurative image, implies the location of the protected threshold and in so doing sets the porch beyond the limits of the church. At this period, even when built in conjunction with the rest of the church, porches were seemingly peripheral locations, a suggestion also supported by the large entrance arches and small side openings which are common

---

[5] Blomefield, *Topographical History*, vol. 1, 490–1.

19 Exterior view, south porch, Gooderstone

features in the early fourteenth century. Each of these formal elements would change in character in the second half of the century, questioning the extent to which the porch was a covered place beyond the confines of the church or integrated with the church building as a single unit.

By the 1340s the simple, box-like porches of the early century were being surpassed by greater architectural elaboration and a developmental trajectory is identifiable around the mid-century. A good example of this is Gooderstone (fig. 19). The porch's design closely resembles that at Besthorpe and the wing-like buttresses and plain entrance arch would not be out of place on a porch built c.1310. Gooderstone porch was, however, built along with the south aisle c.1342.[6] The main feature differentiating this porch from its earlier counterparts are the large, circular reticulated windows of finely cut ashlar in the east and west walls. Judging by the neatly cut glazing grooves in the three trefoils, these originally contained glass. Although of considerably greater depth than Besthorpe, and therefore more commodious, Gooderstone porch remained notionally beyond the confines of the church proper as the keystone at the apex of the church

---

[6] For discussion of the church at Gooderstone see T. A. Heslop, 'The Nave of Attleborough, Norfolk, and the Architecture of Unknowing', in *Architecture, Liturgy and Identity*, ed. Zoë Opačić and Achim Timmermann (Turnhout, 2011), 52–4.

20 Exterior view, south porch, Hunstanton

door provides a plinth for an image. The significant threshold, or point of transition, between the interior and exterior of the church was still perceived as located here, not at the entrance of the porch.

Gooderstone indicates small changes in porch design but other buildings of similar date demonstrate greater shifts, for example, St Mary's, Hunstanton (fig. 20). The date of the rebuilding is not entirely certain. The advowson had been gifted to the Augustinian abbey of Haughmond in Shropshire by Sir John le Strange in the reign of Henry III and the early phases of the building campaign are indicated by the late-thirteenth-century great east window.[7] Judging by the tracery of the circular windows in the porch, this part of the campaign came some years later, perhaps into the 1340s. The entrance is tall and wide, and elegantly elaborated with cusping in the form of a narrow stone cinquefoil which springs from the respond capitals and trims the underside of the arch. This treatment is unique for a porch in East Anglia and owes considerable debt to micro-architectural tomb design. The 1857 renovation of the church did much to the porch but the entrance arch and circular side openings filled with rotated mouchettes

---

[7] Blomefield, *Topographical History*, vol. 10, 324; Pevsner, *North-East Norfolk and Norwich*, 211.

are original features.[8] These paired 'port-hole' windows are more detailed in their patterning than the single openings at Gooderstone and were not glazed. According to the architecture of these two examples, in the 1340s porch apertures – the entrance arch and the side windows – were becoming increasingly elaborate. By contrast, the external walling remains unadorned and the buttresses, where present, are simple lateral extensions to the front elevation. At Cotton (Suffolk) the south porch was built in conjunction with the south aisle c.1340 and with something of the same status. The traceried porch windows have the same reticulated design as in the aisle, although fractionally less ornate in profile, and are of comparable scale. Implicitly the design of this porch casts it as a confident contribution to the church exterior. The porch façade was remade in the fifteenth century when evidence of its original form and decoration was lost and with it potentially early evidence of how porch façades developed around the mid fourteenth century.

The church of St Martin at Thompson was built c.1349 by Sir Thomas and Sir John Shardelowe as part of their chantry foundation served by a college of five secular priests and a master, John Sporle.[9] The porch was part of the church-building campaign and retains the high entrance arch which is commonplace in porches built in the first half of the fourteenth century. The most important feature of the porch is the three-light opening in the front gable (a similar triple-niche is set above the large open arch in the west wall of the tower at Cotton). At Thompson this feature restricts the height of the entrance arch and the apex aligns with the wall plate rather than rising into the gable. Also departing from the existing model are Thompson's angle buttresses – set at 45 degrees to the wall plane they widen the façade (as at Besthorpe and Gooderstone) but also break forward of the main building line. Similarly, although the side openings are still small, they are cusped lancets formed in the tradition of Gothic church windows familiar in the main vessel of churches, and in keeping with the approach taken at Cotton. By contrast, the circular portholes of Gooderstone and Hunstanton are associated with peripheral locations, for example, the clerestory fenestration at Heacham or, on a grander scale, at Cley. Thompson is an early example of a shift towards integration of porches into the church proper, and Cotton also suggests this direction of travel.

The sense of architectural trajectory which is beginning to form around fourteenth-century porches is only part of the story. Also built at the same

---

[8] See John Sell Cotman, *Specimens of Norman and Gothic Remains in the County of Norfolk, Second Series of Etchings* (London, 1838), plate 27.

[9] William Page, ed., *A History of the County of Norfolk*, volume 2 (London, 1906), 461–2.

period are a small number of western porches, around thirty-six lateral tower-porches and, in Suffolk, many timber porches. As will be shown, all three forms contributed to the architectural development of the building type more broadly.

Timber Porches

The architectural debt that West Walton and Great Massingham owe to their relative proximity to Lincolnshire and Northamptonshire – both counties rich in thirteenth century stone porches – cannot be sustained in any other part of the East Anglia. Economically wealthy and highly populated in the century-and-a-half after the Norman settlement, the region saw considerable investment in high quality church buildings in the period preceding the advent of the parish church porch. Conversely, the region boasts very few Early English examples, either owing to a lack of need following Norman investment or rebuilt in the late medieval East Anglian building boom. Stone, whether imported limestone or indigenous flint, was not the only building material favoured in medieval East Anglia and, at the opposite end of the region to West Walton, south Suffolk is rich in timber porches constructed in the fourteenth century.

The density of woodland managed for timber in south Suffolk makes this part of the county comparable to areas of Essex and Kent where timber porches are also well known.[10] Cruck-framed entrance arches give the buildings a domestic, vernacular feel, exacerbated by the effects of time and weathering on the timber. The significance of this corpus of buildings becomes apparent when they are contextualised alongside their stone counterparts. The enclosed flanks of stone-built porches, lacking all but the smallest of apertures, resulted from pragmatic construction of uniform solid walling. The attenuated linear form of timber has greater similarity with the en délit shafts familiar at Massingham, but also the shafts used to elaborate porches of great churches such as Southwell Minster and Tewkesbury Abbey. Timber building technologies and the material's natural form facilitated the building of open, arcaded porches. The weight of masonry is replaced by timber stanchions set on a low stone wall. At Great Blakenham pierced tracery survives in the upper part of each opening, a rare survival of the delicate carved decoration which originally elaborated these porches.

The most architecturally ambitious and visually spectacular timber porch in East Anglia is the north porch at Boxford (fig. 21). This building achieves every attribute of a fully-fledged Decorated stone porch but does

---

[10] Terence P. Smith, 'Three Medieval Timber-Framed Church Porches in West Kent: Fawkham, Kemsing and Shoreham', *Archaeologia Cantiana* 101 (1984), 137–63.

21 Exterior view, north porch, Boxford

so with a remarkable sense of structural lightness owing to the manner of the timber frame. Two pairs of large florid apertures construct the side walls and the entrance arch is framed by shallow niches and blind reticulated panelling above open cusped lancets. Internally the timber frame excels with a web of moulded ribs cast effortlessly over the space.[11] Boxford north porch is a remarkably accomplished architectural set-piece regardless of its material. Widely appreciated as the highest quality timber porch in Suffolk, its exceptional qualities only really become apparent when compared with East Anglia's stone porches of the same period. Boxford porch offers a template for changes which would gradually be seen in lithic porches built from the mid-century, reaching maturity around 1400. Precedents for Boxford porch in timber-based structures are difficult to find. Choir stalls with vaulted canopies share some formal similarities but lack the porch's truly architectural attitude. It is tempting to think that the timber octagon at Ely, erected after the fall of the Romanesque tower in 1322, might have provided inspiration for the inventive approach taken at Boxford.

Unlike the flint-and-stone boxes built in Norfolk in the half-century before the Black Death, Suffolk's fourteenth-century porches are timberwork enclosures within which the sensations and perceptions of the exterior environment are retained. Physical deterioration of early timber porches would have necessitated rebuilding and it is impossible to know how many extant stone porches replace earlier timber ones. The restricted time period for the dating of timber porches in Suffolk is strong evidence for widespread adoption of the porch in parochial Suffolk considerably earlier than is suggested by the grand, elaborate structures which showcase the regional fascination with flint flushwork towards the end of the Middle Ages. Suffolk's early experiments with porch architecture were in timber, not stone.

Western Porches in Fourteenth-Century East Anglia

The porch at Snettisham stretches across the western elevation of the church (fig. 2). It is formed of a three-bay arcade fitted between, and standing very slightly forward of, the west-front buttresses which ascend into pinnacles flanking the gable wall. Snettisham church, including the western narthex, was constructed c.1330, plausibly planned and overseen by John Ramsey, master mason at Ely Cathedral. The porch was a direct design influence on that built by Peter Parler on the southern transept of

---

[11] For constructional context of this vaulting technique, see Robert Beech, 'The Hammer-Beam Roof of Westminster Hall and the Structural Rationale of Hugh Herland', *Architectural History* 59 (2016), 29.

Prague Cathedral.[12] In 1327 Robert Lord Montalt bequeathed the manor of Snettisham to Queen Isabella who, by this date, was resident at Castle Rising.[13] Queen Isabella is regarded as patron of the work at Snettisham, an attribution architecturally supported by the fact that the only building in England which bears comparison with the porch is that at Leeds Priory, Kent, where the adjacent castle had come into the queen's possession in 1327.[14] Although unusual and often termed unique, the Snettisham porch belongs to the long European tradition of tri-arched western entrances, including in England Lincoln Cathedral and its classical allusions.[15] The connection drawn between Snettisham and Leeds Priory raises the point that a western narthex might more commonly be associated with monastic architecture than parish churches. Even so, it shows that design ideas were successfully transferred between the two architectural spheres.

Leeds Priory was an Augustinian foundation, but it is with Cistercian abbeys that west porches are more readily associated, including Byland, Fountains, Melrose, Rievaulx, Roche, Sweetheart and Tintern.[16] The west porch at Tintern Abbey, constructed c.1325–30, is understood from the fragmentary remains to have taken the form of an arcaded narthex, therefore following similar lines to that at Snettisham parish church.[17] Whilst the form may be broadly similar, however, the porch at Tintern was a two-storey structure with an upper chapel, which housed a miracle-working statue of the Virgin and contributed to the abbey becoming a pilgrimage site in the fourteenth century. Nicola Coldstream has posited that west porches (or galilees) at Cistercian monasteries follow the Burgundian and Bernardine plans and hence are found at Rievaulx and Fountains, both founded in 1132. The fourteenth-century resurgence in monastic architecture evoked the 'youthful confidence' of the 1130s and 1140s. Building campaigns at the Scottish Cistercian abbeys of Sweetheart (founded 1273

---

[12] Wilson, 'Peter Parler', 105.

[13] Blomefield, *Topographical History*, vol. 9, 45.

[14] Wilson, 'Peter Parler', 105; Richard Fawcett, 'Snettisham Church', in *King's Lynn and the Fens: Medieval Art, Architecture and Archaeology, The British Archaeological Association Conference Transactions 31*, ed. John McNeill (Leeds, 2008), 142.

[15] Anthony Quiney, '*In Hoc Signo*: The West Front of Lincoln Cathedral', *Architectural History* 44 (2001), 162–71.

[16] Based on the ground plans in David Robinson, ed., *The Cistercian Abbeys of Britain. Far from the Concourse of Men* (London, 1999).

[17] 'Leeds and Snettisham may have been offshoots from the Cistercian tradition of west porches represented in the late thirteenth century by examples at Tintern in Monmouthshire and Neath in Glamorgan, although these differed in projecting well beyond the buttresses of the west front. In so far as it is possible to judge, given that Leeds and the Cistercian examples have been demolished almost to ground level, Snettisham is much the closest in form to Prague.' Wilson, 'Peter Parler', 105 n.26.

and rebuilt in the fourteenth century) and Melrose (founded in 1136 and rebuilt in the 1380s) included western porches designed in deference to the earlier tradition.[18] At Holm Cultram, Tintern and Newminster, a west porch was also added to the existing abbey church. Cistercian west porches were places appropriated for high status burials. No documentary evidence is known for interments in the porch at Snettisham but the architectural exchange makes the suggestion plausible.

The west porch at North Elmham, built c.1350, is entirely different in conception to that at Snettisham, although similarly located. At Elmham, the front-facing buttresses of the tower are greater in depth than the porch and therefore, although the porch projects westwards from the tower wall, it does not protrude beyond the primary building line. The porch is bounded on three sides by the tower and the only open element is the front entrance. The porch and tower appear integral, but the porch is only partially over-sailed by the tower and does not constitute its ground storey. The porch is faced in ashlar, not flint, which differentiates it from the tower. A moulded string course above the entrance, decorated with fleurons, serves as the edge for the roof and encourages the porch to be seen as a discrete element distinguished from the large west window and the mass of the tower above. The keystone at the apex of the entrance hood-mould is of a piece with the base of an image plinth upon which a sculpture of the Virgin is likely to have stood, directly aligned with the central light of the window behind. The image of the church's patron saint was positioned directly above the entrance into the porch, not set in a niche in the façade. Although this is a very different type of building to that at Thompson, it is further evidence of the gradual enhancement of church porch exteriors in East Anglia around the mid fourteenth century. Porches were starting to be conceived as part of the main vessel of the church; more integral, less peripheral.

Three western porches are known in Suffolk, plausibly built in the fourteenth century. Western galilees at Debenham and Cavenham (now lost), and the surprising arrangement at Mutford, where a deep western porch with wide, open front arch and side windows, was uniquely built against a tall twelfth-century round tower. The Mutford porch was part of a campaign of church renewal which included the addition of an octagonal belfry, a remade tower arch, new south aisle and chancel. Mutford porch adheres to the basic template for East Anglian porches built in the first half of the fourteenth century but stands out because of its unusual location. Although not an approach widely employed, it might be that this porch

---

[18] Nicola Coldstream, 'The Mark of Eternity, The Cistercians as Builders', in *The Cistercian Abbeys of Britain. Far from the Concourse of Men*, ed. David Robinson (London, 1999), 50.

was simply built over a pre-existing door in the base of the round tower. The suggestion gains credence if the chevron arch over a later tomb now in the north nave wall originates from a lost opening which once led from an earlier Romanesque western galilee into the tower.[19]

Tower-Porches

The fourteenth-century porches considered up to this point are single-storey buildings, but full height towers were also constructed over the lateral doors of parish churches from the end of the thirteenth century into the early fifteenth. The open-fronted ground-floor levels of these structures were formed as porches, externally accessed and set before the church door. They exemplify the appetite for architectural hybridisation and experimentation in England from the late thirteenth to early fifteenth century. Architectural history's tendency to segregate buildings into nominal types is challenged and unsettled by tower-porches, but the defining formal attributes of both parents were successfully integrated to new effect. Neither porches nor towers were location specific, and whilst the majority of East Anglian tower-porches abut the north or south side of the church, occupying the traditional porch location, a small number of western towers with an open ground-floor stage were also built. One such example is at Wighton, where the porch exists beneath the tower, a solution rather more elegant than the protruding western galilee at Mutford. Tower-porches have received little attention to date, and the interpretation offered here is the first detailed attempt to analyse the significance of their architectural appearance and its development. At least thirty-six lateral tower-porches of medieval date are extant in East Anglia, eighteen in Norfolk and eighteen in Suffolk, as listed in the table below.

Tower-porches are not confined to East Anglia, with examples elsewhere including Sutton-under-Brailes (Warwickshire), Melbury Bubb (Dorset), All Saints Canterbury (Kent), Ringmore (Devon), Yeldham (Essex), Tutbury (Staffordshire) and Norbury (Derbyshire).[20] Counties with several

---

[19] 'St Andrew, Mutford, Suffolk', *Corpus of Romanesque Sculpture of Britain and Ireland*: http://www.crsbi.ac.uk/site/348/; Nikolaus Pevsner and Enid Radcliffe, *The Buildings of England: Suffolk* (Harmondsworth, 1975), 369.

[20] 'The tower of Norbury church, Derby, the mausoleum of the Fitzherberts, occupies a unique position, situated as it is between two chapels on the south side of the nave. In the first half of the 15th century, when the church consisted of an unaisled nave of the 12th century and a chancel of the 14th, the tower was built against the south wall of the nave. The ground floor served as a porch which communicated with the manor house west of the church.' Cook, *English Medieval Church*, 138.

East Anglian Tower-Porches

Norfolk	Suffolk
Briningham	Akenham
Colkirk	Brettenham
East Barsham	Burgh
Hardingham	Clopton
Holkham	Culpho
Holme-next-the-Sea	Gosbeck
Little Cressingham	Grundisburgh (medieval original replaced in 18th century)
Little Ellingham	Haughley
Mileham	Holbrook
Norwich St Stephen	Little Bealings
Norwich St John Maddermarket	Mickfield
Roudham	Newbourne
Sculthorpe	Playford
Stanhoe	Shelley
West Bradenham	Stonham Aspal
Whinburgh	Stutton
Wighton	Witnesham
Wicklewood	Wickham Market

examples are Somerset, with at least twelve, and Wiltshire with at least ten.[21] East Anglia offers the largest concentration of these buildings in England, however, and is the focus of attention here.

The geographical distribution of tower-porches connects the Suffolk coast near Ipswich with the north Norfolk coast at Holkham, cutting a swathe through the region. Based on the style of its architectural detailing,

---

[21] Data collated from Nikolaus Pevsner, *Buildings of England: Somerset and Bristol* (Harmondsworth, 1958) and Nikolaus Pevsner, *Buildings of England: Wiltshire* (Harmondsworth, 1975, 2nd edition revised by Bridget Cherry).

the earliest Suffolk example may be that at Witnesham, plausibly constructed in the late thirteenth century. Most of the Suffolk tower-porches were built between c.1300 and c.1350, with the examples at Stutton and Playford built in the fifteenth century. This date range is mirrored in Norfolk. Hardingham was built c.1280, the majority can be dated to the early to mid fourteenth century, and Holme-next-the-Sea and Wicklewood were constructed in the first quarter of the fifteenth century.

East Anglia's thirty-six tower-porches present some interesting consistencies and variations. The majority of tower-porches are sited on the south side of the church; whilst this is true for porches in general (78% on the south side), a still larger proportion of tower-porches are sited on the south, with just four examples on the north side. In terms of their relationship with the church, tower-porches also correspond with standard features of East Anglian porches more generally. Over two-thirds abut the westernmost bay of the main church vessel, with the others positioned one bay to the east, and a window to the west of the tower-porch. Their structural relationship with the aisle or nave is variable, however. Whilst the example at Holme-next-the-Sea was originally flanked by an aisle, Briningham church is aisleless and the tower-porch is recessed into the nave. There is simply no meaningful correlation between the form of the church's main vessel, including the presence or absence of aisles, and the decision to build a tower-porch.

All tower-porches, of course, exceed the height of the church to which they are attached, and their height and necessary structural solidity define them as towers. Comparisons can be made with other forms of coeval porches, however. The lateral tower-porch at Stanhoe, built c.1300, presents similar architectural simplicity and an absence of detail to the single-storey porches at North Creake, Besthorpe and Honingham, all built around the turn of the fourteenth century. Unmoulded portal jambs, a simply-chamfered arch moulding, and the absence of even a hood-mould define this building as austere but also solid, powerful and permanent, a form of bastion. The notion of its design connoting a stronghold is reinforced by the 'arrow-slit' aperture in the upper storey and the crenellated parapet. Perhaps this reading of Stanhoe's strength in restraint can be usefully transferred to the other unelaborated early-fourteenth-century East Anglian porches already discussed above.

One possible explanation for why towers were combined with porches is as a straightforward building solution which worked for the interests of the patron and the mason's knowledge. Placing a tower laterally rather than axially enabled a large window to be set into the west wall of the nave. This maximised the amount of direct light coming from this direction and provided the opportunity for painted glazing schemes on an axis with the centre aisle, chancel and high altar. The double-height arch in the tower base at St Andrew's, Cotton, was an alternative but rarely adopted way to let light reach a window in the west wall of the nave. Few north and south church doors of this date have windows over them, so situating a tower on the nave's flank did not block light from the church interior. Prominent examples of East Anglian tower-porches which coincide with sizeable west windows are found at Clopton and Little Cressingham. Elsewhere, for example at Burgh, the position of the tower-porch made possible the subsequent insertion of a nave west window. Unfortunately, in many cases time has not been kind and arrangements at the church's west end have been altered or lost. As a result, it is difficult to draw solid conclusions about the relationship between the presence of large west windows and the building of lateral towers.

Ground plans of tower-porches tend to be square as opposed to the predominantly rectangular plan of other East Anglian porches. At Little Ellingham, constructed c.1300, the rectangular interior space is disguised within a square-plan tower because the thick, structurally substantial east, west and south walls are not repeated on the north side where the porch and nave are integral. The size of tower-porches ranges quite considerably – Roudham measures a little over 61 sq ft, Holkham measures 384 sq ft.[22] However the average – 122 sq ft – diverges little from that of all East Anglian porches. The thick tower walls result in buildings of more substantial external width although the internal plans of tower-porches are no greater than other forms of porch.

Tower-porches successfully hybridise the form of their two constituent building types. The ground-floor stages adhere closely to East Anglian porches more generally; for example, in all cases the external arch is larger in width and height than the frame of the church door within. The grand scale of the entrance arches relative to the quantity of masonry is less visually apparent in tower-porches than early-fourteenth-century single-storey porches. It can, however, be hinted at if we exclude the upper stages of the tower and concentrate on the building's breadth. On average the open entrance of a tower-porch accounts for 60 per cent of the building's width, with some less than 50 per cent, as at Whinburgh, and the largest, at Briningham, reaching nearly 80 per cent. The range is considerable, but the early-fifteenth-century tower-porches at Playford, Holme-next-the-Sea and Wicklewood are three of the smaller examples. This suggests the proportionate scale of open entrances diminished into the fifteenth century.

---

[22] The tower-porch at Holkham was rebuilt in the nineteenth century but Ladbrooke's print of the church before rebuilding shows it to be based on the original plan. See Robert Ladbrooke, *Views of the Churches in Norfolk* (Norwich, 1823). However, caution is recommended as the ground plan is considerably larger than other East Anglian tower-porches.

The plain exteriors of the earliest tower-porches encourage comparison with the designed character of single-storey porches built in the early fourteenth century. As already mentioned, the façades of tower-porches were given little priority over the other elevations except surrounding the entrance arch. At Holme-next-the-Sea and Playford, multi-ordered archways with complex mouldings are framed by deeply carved spandrels, but the articulation and decoration does not escape from the entrance onto the surrounding masonry. These buildings mark and emphasise the primary way into the church through a combination of height and an elaborated open entrance arch.

East Anglian tower-porches adhere to the formal pattern of west towers in the region. Several examples built in the early fourteenth century are unbuttressed and have little external elaboration to differentiate between the storeys, either being completely undivided, as at Briningham, or having a string course demarcating the top stage and visually emphasising the location of the bells, as at Colkirk. Alternatively, tower-porches are divided into stages which decrease in girth from base to parapet. The tower-porch at Little Ellingham, built c.1300, is unbuttressed but the small reduction in width at each stage externally articulates the arrangement of the interior spatial divisions. Whether for structural or aesthetic purpose, buttressing frequently enhances the exterior effect of East Anglian parish churches from the late thirteenth century and became ubiquitous by the mid fourteenth century. Tower-porches are no different, and their structural solidity is certainly enhanced by buttressing, especially where decoratively elaborated as at Playford.

Despite its formal simplicity, the south tower-porch at Little Ellingham was decorated in a manner of considerable sophistication rarely seen at such an early date (fig. 22). Immediately over the entrance arch, set flush into the rubble flint walling, is a lustrous black flint cross. Whether a form of consecration cross or a singular apotropaic motif to protect the entrance, this cross is an early East Anglian experiment with decorative flint-work. The uppermost stage of the tower is even more remarkable – framing the cusped Y-tracery sound holes is a pair of elaborately pinnacled blind-niches constituted purely through the laying of dark knapped flints in contrast to the paler surrounding walling. This tower-porch pre-dates the flint flushwork of the Ethelbert Gate in Norwich by more than a decade and deserves recognition as amongst the earliest iconographic experiments using this craft technique to elaborate an entrance building in the region.

Tower-porches in East Anglia do not follow or adhere to a neat typological trajectory; the presence or absence of the primary architectural elements does not cohere with any apparent consistency. Two late, datable examples, the south tower-porches at Holme-next-the-Sea and Wicklewood (figs 23 and 24), usefully demonstrate how coeval construction does not result in

22 Exterior view, south tower-porch, Little Ellingham

23 Exterior view, south tower-porch, Holme-next-the-Sea

24 Exterior view, south tower-porch, Wicklewood

architectural similarity. The chancel at Wicklewood was remodelled in 1412, as recorded in the Norwich Cathedral Almoner's Roll.[23] The material evidence supports the suggestion that the tower-porch was constructed as part of the same programme of works. The dating of the tower-porch at Holme-next-the-Sea is also known, in this instance through a memorial brass dated 1405: 'Henry Notyngham and hys wyffe lye here Yat maden this chirche stepull and quere'.[24] Thus these two tower-porches were constructed within a few years of each other but designed very differently. The powerful, half-drum jambs surmounted by shallow capitals at Wicklewood contrast the more delicate multi-ordered shafts of the entrance at Holme. However, it is not simply a case of the latter example being a more 'ambitious' piece of architecture. At Wicklewood, the diagonal buttresses are faced with a combination of regularly cut black flint and ashlar set with exquisite precision. This attention to detail is again seen in the string course which runs around the tower-porch and continuously around the church. It is delicately treated at the point where it rises to form the hood-mould of the entrance archway, resulting in a form of voided label. The walls surrounding the hood-mould are equally detailed and well executed – an alternation of narrow red bricks with almost jet-black flints set to the same width and length, the bricks emphasising the canopy under which one walks when entering the church. The treatment of the same element at Holme is different but results in similar effect. Spandrels are formed by the outermost shaft continuing upwards intersecting with a string course which runs horizontally from the apex of the arch's outer order. The spandrels are carved with a regular geometric pattern, the main element is an encircled quatrefoil with a blank shield at its centre. Two contrasting designs both serve to emphasise the arch of the entrance. These two tower-porches, constructed within a few years of each other, present contrasting architectural forms and decorative details. By implication no standard template for East Anglian tower-porches ever emerged.

Tower-porches, vertical structures built over the lateral doors of churches, have practical and appealing logic – combining the tower with the porch focuses attention on a single point of entry, and does not restrict light reaching the nave through a west window on an axis with the high altar. Greater significance can be bestowed on these turriform buildings when contextualised as porches, rather than as towers. Tower-porches sit between two other phases of tower building – antecedent western towers which only communicated with the church interior, and later grand

---

[23] Cattermole and Cotton, 'Church Building in Norfolk', 273. For historical information which offers further circumstantial evidence of why work would be conducted at this time see Blomefield, *Topographical History*, vol. 2, 461.

[24] Cattermole and Cotton, 'Church Building in Norfolk', 252.

'processional' entrances where substantial west doors are surmounted by an impressive traceried window. That this new arrangement facilitated large west windows in church naves is irrefutable, but another factor perhaps drove the innovation. Regardless of its location, a tower designed also to serve as a porch echoes the biblical description of that built for King Solomon at the Temple in Jerusalem. As discussed in chapter one, according to 1 Kings 6:3 and 2 Chronicles 3.4, this *porticus* was a forebuilding – termed as both *ante templum* ('before the temple') and *ante frontem* ('before the front'). Solomon's Temple porch had a ground plan of 10 x 20 cubits and rose to 120 cubits, approximately 180ft, in height – this *porticus* was a tower, erected on a 2:1 rectangular plan. The first-built tower-porches in East Anglia are amongst the earliest surviving porches in the region. In the late thirteenth century the form that church porches could take was far from settled and the integration of towers with porches was one solution. It is tempting to speculate that the invention of tower-porches owes much to the cultural awareness of and desire to honour King Solomon's architectural works. This uncomplicated application of the Solomonic motif cannot be proven beyond doubt, but neither can it be easily discounted.[25]

Church Porches in East Anglia c.1380–1540

The architectural identity of East Anglian church porches shifts perceptibly in the second half of the fourteenth century, moving away from the simplicity of those built before the middle of the century. Exemplification of these changes is seen in the south porch at North Walsham (fig. 25), a dramatic composition associated with John of Gaunt, duke of Lancaster. The duke's heraldry is displayed carved onto shields set within elegantly cusped roundels in the spandrels of the large entrance arch. The arms in both spandrels are of England quartering France Ancient, English royal heraldry pre-dating Henry IV's 1406 reduction of the coat's fleur-de-lis to three. The shield in the sinister spandrel denotes King Edward III, that in the dexter spandrel is differenced by a label of three and denotes Edward's son John of Gaunt.[26] The porch was likely constructed following John of Gaunt's acquisition of the manor at North Walsham in 1382. A construction date between 1382 and 1406 is therefore reasonably secure, and between 1382 and Gaunt's death in 1399 plausible.[27]

---

[25] Lunnon, 'Inventio Porticus'.
[26] Munro Cautley, *Norfolk Churches* (Ipswich, 1949), 260.
[27] Further supporting evidence is Alan Wale's testamentary bequest of 40s to the emendation of the tower in 1380. NRO NCC Heydon 182.

25 Exterior view, south porch, North Walsham

This detail alone – the decoration of the façade with coats of arms – composes this porch in radically different mode to earlier examples. The building confidently projects its earthly and divine patronage through the proximity on the façade of royal heraldry and three large image niches. The façade's composition carefully lays out an iconographic arc which alternates saintly and earthly authority to frame the portal, powerfully promoting the sanctity of the English Plantagenet monarchy. The design astutely harnesses the opportunity offered by church porches to express power and piety architecturally to a mass public.

Built in the 1380s, North Walsham porch was an early instance of a parochial entrance façade designed as an individualised object to enthral and fascinate the viewer. Architectural primacy in the English medieval parish resided in the church, the largest stone building with which all members of the community were intimately involved. The church dominated its environment, ever present in daily life. Porches were directed towards the people, set to face the working habitat. Before the mid fourteenth century non-figurative forms connoted the aesthetic character of a porch; after that date significant imagery dominated porch composition. The immediate stimulus for this shift was architectural experimentation with the form and decoration of monastic gatehouses through the fourteenth century. Elaborate façades comprising contrasting materials, the display of religious iconography and secular heraldry, were well established for entrance architecture throughout England at least from the late thirteenth century, for example, the gatehouse to Kirkham Priory (North Yorks.), but East Anglian gatehouses including the Ethelbert Gate in Norwich and Butley Priory gatehouse close to the Suffolk coast, provide more immediate contextualisation for this change in the character of church porches and the move to elaborate their exterior surfaces.[28]

Transmission of gatehouse motifs is concentrated in the design of porch façades, as exemplified at North Walsham; but the bodies of the buildings also have similarities. Internal spaces are divided into bays by vertical wall shafts and integral stone benches run horizontally along the interior walls. Side windows at ground-floor level differentiate church porches from most gatehouses, not only in design terms but also in their influence on the environment within. At North Walsham the paired windows in the flanking walls are large and low, positioned and scaled to imply the level of a notional division of the lower chamber from a fictive upper space. The elevations of this lower section are composed of more glass than masonry. The relative austerity of castle gatehouses contrasts with the exuberant richness of porch exteriors, their elaboration riffing on a basic model in much the same way as the rich ornamentation of monastic gatehouses in

---

[28] Luxford, 'Architecture and Environment', 31–72.

26 Exterior view, south porch, Lynn St Nicholas

the fourteenth century.[29] Domestic, civic and monastic gatehouses were architectural expressions of status, confident announcements to every resident, visitor and passer-by. Church porches were the ecclesiastical equivalent, set-piece edifices defining the strength of Christian faith and the Roman Church in England.

Emphasis on the façade, so evident at North Walsham, is also a characteristic of the porch at Lynn St Nicholas (fig. 26) built along with the body of the church in the first two decades of the fifteenth century and referred to as '*de novo edificata*' in 1419.[30] The architecture of the ashlar façade plays with actual rather than implied surface modulation. Visual texture is created through the fall of light on different planes rather than by means of differently coloured and surfaced materials creating a comparable effect. There is little reference between Lynn and North Walsham and one cannot be considered as the genesis of the other. Two key elements are found at Lynn for the first time: it is the earliest extant two-storey porch in East Anglia (excluding tower-porches), and the earliest surviving instance in the region of a full programme of figurative bosses integrated in a porch vault outside Norwich.[31] The ground plan measures 136 sq ft, a little larger than the East Anglian average of 122 sq ft, but considerably smaller than Walsham (253 sq ft). Its height is far greater than its width or depth. The angle buttresses are narrow and only present at ground-floor level, the upper storey is unbuttressed. The proportions of the porch are, if anything, a little ungainly and this is exacerbated by the horizontal divisions of the façade. The lowest stage appears to finish at the apex of the entrance arch, above which a string course differentiates the arch from a row of ten identical image niches. This tier is then surmounted by a third level with three niches, the central one being the largest and most ornate, set within a field of blind tracery detail including a row of small shields. The porch is set under a low-pitched gabled parapet with small-scale blind arcading running along it. Not only is the external three-tier division unrelated to the internal arrangement of two storeys but also the restricted height of each tier creates a sense of vertical compression. The generous expansive proportions of Walsham are not part of the design at Lynn.

Whereas contemporary heraldry is designed into the porch at North Walsham, at Lynn the spandrels display large shields carved with the Arms

---

[29] For discussion of the relationship between gatehouses and porches, see Goodall, 'The English Gatehouse', 6.

[30] Cattermole and Cotton, 'Church Building in Norfolk', 253.

[31] Whilst the Virgin boss at North Elmham dates from the fourteenth century it is not part of a group or cycle. Two earlier examples in Norwich are the two c.1300 bosses of the martyrdom of St Stephen at Norwich St Stephen, and the south porch at Norwich St Gregory, built in the 1390s.

of the Passion and Trinity and the plethora of niches present opportunities for a complex scheme of statuary to be displayed. Internally the central vault boss shows God the Father, and on the surrounding ring of eight bosses angels hold shields and scrolls. The imagery is not singularly religious, however. The vault corbels and arch headstops are representative of contemporary figures, potentially those who were responsible for building the porch. The porch at Lynn is a complicated, multi-layered, composition with little sense of unity. It is a more domestic, more human space than that at Walsham, and gatehouse allusions are present but tempered. There is no readily identifiable precedent for the porch at Lynn whereas that at Walsham sits with reasonable comfort within a wider tradition of entrance architecture.

The south porch at Cley-next-the-Sea, built c.1414 under the patronage of Lady Beatrice Stafford, is entirely clad in ashlar (figs 27, 48). Newly seen in this porch is fenestration in the upper chamber contributing to the composition of the façade. As at Walsham and Lynn architectural emphasis is loaded on the front elevation, consciously constructing the porch as a façade to the church. It is this design decision which links all three buildings and clearly differentiates them from earlier porches. Cley porch was built approximately eighty years later than the aisle into which it leads.

27 Arch detail, south porch, Cley-next-the-Sea

A major campaign of refenestration was undertaken in the first quarter of the fifteenth century which encompassed the north and south aisles, the chancel east window and the nave west window. The embattled transoms of these east and west windows, although not present in the aisles, are replicated in the south porch. This detail indicates that the porch was constructed as part of the same building campaign, and it is notable that only the apertures at the extremities of the church are crenellated. Implicitly the porch was conceived as part of the architectural envelope of the church. Internally Cley porch comprises two bays, the division emphasised by a wall shaft running vertically between the windows and connecting with the rib vault. This building was designed as a sumptuous space: deep stone benches, large multi-light glazed windows in the entrance bay, an elaborate vaulted ceiling adorned with carved figurative bosses. It brings together forms which were experimented with at North Walsham and Lynn and resolves the issues of architectural form and its elaboration which were being tackled around the turn of the fifteenth century.

High-ranking personal commissions were the impetus for architecturally ambitious early-fifteenth-century church porches in East Anglia. These entrance buildings became vehicles for the visual combining of patronal and commemorative motifs located prominently at the threshold of a parish church with which their patron was intimately associated. Other examples make the same point, such as the south porch at Fressingfield. This showpiece façade aesthetically dominates the whole church (fig. 28). Tiers of dark flint-filled ashlar frames cover the first two stages and emerge as shallow ashlar image niches in the upper register. Although heavily restored, the iconography supports the tradition that this building was constructed for Katherine de la Pole, c.1415–1419. Katherine's husband, Michael de la Pole, 2nd earl of Suffolk, died of dysentery at Harfleur in 1415, her son died a month later at Agincourt.[32] The porch can be read as monumentalising her husband, his familial kinship and their shared piety. The eroded key stone of the porch entrance can just be made out as an angel with flowing curls holding a shield bearing the impaled arms of Wingfield and de la Pole. The reference is to the dynastic marriage of the second earl's parents, Michael de la Pole, 1st earl of Suffolk, and Margaret Wingfield. The bold panels of roses have been interpreted as Lancastrian emblems, but the Annunciate Virgin carved on the central boss of the porch vault makes a Marian motif on the porch exterior more plausible. Crowns frame the entrance arch, an expanded and repeated notation of the arms of Bury Abbey (which held a portion of the rectory of Fressingfield). The Bury arms are also carved on the interior keystone of the entrance

---

[32] Rowena E. Archer, 'War Widows', in *The Battle of Agincourt*, ed. Anne Curry and Malcolm Mercer (New Haven and London, 2015), 221–2.

28 Exterior view, south porch, Fressingfield

arch. The Fressingfield porch speaks in the late medieval visual language of memorial, interweaving ancestry, privilege, affiliation and devotion. Although these themes are familiar in a range of artistic media, the scale, prominence and permanence offered by a porch façade expanded the field of commemorative arts from primarily interior forms directly into the gaze of a collective mass public.

In little more than half a century the design concept of a church porch built in East Anglia by a wealthy patron had altered considerably. As has been seen at Gooderstone, under the direction of Marie de St Pol, countess of Pembroke, a neat single-storey porch with a plain external elevation and perfectly designed and executed circular traceried windows had been constructed. Lady Stafford's porch at Cley could hardly be more different, and the variations are not simply a matter of style. As an expression of social standing and religious devotion Cley porch is demonstrative and relatively easy to understand, or at least to appreciate. At Gooderstone, and in keeping with the countess's other commissions, the build quality is faultless, but the architecture is very straightforward.[33]

By the second decade of the fifteenth century parish church porches in East Anglia were relatively numerous but still rarely built with the ambition evident at Walsham, Lynn, Cley or Fressingfield. If Walsham is the earliest of the four it may be considered to mark the inception of a new architecture for porches which was to remain current throughout the rest of the medieval period. However, those at Lynn St Nicholas, Cley and Fressingfield all introduced elements not used at North Walsham, including the upper chamber and figurative bosses in combination with a vaulted interior. Perhaps because of the clarity inherent in personal commissioning, these buildings reconstructed how a church porch could act. They were exploited as vehicles for in-life or post-mortem commemoration in an architectural setting drenched in significance as occupying the liminal threshold between worldly sin and eternal salvation. The later elaborate porches for which East Anglia is well known, magnificent preludes to the church beyond, all owe a debt to the architectural bravery of elite patrons and the masons they employed in the period from c.1380 to c.1420.

Vaulted Porches and the Iconography of Burial

Church porches and vaulted ceilings have a long history of association. The mason of the early-thirteenth-century porch at Barnack (Northamptonshire) faced the challenge by constructing a domical groined vault; the porch at Malmesbury Abbey displays a more convincing achievement. Vaults and canopies universally promote, they designate whatever is beneath as special, confirming the status of the space, image or effigy as worthy of distinction, honour and protection. Although the association might not have been foremost in the mind of a late medieval commissioning patron or designing mason, vaulted porches have their origins in the throne of King Solomon and his royal *porticus* (see chapter one). Medieval church porches built throughout England feature vaulted ceilings. Those in East Anglia are an important part of the wider practice, especially given the absence of indigenous freestone and the prevalence of ornate timber roofs which cover many of the region's nave and chancel spaces. Building a

---

[33] For discussion of Marie de St-Pol's architectural and artistic patronage see Heslop, 'The Nave of Attleborough', 54.

vault in an East Anglian porch was a financially ambitious project, indicative of the building's perceived importance. There is no better example of this than Sir Ralph Shelton's fan-vaulted brick porch. The vault remains incomplete, construction having ceased when the exuberant and lavish patron died, despite his testamentary instruction for his executors to continue the building work he had started at Shelton parish church.

Vaulted ceilings are an architectural device which characterises a place. 'Vaults ... have a deeply symbolic significance: the emperor's canopy in Imperial Rome, the Vault of Heaven in a Christian church, or simply as a demonstration of the financial power and status of a patron.'[34] Such cultural significance and economic prowess underpin how the prevalence of vaulted ceilings in porches is evidence of the import with which these buildings were designed.

In East Anglia stone vaults prominently feature bosses carved with figural and foliate forms, iconographic appendages to the web of ribs. Occasionally, however, porch vaults are unadorned, lacking representational imagery. Examples include Ingham, Outwell, Upwell and Little Walsingham. The type is more prevalent in Norfolk than Suffolk, and also in Norwich than in the county at large. Of the seventeen vaulted porches in the city, eight have bosses (and these are found at only five churches) but nine do not.[35] This corpus of buildings warrants close attention.

The day after the feast of the angelic Annunciation to the Virgin in 1455, John Brosyard wrote his final testament and just two weeks later, on 10 April, the document was proved. In his will Brosyard bequeathed his soul to almighty God, Blessed Mary and All Saints and requested that his body be buried in the porch of St Giles parish church in Norwich.[36] Implicit in John Brosyard's specification of his burial location is his awareness of the type of place the porch was; possibly he also had some influence on its design. The porch is of two storeys with an ashlar façade to the south (fig. 29). Knapped-flint walls east and west have centrally placed traceried windows, the sills of which align with a base course present only on the buttresses. These diagonal buttresses have three off-sets, the middle one aligns with a string course running directly beneath the large first-floor window which is flanked by niches. A second string course is set in line with the apex of the entrance portal and forms the upper limit of the spandrels

---

[34] Jane Turner, *Grove Dictionary of Art*, volume 32 (Basingstoke, 1996), 86.

[35] Vaulted porches in Norwich which do not have bosses are St Helen, St Gregory (north porch), St George Tombland (north porch), St Giles, St Laurence (north porch), St Mary Coslany, St Margaret Westwick, St John Timberhill and St John Sepulchre. The vaulted porches with bosses are listed below, p. 000.

[36] He left the customary 6s 8d to the high altar and 20s for the reparation of the church, but nothing to the porch. NRO NCC Brosyard 1.

29 Exterior view, south porch, Norwich St Giles

which frame the shoulders of the arch. This string course extends only to the width of the arch where it is met by vertical mouldings rising from the label stops. The enhanced entrance is isolated within the ashlar façade, it does not connect with any other feature of the porch (the elaborate niche immediately above is a later addition). Inside, the porch is well lit from the open entrance and two relatively large, low, side windows. The door into the church is framed by a flat four-centred arch, the mouldings of which run without alteration or interruption from the plinth to the apex and even the label protrudes only ever so slightly beyond the arch. The ceiling is fan-vaulted, the conoids of which are formed of trefoil-headed cells arranged in two tiers delineated by horizontal bounding ribs. Each of the four roundels which are recessed within the centre circle is composed of a regular quatrefoil with cusped lobes which are recessed further still. Between the large framing circle and this cusping, the surface is set back four times which, with the addition of mouldings and angled surfaces, creates a fluid and undulating effect; innovative plays are made by contrasting geometric formality with curved mouldings and subtle layers of detail.

The interior space of the porch at Norwich St Giles is rectangular, measuring approximately 13ft north-south by 10ft east-west. The vault, however, is constructed on a square plan. The void between the northern edge of the ceiling vault and the hood-mould of the church door is filled with an arch-of-shields reminiscent of other entrance buildings, including the outer arch of the south porch at Cley. This combination of fan-vault and arch-of-shields was well established in the architectural repertoire of entrance buildings, but it was also closely associated with monuments. The earliest extant experiment with the principles of fan vaulting in England is in a memorial setting – the canopy over the mid-fourteenth-century tomb of Hugh Lord Despenser in Tewkesbury Abbey.[37] Similarly, frames of shields decorate the canopy-arch of tombs such as that of Lord Morley (d.1435) in the chancel at Hingham. Thus, the design of the porch at St Giles is drawn from a repertoire of architectural forms which enables it to serve as both an entrance and as John Brosyard's sepulchral monument.

The vaulted north porch at Norwich St Laurence also served as a tomb canopy. It was constructed in accordance with the terms of the 1459 will of Richard Playter (fig. 30). He gave 46s 8d and 40 stone of lead for the roof, the monetary part of which is almost the same as the mean recorded bequest to porch fabric in medieval Norfolk.[38] At first glance there is nothing particularly unusual about this porch, however, the rather understated

---

[37] Walter C. Leedy, *Fan Vaulting: A Study of Form, Technology, and Meaning* (London, 1980), 8. Leedy also notes that 'the first stone fan vaults probably influenced the wooden tester of the tomb of Edward III'.

[38] Blomefield, *Topographical History*, vol. 4, 269.

external treatment makes little preparation for the stone vault within (fig. 31). This is where the architectural emphasis is placed; an intricate web constructed of slender, delicately-moulded ribs not only supports an upper storey but provides a canopy over the benefactor's tomb. Porches constructed as tomb canopies are discussed in chapter two, and vaults were the principal architectural means by which monumental forms were connoted. It would be going far too far to suggest that the only impetus for vaulted porches was monumental, yet the recurring popularity of being buried in a church porch needs to be acknowledged, and the potential for

30 Exterior view, north porch, Norwich St Laurence.
Reproduced with thanks to The Churches Conservation Trust

3. ARCHITECTURE AND DECORATION

31 Vault canopy, north porch, Norwich St Laurence.
Reproduced with thanks to The Churches Conservation Trust

quasi-monumental design elements increased their desirability as burial places over an extended period.[39]

The porch at the parish church of St Stephen in Norwich, constructed c.1300, is the finest tower-porch built in East Anglia and the earliest extant vaulted porch in the city (fig. 32). Its form and design, and the quality of carving displayed on the bosses, are first class and it is an important antecedent to the wider tradition of vaulted porches in the city. High status buildings in fourteeth- and fifteenth-century Norwich were something of a hot-bed for the development of stone vaults. The canopy at St Stephen's is a key piece in the puzzle which saw masons investigating possibilities of composing and constructing vaulted forebuildings. The cathedral cloister, the Ethelbert Gate and Bishop Salmon's palace porch are all roughly contemporaneous with St Stephen's. It is also worth noting that the cathedral priory was patron of St Stephen's.[40] Although other fourteenth-century porches may have been lost or rebuilt, the extant evidence presents a gap

---

[39] Helen E. Lunnon, '"I will have one porch of stone … over my grave": Medieval Parish Church Porches and their Function as Tomb Canopies', *Church Monuments* 27 (2012), 53–65.

[40] Blomefield, *Topographical History*, vol. 4, 145–6.

32 Exterior view, north tower-porch, Norwich St Stephen

of nearly a century before the next vaulted porch was constructed at St Gregory's, c.1394.[41] This building evidently picks up the themes of St Stephen's both in terms of the use of bosses for narrative visual schemes (although near impossible to make out in their current state) and in its form, being two bays deep with the vaulting divided accordingly.

Of the vaulted porches in Norwich, just eight have carved bosses at the rib intersections: St Stephen, St Gregory (south and west porches), St George Tombland (south porch), St John Maddermarket (north and south porches) and St Peter Mancroft (north and south porches). There seems to be a fundamental difference between the fourteenth-century vaulting model (seen in the north tower-porch at St Stephen and the south porch at St Gregory, and built in conjunction with projects including the Ethelbert Gate and the cloister vault) and the fifteenth-century focus on geometric vault design (as opposed to its possibilities as a vehicle for narrative sequences). Ultimately a simpler reworking of integral, figurative vault bosses was introduced at the end of the fifteenth century, as at St George Tombland (c.1495) and St Peter Mancroft (c.1500). It is perhaps not coincidental that these later porches were built after Bishop Lyhart's vaulting in stone of the cathedral nave roof following the fire in 1463. The earlier fifteenth-century stone-vaulted porches emanate from an independent tradition in which architectural confidence is placed in the geometric design of the vault – the rib patterns and the articulation of the walling – as opposed to figuratively-carved bosses. Rather than in any sense being the inferior partner, the unadorned vaults reference tabernacles, image niches and other such honorific structures. In this sense it is appropriate to see them as enlargements of micro-architectural forms not as diminutive versions of larger buildings.

The combination of ribs and bosses at St Peter Mancroft demonstrates, however, that the two priorities were not mutually exclusive. The profile of the ribs in the north porch at St Peter's is highly elaborate in cross section and even more so where the outer two orders split from the core, the inner moulding breaking into a single cusp and the outer into a tri-cusped adornment of the inner one. Archaeological and documentary evidence suggests this porch was built c.1500 and therefore is a late example of a vaulted porch in Norwich (fig. 33). This design prioritises, and thus emphasises, the vault rather than the imagery, the latter essentially doing little more than reinforcing the presence of the dedicatory saint at the entrance to the church. The conception of historiated sequences explored in the nave of the cathedral or

---

[41] It is coeval with the rebuilding of the nave (c.1394) and therefore likely to have been designed by Robert Wodehirst, cathedral mason (d.1401). John Harvey, *English Medieval Architects: A Biographical Dictionary down to 1550* (Gloucester, 1987), 342.

33 Vault canopy, north porch, Norwich St Peter Mancroft. Reproduced with thanks to the Vicar and Churchwardens of St Peter Mancroft church

narrative cycles depicted in several fifteenth-century East Anglian porches is absent from this most ambitious of Norwich buildings. Whilst this could be construed as evidence of conservatism and reserve, I suggest that deliberate emphasis is placed on the display of sophisticated technical virtuosity. The success of the geometry, the precision with which the porch is built, the cutting and jointing of the rib stones are all on show and they are made even more evident by being set at an easily viewable height.

Association and Attribution

At various stages in this chapter the apparent tension in porch design, between the individual architectural form and a sense of an overarching typology, has been hinted at. In different contexts it has been possible to recognise divergence as easily as continuity. Porches built in East Anglia before c.1420 are notable for their variety – one does not need to seek out difference amongst obscure details. By contrast, from the second quarter of the fifteenth century a greater number of porches were built than previously but collectively they present a much greater degree of architectural conformity than can be evidenced in the earlier period.

Biographical information about the architects of medieval buildings below the most prestigious commissions is scarce but has been overcome by architectural historians who utilise buildings as the evidence of their own creation. Art history's attribution of works to artists based on visually observable individuality, the quirks and idiosyncrasies of the artist's technique, has been adapted and applied to medieval buildings, including church porches. The study of moulding profiles has been central to the classification, identification and characterisation of medieval buildings by historians throughout the twentieth century. Attributing the design of multiple buildings to a single unnamed mason can start with recording the mouldings of cut-stone details. Masons' assemblages of templates, developed and used over an extended period by their workshops, were the way in which key design elements were transferred from one building to another (fig. 34). These thin, wooden, full-scale templates were the most important means of transposing drawn design to cut stone, and master masons invested much in their precision. The specially selected raw material from which the templates were cut was often imported to England from continental Europe and skilfully shaped to ensure masons

34 Design templates, masons' loft, York Minster
© Chapter of York: Reproduced by kind permission

35 Exterior view, south porch, Walpole St Peter

36 Exterior view, north porch, Wiveton

37 Exterior view, south porch, Great Cressingham

38 Exterior view, south porch, Hilborough

39 Exterior view, south porch, Norwich St Mary Coslany

had accurate guides for every piece of stone.[42] These most practical of objects are fundamental to establishing an architectural chain of ancestry and continuity between buildings. In East Anglia near-identical moulding profiles encouraged Richard Fawcett's exploration of 'a group of buildings ... which appear to show sufficient points of similarity to be attributable to one mason'.[43] The buildings and monuments in this group include several porches, all constructed between c.1435 and c.1466 – the mouldings of the exterior jambs and arches are near-identical at Walpole St Peter (north porch), Wiveton, Great Cressingham, Hilborough and St Mary Coslany, Norwich (figs 35–39).[44] A robust case was made by Fawcett using the detailing of arches, capitals and jambs, but the study also reveals how, even amongst buildings with shared details, other facets of their form break away from the notion of continuity. The porches at St Mary Coslany, Wiveton and Great Cressingham share near-identical moulding details but 'in other respects the porch [at St Mary Coslany] could hardly be less like those at the other churches'.[45] Despite the centrality of moulding profiles to the master mason's working method, carved masonry features do not define any building in its entirety. The major differences which are observable in the architecture of porches with shared carved details hint at the specific circumstances of each project, and by association the interests of the mason's patron.

The counterbalance to the diversity of approaches taken to designing porches, even those which apparently share a designing mason, are buildings with more immediate formal similarity. The first group are those related by design details as already mentioned. The second group, related by formal features, comprises Colby (c.1435), South Walsham (c.1454), East Tuddenham (c.1458) and Acle (c.1497) (figs 40–43). St Mary Coslany (c.1466) is a pivot-point between the two different groups of porches as it relates to both. The porches affiliated by having shared detailing include St Mary Coslany but formally it bears little similarity with the others. It is akin to the Colby group, where structural similarities are evident but detailing differs. The initial impression one gets of these five porches is overriding similarity, and formally they are about as similar as East Anglian porches get. (Others could be added, for example, St Michael at Pleas and St John Sepulchre in Norwich, Rickinghall Inferior and Rickinghall Superior in

---

[42] Lon R. Shelby, 'Medieval Mason's Templates', *The Journal of the Society of Architectural Historians* 30.2 (1971), 140–54.

[43] Richard Fawcett, 'St Mary at Wiveton in Norfolk, and a Group of Churches Attributed to its Mason', *Antiquaries Journal* 62 (1982), 35.

[44] Richard Fawcett, *The Architecture and Furnishings of Norfolk Churches* (Fakenham, 1974), 17–18.

[45] Fawcett, 'St Mary at Wiveton', 42.

40 Exterior view, south porch, Colby

Suffolk, but they begin to diverge from the formal identity of the main group.) Yet the architectural content of each building – the way each constitutive element is treated – demonstrates how choice and opportunity were retained during the design process. Whilst masons' cutting templates facilitate identical repetition, it is variety that characterises the buildings, even though they would look very similar presented as design-drawings. A few observations serve to make the point. The use of pale-coloured, square flints laid in neat horizontal courses at Colby (the earliest in the group) is only repeated at South Walsham, the pale ashlar façade at St Mary Coslany being related in tone but not effect. Above the entrance at East Tuddenham is a technically accomplished frieze with a flint flushwork inscription, setting it apart from the others. They all have friezes above the entrance arch, but these are either blank panels or, as at Colby, hung with shields. The closely similar porch at Rickinghall Superior is another example of this form of porch which presents graphic flushwork motifs, here referring to the Virgin Mary and Jesus Christ. A central image niche set between two windows is common to all five (not featured at either of the Rickinghall porches), but the scale, detail and placement are different in all cases. For example, the canopy of the niche at Colby is unique in breaking forward beyond the plane of the porch façade.

41 Exterior view, south porch, South Walsham

These two distinct ways of establishing groups of related buildings draw out tensions in fifteenth-century porch design. On the one hand, the close dating of several examples aids the argument that moulding profiles can be attributed to a single designing mason, even if the buildings are fundamentally inconsistent in their overall form. Conversely the group of five porches

42 Exterior view, south porch, East Tuddenham

identified here as displaying much greater architectural reliance on each other span a much longer period and are unlikely to have been designed by the same person. What conclusions can be drawn? Predominantly, that both models are appropriate. Porches which present great formal variety were built under the direction of a common designing mason; visually similar porches were designed by numerous master masons. The latter conclusion, that imitation of pre-existing buildings was part of the medieval design-build process, is widely recognised on the basis of the terms written in to building contracts. Less well-observed is that buildings themselves are equally reliable documents for information on the late medieval nexus of architectural influence.

As much as commissioning patrons and designing masons could, and did, travel to see for themselves the new architectures of their own time, proximity occasionally negates any need for complex patterns of association or influence. Two Suffolk porches demonstrate this well. The south porch at Rickinghall Inferior (fig. 44) was built in the early fourteenth century; the cusped trefoil portholes set within low two-bay wall arcades are quintessentially of that period. Just half a mile away to the south, the nave at St Mary's, Rickinghall Superior (fig. 45) was rebuilt in magnificent style around 1442, fitting between the fourteenth-century (therefore pre-existing) west tower and chancel. The porch at Rickinghall Superior is two-storeyed, with blank shields flanking the entrance and a flushwork frieze alternating the crowned

43 Exterior view, north porch, Acle

trigram of Christ and the Virgin's monogram, also crowned. The chequerwork flint of the base course marries with the rest of the nave, creating a sense of formal continuity between the porch and the main vessel. Around the same time, the porch at Rickinghall Inferior was architecturally brought up to date, heightened by the addition of a second storey and aesthetically renewed with a façade approximating that of its near neighbour. The

44 Exterior view, south porch, Rickinghall Inferior

two Rickinghall porches strongly suggest direct imitation or transference between the two parishes, and most plausibly Inferior followed the model of Superior. No written contract survives for either porch, it is the buildings themselves which imply the specification and design process involved in their making. In this way the architectural narrative closely adheres to numerous medieval building contracts specifying that the proposed new building should take the likeness of an existing one, but with variation introduced by certain specified adjustments.[46]

[46] Gabriel Byng, 'The Dynamic of Design: "Source" Buildings and Contract Making in England in the Later Middle Ages', *Architectural History* 59 (2016), 123–48.

45 Exterior view, south porch, Rickinghall Superior

Making Boundaries

The surface finish of porch elevations also identifies similarity and difference between buildings. For example, a feature of Norwich porches, although many are unremarkable buildings, is a tendency to be finished in neatly knapped dark flints. The external 'wrapping' of the building also constitutes the boundary, the point at which the building and our engagement with it commences. Materials and their external application are a fundamental means by which the purpose or nature of a building is conveyed. The following architectural analysis is offered as a complement to the investigation of function offered in chapter two.

In the design of East Anglian porches different materials are frequently used *en masse* or in decorative combinations to distinguish the façade from the other elevations. The ashlar-clad façades of the Norwich porches at St Giles and St Mary Coslany contrast the snapped flint walling of the other elevations and the body of the adjacent church. At St Margaret, St Laurence and St Gregory all elevations are made in the same material, but otherwise they present incremental stages in façade design. St Gregory's is essentially unelaborated, at St Laurence spandrels are introduced, and at St Margaret's a frieze is inserted between the apex of the entrance-arch hood-mould and the sills of the upper windows. At St John Sepulchre all three elevations are flint but the façade is a two-tiered frieze surmounting the entrance. The lower register is set with four panels: two flushwork 'I' (or 'J') monograms interchanged with blank shields framed by star-burst quatrefoils and the upper register is a band of low-relief shields carved into ashlar panels. Such decoration is unusual in Norwich, where the porches are remarkably devoid of emblematic exterior decoration, with St Michael at Pleas being another notable exception (fig. 46). The front face of each of these Norwich porches is individually treated and are examples of the widespread use of porch façades to represent and visually introduce the entire church.

Many other examples exist throughout East Anglia where special finishes and materials are reserved for the façade and the less important elevations are made of lower quality, cheaper materials. The front elevation and west wall of the porch at Great Cressingham are those seen as people approach the building. Both are clad in ashlar and the base course comprises flushwork panels of crowned 'M's and erect swords. Neither of these fine details is present on the east side, the elevation of the porch less frequently seen. This wall is built of flint rubble and the base course has blank ashlar shields. All details of the façade of the tall, elegant porch at Woolpit – the surface, niches and low-relief sculpture – are uniformly made of cut ashlar giving the building a visually smooth and coherent appearance. The west wall, although much repaired, was originally finished in casually laid flint and ironstone, and the east wall is finished in knapped-flint and ashlar chequerwork. This surface decoration unites the east side of the porch with the clerestory and chancel parapet. It faced towards the rectory, located to the east of the church, and would also have been seen by pilgrims who visited the sacred image of the Virgin Mary in a churchyard chapel to north of the chancel.

At Gissing, the surface of the front elevation is elaborately decorated (predominantly flint flushwork); the side walls are austere by comparison. Here, detailing is loaded on the entrance, promoting the status of the space within and emphasising its contrast with the open churchyard. The buttresses at Gissing are treated in a way which also makes a contribution

46 Exterior view, south porch, Norwich St Michael at Pleas

to the façade, creating and exaggerating its breadth and solidity. The buttresses and south wall have a shared base course or plinth, the side walls do not. The selection and combination of varied stone types and masonry techniques imposes a hierarchical system onto the porch's architecture. Money cannot explain the phenomenon. If expense primarily dictated porch design, there would be no reason against equal distribution of value throughout the building. Porch elevations were materially differentiated with a level of sophistication appropriate to the site-specific context of how the building occupied its environment.

The grandeur and magnificence of many East Anglian church porches encapsulates the late medieval commitment to displaying piety and honouring the Divine through material and visual splendour. From the late fourteenth century, church porch façades publicly exhibited the timeless Christian principles which cohered medieval communities in a thoroughly contemporary mode. Wealthy, populous communities of medieval East Anglia were committed to architectural notions of the well-built earthly city as mirror of the heavenly. Church porches became expressions of religiously framed morality. The architectural mode in which they were conceived observed the medieval European Christian tradition of church portals as sites for the public sculptural arts.[47]

The change in how porch façades were decorated from the late fourteenth century to the early sixteenth century also implies a shift in the status of the building type. Before c.1380 exteriors were adorned with architectural forms rather than representational images or motifs. As we have seen in some early cases already discussed, an image niche is found over the church door within the porch, suggesting that the porch existed beyond the confines of the sacred envelope. Heightened visual richness of the façade and the relocation of image niches (and their attendant statuary) to the exterior transferred the significant threshold of the 'church door' to the porch entrance. The ornamentation and decoration of church exteriors which involved imagery, representational motifs, surface textures and patterning were ubiquitous parts of late medieval Perpendicular style. The skin, or periphery, of these churches acted to create architectural objects which demanded and rewarded visual contemplation from beyond its walls as well as within.

How porch exteriors were elaborated in combination with their architectural content conveyed the status of each church porch. The north elevation of the nave at Mildenhall in Suffolk, constructed in the 1430s, was designed as the church's showpiece façade, the means by which the church

---

[47] Conrad Rudolf, 'Inventing the Gothic Portal: Suger, Hugh of Saint Victor, and the Construction of a New Public Art at Saint-Denis', *Art History* 33 (2010), 568–95.

47 Exterior view, north porch, Mildenhall

communicates with the town and those approaching it (fig. 47). The embattled parapets on the porch, aisle and clerestory have a carved shield on each merlon and both motifs (crenellations and shields) are culturally symbolic of strength and defence. Their use at Mildenhall establishes a sense of architectural and structural cohesion and singularity around the building. Yet the architectural relationship between the north porch and the aisle is intriguingly varied. The buttresses of the porch are plain ashlar, those of the aisle have panels infilled with dark knapped flint. The lowest level of base course runs continuously from the aisle to the porch, but the upper plinth is exclusive to the latter. The shields set within traceried panelling on the aisle are small by comparison with those which run across the front of the porch, and the disparity in size is increased by the comparative distance of the shields from the human eye at ground level. The porch is an incrementally bolder architectural statement than the aisle. The whole porch, every element, is lifted a little and quietly dominates.

Freely-open large porch entrances were constantly at risk from malevolent infiltration and by implication needed a greater level of protection than the enclosed body of the church.[48] The threat of infiltration and need for apotropaic protection was not always the paramount design concern. The aisle parapet at Harpley closely resembles that at Mildenhall yet the porch is not embattled or seemingly defended by any other means (apart, perhaps, from the statuary which once occupied the three niches). Formal variations in porch parapets across East Anglia show that a defensive mode was an option, but not the only one. The south porches at Cley and Pulham St Mary exemplify this diversity (figs 48 and 49). Open quatrefoils drawn upwards, and evidently sprouting, form the parapets of these two porches. The Pulham example is gabled and the foils, with small crockets, are turned to follow the line of the roof. At Cley the parapet is horizontal and each heavily crocketed foil stands vertically. The curved forms, broken lines and lace-like piercing is more delicate, perhaps more feminine, even less 'Perpendicular', than the panelled crenellations at Mildenhall and Harpley. In whatever way the tone of the forms at Cley and Pulham is understood, the parapets are distinct from the rest of the church – a lily-like crown bestowed on this part of the church only. The

---

[48] 'Liminal situations and roles are often regarded as dangerous and inauspicious … This is due to the difficulty of classifying the liminal subject, experience or place in terms of traditional criteria of classification: in fleeing the definitive the liminal in unstable and may be regarded as polluting as well as sacred … Such a fundamental threat to cultural and individual order, the removal of the basic points of reference which guide and ground us in the phenomenal world, must be well-protected if social stability is to prevail.' Alex Woodcock, *Liminal Images: Aspects of Medieval Architectural Sculpture in the South of England from the Eleventh to the Sixteenth Centuries* (Oxford, 2005), 15.

desirability of including notionally defensive elements in the design of a porch was seemingly a matter of choice and judgement, not a universally adopted standard. Yet both Cley and Pulham do feature motifs which can be read as notionally protective, even if the parapets cannot. To greater or lesser extent protective motifs were commonly integrated into porch exteriors designed in fifteenth-century East Anglia. Shields, blank or otherwise, evoke the church militant and their presence on porches should be seen in the wider context of including martial forms in the architecture of English parish churches.

As well as rows of blank shields, such as the frieze above the portal at Colby, quasi-heraldic motifs are also a feature of East Anglian porches. Examples including Aldeby, Cley, Geldeston, Huntingfield, Lynn St Nicholas and Wisset display low-relief carvings of the Arms of the Passion and/

48 Exterior view, south porch, Cley-next-the-Sea

49 Exterior view, south porch, Pulham St Mary

or the Trinity symbol in the spandrels. Trinity and Passion symbols were common in late medieval East Anglia, with a regionally specific catalyst for widespread Trinitarian devotion being the diocesan cathedral at Norwich, dedicated to the Holy and Undivided Trinity.[49] The pairing of the Trinitarian motif with emblems of Christ's human suffering on the cross defines the scheme's implications as appropriate to the union of earthly

---

[49] Ann Nichols has commented that 'the arms of the Trinity were one of the most common symbols that Norfolk parishioners saw in their churches.' Ann E. Nichols, *The Early Art of Norfolk: A Subject List of Extant and Lost Art Including Items Relevant to Early Drama* (Kalamazoo, 2002), 7–8.

and heavenly realms at the church porch. Imagery and setting are mutually appropriate, and recognition of their significance is reinforced through repetition and familiarity. Representations of Christ's Passion and the Holy Trinity, expressed in heraldic mode and situated at the church entrance, connote the prospect of salvation within. The conjoined signs mnemonically express the message and means of Christ's humanity, crucifixion and unity with the Trinity, and reconfirm the metaphor of Christ as door (John 10.9). Imagery of such power flanking the porch entrance demonstrates that in fifteenth-century East Anglia this place marked the spatial limen of many parish churches.

Populating the Threshold

As early as 1866 John Henry Parker observed the prevalence of ornamentation associated with porches, noting that the Romanesque and Early English tendency to emphasise the doorway and interior contrasted with the later external enrichment.[50] Parker's appreciation of the shift from internal to external decoration is borne out in East Anglia. It is a register of aesthetic preference but the observation also allows us to locate the church threshold, as already mooted.

An image of the church's patron saint is widely recognised as the foremost iconography of porch façades.[51] Integrally carved into the central stanchion of the timber porch at Great Blakenham is the figure of the Virgin Mary holding the Christ child high against her left shoulder. This and the small number of stone figures surviving in porch niches, for example, at Great Cressingham, Loddon and South Walsham, all conform to the tradition of the patronal saint protecting the porch entrance.[52] Yet the number and arrangement of niches on many façades hints at the more interesting story that can be told about porch imagery.

---

[50] John Henry Parker, *A Concise Glossary of Terms Used in Grecian, Roman, Italian and Gothic Architecture* (Oxford and London, 1866), 196.

[51] Wall, *Porches and Fonts*, 56–60. For a general discussion of patronal images, see Richard Marks, *Image and Devotion in Late Medieval England* (Stroud, 2004), 64–85.

[52] It appears from the diary of William Dowsing that statuary which occupied porch image niches was already absent by the mid seventeenth century. This implies that the statuary was removed in the mid sixteenth century and written records of subject matter of this category of imagery are very limited. Dowsing notes instances of imagery on porch façades including in the spandrels, but makes no reference to statuary in niches. C. H. Evelyn White, ed., *The Journal of William Dowsing* (Ipswich, 1885).

Fifteenth-century church porches in East Anglia frequently feature multiple niches and speculating on the imagery which would have been displayed is not a straightforward task. Difficulties are particularly acute if no distinction or hierarchy in style, size or position exists between the niches. A set of three horizontally arranged niches where the centre one is larger than those at the sides suggests a patronal image flanked by angelic supporters. Speculatively, the porch at Holy Trinity, Long Melford, perhaps featured a *Gnadenstuhl* Trinity (the Father seated, holding a cross with the Son's body still nailed to it and with the Spirit hovering over in the form of a dove) in the central niche venerated by a brace of accompanying angels. Conversely, above the entrance arch of the north porch at All Saints Mattishall are three identical, canopied niches but as there is no apparent tradition of how the company of heaven would be represented in three equal parts the likely iconography is difficult to construe. A rather more sophisticated arrangement is the façade at Lynn St Nicholas which we have already considered. The façade has a total of fifteen niches. Presumably an image of St Nicholas occupied the largest central niche, but this would have been only one part of a large collective scheme. A distant but pertinent architype was the tripartite porch of the north transept at Henry III's Westminster, which survived into the modern era. Here twelve image niches were designed to house figures of the apostles, and the Last Judgement fitted into the interstices of a complex blind tracery design.[53] A plausible reconstruction of the arrangement at Lynn would be to flank Nicholas with censing angels, place Peter and Paul in the buttress niches to the right and left of the entrance, and the remaining apostles could occupy the row of ten niches which form a frieze above.

In the absence of the saintly statuary which once populated the niches of East Anglia's medieval church porches our attention can be directed towards the larger corpus of figures, saintly or otherwise, which were integral to the building's structure. Roof pinnacles carved in figurative form, mythical beasts and wildmen were part of a widespread repertoire of apotropaic imagery. Extant examples can be seen at Pulham St Mary, Salle, Yaxley, East Bradenham, Gressenhall, Lynn St Nicholas and Barton Turf. We cannot know with any certainty how individuals interpreted specific images, but medieval conventions for visual imagery and textual traditions provide a context within which their significance can be set.

Apotropaic beasts guarded entrances to protect the elect and challenge the sinful. The tale of St Ethelburgha, the seventh-century founding abbess of Barking, establishes the tradition. During the Danish invasions of England in Ethelred's reign,

---

[53] Wilson, 'Calling the Tune', 70–1 and n.39–44.

there came an enemy troop to the monastery of the blessed Ethelburgha, not so much to fight as to pillage. For everyone had fled to the nearest city, London ... and they left the church and the bodies of the saints without protection, abandoning everything to the care of the God of heaven. Drawing near to the holy place, the Danes saw a huge wolf before the doors of the church instead of a doorkeeper, on guard like a pricked soldier, terrifying in appearance, and of itself it made an unprovoked attack on the mob. ... They looked for a safer entrance but a bear as defender drove them away more fiercely from the other door. Next a huge lion stood in the way when they were trying a third entrance and, growing savage, kept them at a great distance as they fled from its roaring and attack. At length, tamed by beasts from beastly savagery, and perceiving that they had been driven out by divine influence, they prayed to the guardian saints of the place to let them go in peace. Straightway, the guardian beasts allowed them entrance, now bringing peace to the cherishers of peace and they who had by no means been able to enter by violence, now entered with devoutness. ... So thus, the holy Ethelburgha who watched with her lamp for the coming of the Lord was worthy to guard vigilantly her own dwelling and in the beasts to have the Lord as her defender.[54]

Wolves, bears and lions, all beasts with savage potential, worked as protectors of the sacred place, defending the multiple doorways from incursion by non-Christian Danes. The bodies of the saints are described as 'without protection' yet the guardian beasts are there when all others have left the place unguarded. The end of the passage makes apparent that God's presence, working through the beasts, and St Ethelburgha's vigilance and faith in him as defender maintained the sanctity of the church and resulted in the conversion of the raiders.

Related apotropaic applications are evident in late medieval East Anglia, for example, the twin porches at SS Peter and Paul, Salle (Norfolk). Both adorned with pinnacles, these porches show how, and perhaps why, two coeval porches at the same site are architecturally singular (figs 50 and 51). The major early-fifteenth-century (re)building campaign is reasonably well recorded in primary written sources.[55] The south porch was built by Thomas Brigge, his heraldic coat displayed above the entrance arch, and can be dated to c.1444, the year of his death. The building of the north porch was associated with Geoffrey and Agatha Melman. An incomplete record of a now lost memorial brass once in the north porch read, 'Pray

---

[54] Vera Brown with Jocelyn Wogan-Browne, trans., *Guidance for Women in Twelfth-Century Convents* (Cambridge, 2003), 146–7.

[55] Cattermole and Cotton, 'Church Building in Norfolk', 263.

50 Exterior view, south porch, Salle

51 Exterior view, north porch, Salle

for the souls of Geoffrey Melman and Agatha his wife at whose expense, for both timber and carpentry, this whole porch ...'. Geoffrey died in 1404; the year of Agatha's death is not known, but their sons, William and John, were involved in the building campaign up to the 1440s. It is probable that the sons oversaw the building of the porch and subsequently laid a brass memorialising their parents.[56] Evidence in the fabric indicates that both porches were at least set out at the same time as the aisles, c.1405–20, even though their erection probably came several years later, once a suitable benefactor had been identified.

The figure sculpture on the parapet of the north porch is extant and in reasonable condition. Two wildmen stand, legs slightly apart, with a tree trunk at their backs, facing directly out from the porch. Each figure is posed as a mirror image of the other. They hold a head of the club in the hand closest to the centre, whilst the shaft is supported by the other hand. On the central plinth a griffin looks straight ahead, its wings raised but not unfurled. The posture of both wildmen and the griffin is not overtly aggressive; the men do not hold their clubs high above their heads nor clench their teeth in rage. Their stance evokes that of sentinels or guards; armed for action and alert but not yet engaged in combat. Their posture is reminiscent of the 'huge wolf before the doors of the church, on guard like a pricked soldier' which defended St Ethelburgha's church from the Danes.

Interpretations of wildman imagery are many and varied, but in the context of porch sculpture their primary significance is as a modification of a heraldic tradition which employs them as supporters, guardians or protectors, their super-human attributes harnessed for the good of their patron. In the conventions of heraldic protectors (figures which hold or guard a coat of arms) the charge was originally given to angels and patron saints, and 'through a process of artistic extrapolation' came to include 'unicorns, lions, griffons, and other savage beasts which had left their place within the heraldic shield to take up their station beside it. In this process of progressive secularization the wildmen came almost last.'[57] Savagery may be inherent in figures such as the wildmen and griffins which adorn the north porch at Salle but their containment in sculptural form, bonded to the fabric of the church, yokes their aggressive strength and assigns it to the service of God.

The north and south porches at Salle were laid out coevally but designed differently. The flat-topped, square plinths on the corners of the

---

[56] W. E. Parsons, *Salle: The Story of a Norfolk Parish, its Church, Manors and People* (Norwich, 1937), 24–5. The Latin original reads, '*sumptibus tam in memerio quam carpenta ... ac totum porticum*', as recorded by Martin and cited in Roger Greenwood and Malcolm Norris, *The Brasses of Norfolk Churches* (Holt, 1976), 50.

[57] Richard Bernheimer, *Wild Men in the Middle Ages* (New York, 1970), 178.

south porch parapet have lost their sculpture but something of its nature is recoverable. The crenellation sequence of the southern parapet lacks a central merlon or plinth, unlike the north parapet. The centre point of the parapet is a low crenel and an image could not have been set directly over the entrance arch of the south porch. No sentinel was centrally placed on the parapet, but there is an elongated image niche immediately above the entrance arch flanked by two small windows. As a result, in spite of the different designs of the two porches the boundaries of both are notionally protected by a combination of sacred and profane figurative imagery which was integral to the fabric and function of the building.

The porch at Pulham St Mary is also populated with figurative pinnacles, including a wolf guarding the head of St Edmund, and a wildman holding a club and seated cross-legged directly over the apex of the entrance arch. The façade combines several different themes: guardian beasts on the parapet, the arms of the Trinity and Passion and those of Bury Abbey, the Annunciation to the Virgin flanked by an angelic orchestra, as well as blank shields, empty niches and coroneted capitals. There can be little doubt that the outer surface of the porch marks the threshold of the church. The corollary to the risks associated with thresholds and boundaries were the possible opportunities and revelations. Michael Camille made the point well: 'If ... edges were dangerous, they were also powerful places ... the edge of the water was where wisdom revealed itself ... Openings, entrances and doorways, both of buildings and the human body ... were especially important liminal zones that had to be protected.'[58] Through a detailed programme of architectural forms the design of the building conveys notions of defence and protection whilst presenting the foundation of Christian salvation.

The Company of Heaven

In guarding the porch, pinnacle sculptures ward off evil; they ensure the place within is a sanctuary for those who are permitted to enter. The same theme also characterises the range of imagery which flanks porch entrances and takes the traditional position of sentries. In being permanently open porches were always at risk. The portal between porch and nave was closed by a door, windows could be protected by glazing, but the universal characteristic of porches is their openness, leaving them vulnerable. Examples of early-fifteenth-century porches, including Lynn St Nicholas and Harpley, have niches flanking the entrances and although the subject matter of

---

[58] Michael Camille, *Image on the Edge: The Margins of Medieval Art* (London, 1992), 16.

the statuary they once held is unknown, they allude to the form and social relevance of gatehouses, including the Ethelbert Gate in Norwich.

In many cases, the images placed closest to the entrance arch (i.e., those in the spandrels) continue the theme of guardianship and protection from evil, but these locations are occupied by saints rather than beasts as protectors. Warriors Michael, George and Margaret, all reputed dragon-slayers, are the most prevalent saints to inhabit porch façades, except for the Virgin. The church of St Giles at Colby (Norfolk) is an example where the spandrel imagery is not related to the patron saint but shows dragon-slaying saints, in this case St George and St Michael. The protective characteristic of both Michael and George is shown, for example, in the popular thirteenth-century text *The Golden Legend*, translated into English by Caxton in 1483. The protective, salvatory role of St George is established in the legend and ultimately realised in his defeat of the dragon:

> While they were talking, the dragon reared his head out of the lake. Trembling, the maiden cried: 'Away sweet lord, away with all speed!' but George, mounting his horse and arming himself with the sign of the cross, set bravely upon the approaching dragon and, commending himself to God, brandished his lance, dealt a grievous wound, and forced him to the ground.[59]

An extract from the same author's tale of St Michael is also resonant of protection:

> The owner, annoyed at the bull for having wandered off alone, aimed a poisoned arrow at it, but the arrow came back, as if turned about by the wind, and struck the one who had launched it. This dismayed the townsmen, and they went to the bishop and asked him what he thought of the strange occurrence. The bishop bound them to a three-day fast and admonished them to direct their questions to God. They did, and Saint Michael appeared to the bishop and said: 'Know that it was by my will that the man was struck by his arrow. I am the archangel Michael, and I have chosen to dwell in that place on earth and to keep it safe. I wished by that sign to indicate that I watch over the place and guard it.'[60]

The closing words of this extract are crucial – St Michael guards the place 'to keep it safe' whereas St George's salvatory protection is for the benefit of the maiden. Together the two saints guard places and people, a powerful combination which, when displayed at the entrance arch, emphasises the protective resonance of church porches.

---

[59] Jacobus de Voragine (c.1229–98). *The Golden Legend: Readings on the Saints*, volume I. trans. W. G. Ryan (Princeton, 1993), 239.

[60] De Voragine, *Golden Legend*, 201–2.

Colby is not the only example. In the dexter spandrel of the south porch at Palgrave, a figure wearing a feathered tunic and with large outstretched wings brandishes a spear, the tip of which is directed towards the apex of the entrance arch. In the sinister spandrel the image of a dragon is scaled to fill the space to such an extent that the wings are folded and the legs tucked tightly under the body. Depicted in the act of breathing fire, the flames are contained by the corner of the spandrel before having a chance to become expansive or dangerous. Caged by the architectural space it inhabits, the dragon's battle with saintly goodness is over before it even begins. The image niches which flank the spandrels at Palgrave are also notable as they indicate the identity of their now lost occupants. The dexter niche features the crossed keys of St Peter and the sinister the crossed swords of St Paul. Therefore, accepting that figures of Peter and Paul are likely to have occupied these niches, they stood as guards or sentinels of *their* church, but the ever-open arch itself (the potential battle ground) needed a protector with the capacity to quash satanic rebellion.

The iconography of a warrior figure in combat with a dragon, often identified as St George, was firmly associated with gateways and entrances. The instances of this imagery flanking porch entrances are part of a much wider cultural phenomenon. Perhaps the best-known example of combatants inhabiting gatehouse spandrels in East Anglia is the west front of the Ethelbert Gate at Norwich Cathedral, as discussed in chapter one. Direct influence of one building on another is always difficult to prove, but the pertinence of this imagery to gates and porches strongly suggests a shared significance between the two building types. A porch which was plausibly influenced by the design of the Ethelbert Gate is that built by John Bacon at Hessett in Suffolk (fig. 52). In one spandrel at Hessett a human figure brandishes a sword directed towards the apex of the arch. In the opposing spandrel a dragon rears up, mouth open, apparently roaring at the warrior. This porch is certainly not unique in having this sort of conflict scene flanking the point of entry, however, the dedication of the church to St Ethelbert and the combatants in the spandrels makes a connection with the cathedral gate more apparent than elsewhere. Warrior figures addressing a dragon or serpent-like aggressor across the void of an arch should not necessarily be identified as St George, particularly if not obviously vested in armour. The figure in the sinister spandrel of the c.1480 porch at Badingham brandishes a club-like object and wears a short tunic with no apparent armour protecting his legs. The church is dedicated to St John the Baptist. Although heavily eroded, the figure in the same location at St Mary's Ufford appears to have an animal fur draped over his shoulder and his weapon is difficult to decipher but appears not to be a sword. His opponent is not a dragon but a basilisk – against which a sword would be an ineffective weapon. Whatever the weapon used, victory is hinted at by

52 Exterior view, south porch, Hessett

the beast's knotted tail. A very similar composition is found at Ardleigh, but the figure here is clearly vested in feathers and sits astride the branch of an oak tree. Such idiosyncratic versions of combative pairings are much more numerous in Suffolk than in Norfolk, vivid examples of imaginative artistic invention twisting and manipulating a conventional mode.

The Virgin Mary – Guardian and Protectress

And the angel being come in, said unto her: Hail, full of grace, the Lord is with thee: blessed art thou among women. (Luke 1. 28)

The Annunciation, in essence a simple composition of two figures meeting, is a subject commonly placed framing an archway. From the twelfth century onwards this iconography is found on the east walls of church naves, with a prominent thirteenth-century example being St Albans Abbey, with the angel and Virgin positioned on either side of the chancel arch, or flanking an altar, for example, the fourteenth-century mural paintings at Little Melton. In appropriating Annunciation iconography, porch design reapplies imagery associated with the potent threshold between nave and

53 Arch detail, south porch, Great Witchingham

chancel onto the entrance of the porch. The common narrative in Annunciation imagery includes the distinction in space between the interior (where Mary is located), the arrival of the angel (from without to within) and the exteriority of the source from which the Holy Spirit descends. The resonance of this spatial narrative to a building which negotiates the transition between inside and outside is clear; the event and the setting are pertinent to each other. It is perhaps surprising therefore that this melding of image and setting was not favoured in Suffolk as it was in Norfolk.

The pose and vesture of the angel Annunciate can have militaristic connotations and share formal characteristics with low-relief sculptural depictions of the 'warrior' saints George and Michael also in porch spandrels. The angel in the sinister spandrel at Great Witchingham (fig. 53) and that occupying the dexter spandrel at Pulham St Mary both have torsos carved with feathers, and belts are slung low around the hips overlaying fashionably short tunics with exaggerated pinked edges. The quasi-militaristic characterisation of the angel is not a feature of Annunciation scenes in other media or other locations. A geographically and chronologically relevant example being the fifteenth-century stained-glass depictions of the Annunciation at Harpley and Bale, both in Norfolk. Equally, there is no sense of battle within the Annunciation story; by implication, depicting the angel in this mode is plausibly a specific response to the inherent dangers of the threshold.

As already mentioned, the porch at Pulham St Mary is richly populated with figures, including a wolf guarding the head of St Edmund and a wildman holding a club, the arms of the Trinity and Passion and those of Bury Abbey, the Annunciation to the Virgin flanked by an angelic orchestra, as well as blank shields, empty niches and coroneted capitals. The Angel of the Annunciation at Pulham St Mary holds a scroll on which is carved '*Ave Marie*'. These are not the opening words of the Angelic Salutation in Luke's gospel (which does not name Mary) but rather of the prayer 'Ave Maria'. Thus, the Virgin is invoked as intercessor, advocate and salvator. According to Miri Rubin, 'Mary was a cure against the deadliness of sin. She earned that power through her role in Christ's birth, but also through her sorrow at his death.'[61] Depictions of the Annunciation in porch spandrels therefore convey the necessity of God being made man through a mortal virgin woman to counterbalance the fall in Eden. Thus, the Annunciation sets in motion a course of events fundamental to human salvation. Occupying the open porch entrance, the Annunciation signifies the salvation which lies within; as only the Holy Spirit can enter the Virgin's womb, only believers can pass through the guarded portal and enter

---

[61] Miri Rubin, *The Mother of God: A History of the Virgin Mary* (London, 2009).

God's kingdom on earth. The notion of protected threshold is once again a recurring theme.

By the fifteenth century porch entrances had become the point of exchange between the profane world and the church within. The conjunction of the heavenly spirit with the earthly body in the event of the Annunciation reinforces this interpretation of that place. A passage from the tenth-century 'Old English Homilies' makes apparent the significance of the Annunciation to such a location. Addressing the Virgin, the angel affirms that '... for a long time, the door of heaven's kingdom, through which I have been sent hither, stands closed through [the sin of] the first persons, but now through thee they shall be unclosed.'[62] Entering the church, via a porch, was made possible by the Virgin having conceived the Son of God. Porches were thus a mode for communicating the contractual relationship forged between humanity and the Divine.

Virginal Vaults

As well as being part of the iconography of exterior spandrels, Mary is also present within church porches, most frequently in the sequence known as the Five Joys of the Virgin: commencing with the Annunciation, and including Christ's nativity, crucifixion and resurrection/ascension, and Mary's assumption/coronation. This figurative image cycle elaborates the sculpted bosses set as though gemstones on a canopy, or stars on heaven's vault. In the East Anglian porches with historiated bosses depicting the Five Joys, the Virgin's coronation is appropriately placed centrally, the highest point within the canopy. This contrasts with known 'Joys' sequences in wall paintings and alabaster altarpieces where the resurrection, not the assumption/coronation, is placed centrally. Whilst these object types evidently emphasise Christ, porches give primacy to the centrally placed Virgin.

Sculpted bosses which show the Virgin Mary as queen of heaven at her coronation can, on the basis of art historical conventions originating in England around 1100, be read as the marriage of Christ to his church, i.e., the Virgin. The subject matter's most obvious pertinence is to the couples united in matrimony before the church door. The significance of the Assumption also relates to transition between earthly and heavenly states. The Virgin's bodily assumption was her resurrection from death and ascension into paradise. When placed at the entrance of the church the subject powerfully conveys the significance of crossing the limen of the church. It is an inescapable observation that the Life (or Joys) of the Virgin

[62] R. Morris, ed., *The Blickling Homilies, together with the Blickling Glosses* (London, 1874–6), 8.

was deemed appropriate to porches not merely as buildings but as places of lived experience, significance and memory. The relationship between image and place is captured by the consistency with which the Annunciation flanks the entrance and the Coronation occupies the highest point of the vault.

Devotion to the Virgin in medieval England was greater than to any other saint, as demonstrated by parish church dedications.[63] It is perhaps not surprising, therefore, that imagery associated with her is a dominant element of parish church decoration in general, and porches are no exception. In the main, Marian imagery in parochial contexts was concentrated in three locations: in the rood group (and occasionally on chancel screens), in the service of altars dedicated to her, and in porches; the location effects the imagery's resonance. The prevalence of imagery associated with the life of the Virgin in and on parish church porches constructs a powerful association between the mother of God/queen of heaven and the entrance to the church, as already indicated by the discussion of spandrels which depict the Annunciation. A few statistics demonstrate the point more clearly. Nineteen church porches in Norfolk prominently feature Marian imagery but only eight of the churches are dedicated to her. Only at Wymondham does the external Annunciation anticipate (and in part duplicate) a Marian vault inside the porch; in all other cases the relationship between subject and location is maintained. The physical hierarchy is apparently reflective of the earthly Annunciation and the heavenly Coronation. This placing of the Coronation in the upper register is replicated by its being positioned not only at the centre of the vault but at its apex. Different arrangements of the events are found, but the relationship is maintained. At South Walsham, for example, an extant Coronation of the Virgin statue fills the niche above the porch entrance and is accompanied by an Annunciation in the spandrels.

The Virgin's Womb and the Throne of Solomon

Spatial distinctions should not, however, be allowed to conceal the integrated nature of these themes. The relationship between the Annunciation, the Virgin's womb, the marriage of bridegroom and bride, and the prefiguration of these events in the person of Solomon is set out in the commentary on 'The Annunciation of Saint Mary'. The text reports the circumstances and significance of the events which leads from annunciation

---

[63] In the regions listed by Richard Marks, parish church dedications to the Blessed Virgin Mary (328) are almost twice that of 'All Saints' (167) which is the next most popular dedication. Marks, *Image and Devotion*, 68.

through nativity, crucifixion, and implicitly the union of Christ and his bride in heaven. The entirety is condensed into a single statement: 'Wherefore the Heavenly King shall prepare thy womb as a bridal chamber for his son'. This is later reaffirmed: 'Let us rejoice then in the union of God and men, and in the union of the bridegroom and the bride, that is Christ and the holy church ...'.[64] The Solomonic prefiguration of these events is also commented on:

> In her [Mary] was fulfilled what was sung in the Song of Songs, thus saying: 'Solomon's bed was surrounded by guards, that is by sixty men, the strongest that were in Israel, and each of them had a sword girt to his hip, on account of the terror of the night. Now then what was Solomon's bed else but the womb of the ever-pure Virgin? The peace-loving king, our lord Jesus Christ, chose and sought that womb.[65]

More commonly Solomon is presented as a type for Christ as judge and his throne for the Virgin. In the words of the Sermon of the Nativity of the Blessed Virgin Mary ascribed to Nicholas of Clairvaux: 'Our Solomon is not only wise but wisdom itself; not only our peacemaker but our peace. He has made himself a throne, even the womb of a pure Virgin where that Majesty sits whose nod shakes the earth.'[66]

Of more immediate chronological relevance to late medieval porches than those early texts are the fifteenth-century Marian N-Town plays, in which the Virgin's corpse as healing relic becomes an enclosed, enshrined body; a performative relic contained within a sacred reliquary. Yet in the subtle mutability of enshrining the sacred, the Virgin's body is also imagined as an enclosing object. The N-Town Assumption play draws on the convention of referring to Mary as a sacred container; God refers to Mary as 'Tabernacle of Joye, vessel of lyf, hefnely temple'. Similarly, the extremely popular Golden Legend terms the Virgin as a 'tabernacle of Christ', a 'vessel of Christ' and a 'sacred living ark'. As Chaganti has expressed, 'some of this language gestures toward Mary's womb as a typological manifestation of the Ark of the Covenant.'[67] Through dramatic performance, the familiar textual metaphor of Mary's body as sacred container was visualised and witnessed, confirming the dynamic relationship between interiority and exteriority, container and contained. As noted earlier, porches do not close,

---

[64] Morris, *The Blickling Homilies*, 8–9.
[65] Ibid., 10.
[66] This passage is cited in Francis Wormald, 'The Throne of Solomon and St Edward's Chair', in *De Artibus Opuscula, XL: Essays in Honor of Erwin Panofsky volume 1*, ed. Millard Meiss (New York, 1961), 543.
[67] Seeta Chaganti, *The English Poetics of the Reliquary: Enshrinement, Inscription, Performance* (New York, 2008), 82–3.

our sense of their interiority is negotiated through the Virgin's containing presence; vessel of Christ, Ark of the Covenant, Throne of Majesty.

These written commentaries and dramaturgical examples support a reading of some late medieval English porches as containers analogous to the Virgin's womb, the tabernacle which held the ultimate judge. The specific imagery applied on and in several church porches encourages linkages to be forged. The relevance of the Annunciation to the open door is clear; that the throne of Solomon is analogous with the door of paradise has been argued by, amongst others, Isa Ragusa.[68] As the architectural and iconographic evidence implies, the location, significance, form and function, of East Anglia's late medieval church porches marks them as places of judgement and salvation.

Conclusion

The purpose of this chapter has been to present and analyse the architecture and ornamentation of church porches so as to understand their design and function. It is apparent that a general developmental trajectory is observable, with shifts coming at the turn of both the fourteenth and fifteenth centuries. The architectural evidence of the manner in which porches were designed has demonstrated that porch entrances became the significant location, the 'church door', from around 1390, with early experimentation occurring from the mid-century. From the late fourteenth century, porch façades were increasingly ornamented and designed as the focus of attention. The threshold between profane and sacred being located at the porch entrance was conveyed very clearly through means of architectural form and decoration.

As well as these generalised findings, individual cases reveal that the demands of designing a parish church porch were specific and apparently reflect as much the input of the patron as of the designing mason. As buildings, porches serve a range of functions, as seen in chapter two, and the architecture had to respond to how and for what they were used. Partly as a result of their function and partly in a more complex network of architectural negotiations, porches are also places which draw ideas from other building types. Their architecture can allude to other contemporary entrance buildings, most notably gatehouses, but also to the biblical model of King Solomon. By considering architecture in an inclusive sense – the structural form in conjunction with the materials, ornament, decoration

---

[68] Isa Ragusa, 'Terror Demonum and Terror Inimicorum: The Two Lions of the Throne of Solomon and the Open Door of Paradise', *Zeitschrift für Kunstgeschichte* 40.2 (1977), 93–114.

and imagery – it has become apparent that porches are fundamental components of medieval churches, establishing the cultural and religious principles which the rest of the building maintains.

Through the employment of architecture as a primary source, the buildings themselves have revealed much more about the manner in which they were conceived than the scant documentation. The consideration of porch architecture and design presented in this chapter implicitly reveals the choices and decisions involved in the planning and building of a porch. But how and by whom were porches commissioned and funded? This question is the subject of the next chapter.

Documenting East Anglia's Church Porches, c.1370 to c.1540

4

Documenting medieval architecture is an exercise in analysing written evidence and architectural detail. Both approaches have been used in the compilation of this chapter. The extant primary textual documentation relating to East Anglian parish church porches provides scant evidence for establishing a generalised understanding of the circumstances of patronage, design or construction. Case studies are, however, possible and some key examples are looked at in detail in the next chapter. The potential of the written evidence is enhanced when correlated with the fabric of the buildings themselves and, as will be seen, important lessons are learnt about the reliability of testamentary evidence. For example, the total absence of a porch indicates that an individual's testamentary instruction to build, or bequeath money to the fabric of, a porch was overlooked by their fellow parishioners after their death. This chapter progresses along a path of various ways to document church porches, presenting the paper trail of their former lives and their enduring architectural attributes.

As has been established in previous chapters, the form of buildings termed porch/*porticus* has historically been diverse. One possible implication is that late medieval porch architecture will also show considerable variety.[1] Investigation of that proposition is based on a survey of the 119 medieval parish church porches in Norfolk and Suffolk for which primary or antiquarian textual information is available.

Late medieval East Anglia benefitted from extensive areas of fertile agricultural land which, when combined with a large population and

---

[1] 'As with towers, the fifteenth century saw the culmination of porch design in this country; the period offers an array of types in different materials that makes a brief analysis seem inadequate.' J. C. Cox and C. B. Ford, *Parish Churches* (London, 1961), 111.

well-ordered social structures, was astutely exploited.[2] With such economic advantage came international trade, political involvement at the highest levels and an equivalent investment in cultural sophistication, including architecture. An index of the region's medieval wealth is the number and quality of its parish churches; it has been estimated that more than 920 were built between the eleventh and sixteenth centuries.[3] They demonstrate a wide range of possibilities and approaches in terms of architectural patronage, design ambition and materiality. Taken as a distinct corpus for current purposes, they provide a detailed inventory of medieval porch architecture in the eastern region.

In terms of available building materials East Anglia lacks major deposits of indigenous building stone, other than flint. Timber was the valuable product of limited, and thus carefully managed, woodland and production of high quality material required long-term investment. Architecture necessarily responded to the specific qualities of the available materials and whilst high status buildings display the benefactor's wealth through the liberal use of imported ashlar, flint rubble is the characteristic component of East Anglian architecture. Locally available flint was often used in combination with ashlar and brick which provided structural stability, particularly as quoins, or for architectural detailing around windows and doorways. Flint was also used in purposeful and sophisticated ways, including the regular coursing of pebbles or snapped flints characteristic of twelfth-century work. From the turn of the fourteenth century flints were carefully selected, worked and applied to create patterned elevations.[4] Ultimately, medieval architecture in East Anglia was very much a product of place and time.

---

[2] Although the picture was not consistent across the region, land values in many areas were high. For example in the early fourteenth century the per-acre value of fertile loam fields of Flegg was 36d, equal to the national maximum. Bruce M. S. Campbell, 'Medieval Land Use and Values', in *An Historical Atlas of Norfolk*, ed. Peter Wade-Martins (Norwich, 1993), 48. For discussion of agricultural technology in Norfolk, see ibid., 50.

[3] Neil Batcock, 'Medieval Churches in Use and in Ruins', in *An Historical Atlas of Norfolk*, ed. Peter Wade-Martins (Norwich, 1993), 60.

[4] It is widely accepted that the earliest example of accomplished flint flushwork was the Ethelbert Gate at Norwich Cathedral (c.1310–17). See Frank Woodman, 'The Gothic Campaigns', in *Norwich Cathedral – Church, City and Diocese, 1096–1996*, ed. Ian Atherton et al. (London, 1996), 161–3. Literature concerned with East Anglian flushwork includes: John Blatchly and Peter Northeast, *Decoding Flint Flushwork on Suffolk and Norfolk Churches* (Ipswich, 2005); Stephen Hart, *Flint Flushwork: A Medieval Masonry Art* (Woodbridge, 2008); Julian Luxford, 'Symbolism in East Anglian Flushwork', in *Signs and Symbols*, ed. John Cherry and Ann Payne. Harlaxton Medieval Studies 18 (n.s.) (Donington, 2009), 119–32.

4. DOCUMENTING CHURCH PORCHES

Primary textual evidence has underpinned several modern studies of East Anglian parish churches. Judith Middleton-Stewart's exemplary work *Inward Purity, Outward Splendour* has at its core the medieval written sources for the deanery of Dunwich, and draws its strength from analytically combining textual and material evidence.[5] Another notable instance is Dominic Summers' unpublished study of Norfolk west towers, which acknowledges the relative wealth of documentary evidence relating to these buildings.[6] Records of donations made to tower building projects often survive in sufficient quantity to indicate the period in which fundraising and/or construction of a single tower took place.[7] An equally fruitful approach was adopted by Richard Fawcett, who produced a series of papers concerned with Norfolk masons and the works attributable to them. Taking written evidence as his starting point, Fawcett drew connections between a wide range of buildings which share identifiable characteristics and plausibly show the hand of a particular designer or other methods of design influence between buildings.[8] Where sufficient or appropriate textual information relating to medieval architecture is available it provides a framework on which to build an investigation of the monuments. It is inevitable, however, that the conclusions which can be drawn from the documentation depend on the nature of the written material; questions posed must take account of the constraints of the evidence. It is therefore necessary for the benefit of the present study to set out the nature of the written evidence relating specifically to East Anglian porches.

---

[5] Judith Middleton-Stewart, *Inward Purity and Outward Splendour: Death and Remembrance in the Deanery of Dunwich, Suffolk, 1370–1547* (Woodbridge, 2001).

[6] Summers, 'Norfolk Church Towers of the Later Middle Ages', vol. 1, 149–83.

[7] For Norfolk there are 586 individual bequests to towers or steeples, the largest number relating to a single parish being 21 bequests to the fabric of the tower at North Walsham, all dated between 1484 and 1522. By comparison 83 individual bequests relate to porches, the largest concentration being the three recorded donations to Swannington between 1452, 1457 and 1478 and all of which are bequests of 6s 8d. These data are taken from Cattermole and Cotton, 'Church Building in Norfolk', 235–79.

[8] Richard Fawcett, 'Sutton in the Isle of Ely and its Architectural Context', in *Medieval Art and Architecture at Ely Cathedral*, ed. N. Coldstream and P. Draper (Leeds, 1979), 78–96; Richard Fawcett, 'A Group of Churches by the Architect of Great Walsingham', *Norfolk Archaeology* 37 (1980), 277–94; Fawcett, 'St Mary at Wiveton in Norfolk'; Richard Fawcett, 'The Influence of the Gothic Parts of the Cathedral on Church Building in Norfolk', in *Norwich Cathedral: Church, City and Diocese, 1096–1996*, ed. Ian Atherton et al. (London, 1996), 210–27.

Documentary Evidence, c.1370–c.1540

In 1983 Paul Cattermole and Simon Cotton published a gazetteer of 'datable references to church building' in Norfolk during the period c.1370–1550. As the authors state, the 'principal sources' used were 'the wills of Norfolk people, supplemented by other sources such as churchwardens' accounts, and inscriptions, many of which were recorded by antiquaries'.[9] In that gazetteer reference is made to seventy-seven porches for which some form of associated primary, heraldic or antiquarian evidence is known. For the present study this list has been augmented with additional references taken from Blomefield's *Topographical History* – a further nineteen buildings.[10] In 2001 and 2010 Peter Northeast published two volumes of late medieval wills from the archdeaconry of Sudbury, Suffolk, dating from 1439 to 1474.[11] Amongst the entries in these volumes are references to church porches, their building, repair and even occasional insights into their use. The two volumes yield thirty-three bequests relating to seventeen church porches. The date range reflects the growth in medieval record keeping and subsequent survival rates. The period of the Sudbury wills closely mirrors the date range in which most extant Norfolk testamentary bequests to church fabric were made and equal caution must be taken when analysing the Sudbury record, as will be demonstrated in discussion of the Norfolk material. However, Northeast's work offers something which the gazetteer of Norfolk evidence lacks. The register entries being published in their entirety retains each bequest's context and this permit something to be said about the reason for and importance placed on the benefaction of porches. The limitations of Cattermole and Cotton's publication is that the evidence has been separated from its original context and whilst conclusions can be drawn concerning the giving to church fabric, there is little to be extracted about the benefactor's interests. This evidence is revealed in the wording of the bequests, not by the hard facts of date, amount and recipient. In addition to Northeast's publications, documentary evidence relating to several Suffolk porches has been drawn from a range of primary sources, published and in manuscript. Compilation of the Suffolk testamentary references has been augmented considerably by Simon Cotton's generosity in sharing his personal research archive. An additional twenty-six pre-Reformation

---

[9] Cattermole and Cotton, 'Church Building in Norfolk', 235.
[10] Many of the additions are references to burials in porches which at the very least provide a *terminus ante quem* for the building. Others are coats of arms recorded by Blomefield but not included in Cattermole and Cotton's article.
[11] Peter Northeast, ed., *Wills of the Archdeaconry of Sudbury 1439–1474: Wills from the Register 'Baldwyne' Part 1: 1439–1461* (Woodbridge, 2001); Peter Northeast and Heather Falvey, eds, *Wills of the Archdeaconry of Sudbury 1439–1474: Wills from the Register 'Baldwyne' Part 2: 1461–74* (Woodbridge, 2010).

references to Suffolk porches are here included. This sample of medieval porches at 136 East Anglian parish churches, which is intentionally non-selective and inevitably not exhaustive, constitutes the central element of the present chapter.

The means of constructing the sample requires a few words of explanation. The 189 separate textual references relating to porches of 136 parish churches in East Anglia are presented in Appendix 1. The majority are testamentary bequests or instructions, with the remainder being made up of coats of arms (mainly antiquarian records of them) and inscriptions displayed on the porch or an associated memorial. For example, at Holme-next-the-Sea Henry Notyngham's memorial records his building of the 'stepyl' which is in fact a south tower-porch and therefore included in the sample. Where it has been possible to identify a particular individual with the heraldry displayed on a porch or recorded by Blomefield it is here taken at face value as a dating tool. Richard Rokelle's bequest of 40s to repair the 'vestibule' at Ludham in 1422 is also included.[12] Although it is the only instance of *vestibulum* being used to refer to a porch in Norfolk this is almost certainly the intended meaning. Whereas *porticus*/porch(e) is almost always used in Norfolk, in Suffolk there are several instances of *vestibula* as well as *porticus*/porch(e). For example, in 1441 Roger Wygenale left 6s 8d to the making of a '*novi vestibuli*' (new porch) at Boxford.[13] Etymologically English 'vestibule' (like its counterparts in other modern European languages) derives from the Latin *vestibulum* and thus pertains to an entrance court or forecourt. In the setting of a late medieval parish church this most plausibly refers to the porch. Ludham is also a case in point of where the text does not specify to which porch it relates and there is more than one at the named church; another such case is Snetterton.

Approximately half of the textual references are concerned with the general building of a porch or a particular element, such as the roof or paving or windows. A small number reference repair or renewal of some kind and include the ambiguous terms 'emendation', 'edification', and 'reparation'.[14] A few simply note a bequest 'to the porch' which could be a gift towards maintenance of the building, but the wording is too general to be meaningful. The remainder of the sample comprises burials in or

---

[12] NRO NCC Hirning 105.
[13] Northeast, *Wills of Sudbury*, 45.
[14] Northeast, among others, has pointed out the need to establish the context of a gift when obscure terminology such as 'reparation' is used. See Peter Northeast, 'Suffolk Churches in the Later Middle Ages: The Evidence of Wills', in *East Anglia's History: Studies in Honour of Norman Scarfe*, ed. Christopher Harper-Bill (Woodbridge, 2002), 94.

close to a porch, coats of arms augmenting the exterior decoration, and inscriptions, often composed in flint flushwork.

Based on the surviving written record, it was in the 1450s that greatest attention (in terms of number of legacies) was directed at porches with more bequests recorded in the extant historical record than any other decade from the 1370s to the 1540s (graph 1). In terms of value, however, it was in the 1480s that the largest sums were bestowed on porch projects (graph 2). After a steep drop in the financial worth of bequests to porches

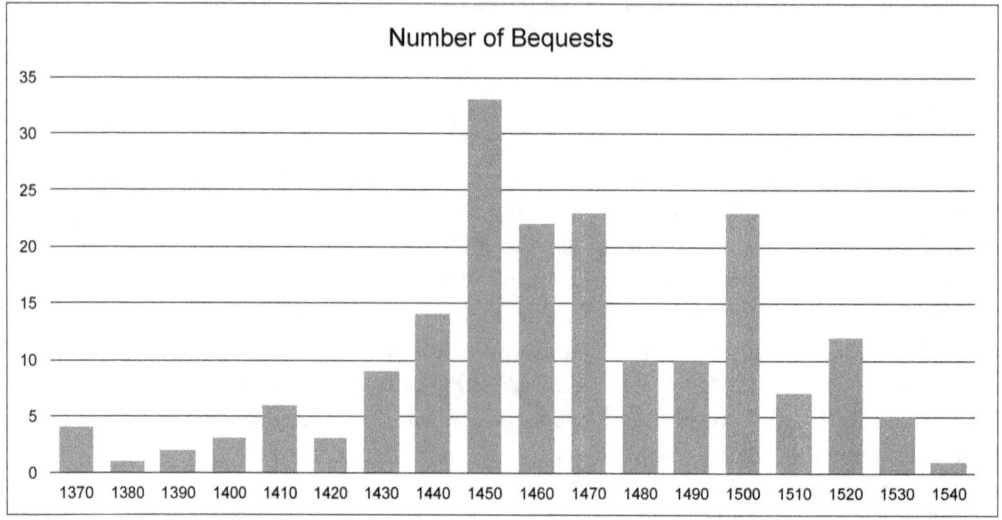

1 Number of bequests to church porches by decade

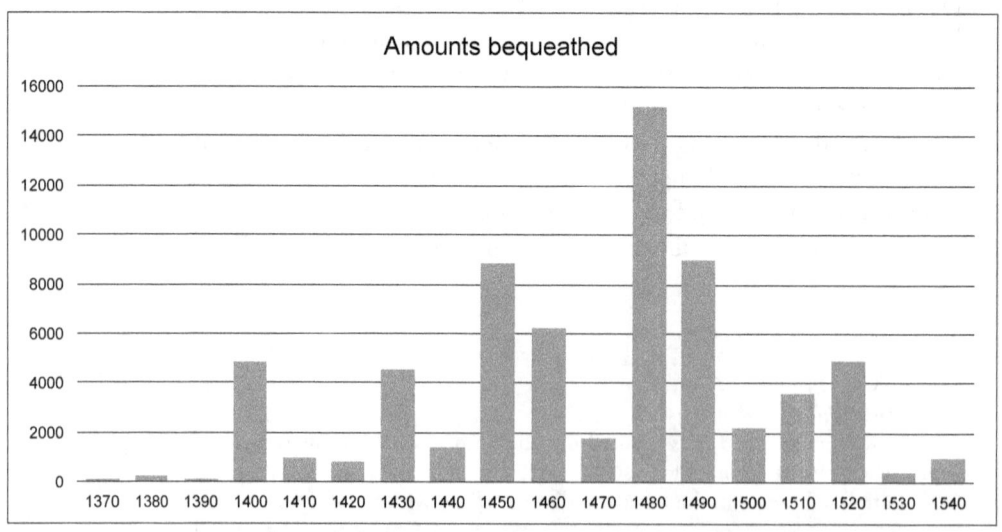

2 Financial bequests to church porches (in pence) by decade

at the turn of the sixteenth century, the subsequent decades saw steady increases until the Reformation. However, such conclusions drawn from the entire body of evidence are perhaps more instructive of the nature of the documentary material than the buildings to which they can be related. There is of course no correlation between the date from which written evidence survives and the occurrence of parish porches.

During the fifteenth century will writing became more common and more widely spread across the population at large than in previous centuries. The relatively low number of testators in England before the late fourteenth century results in an equivalently small number of extant wills. After that date fewer people died intestate than had done previously and testaments from the late fourteenth century onwards are more plentiful. East Anglian wills survive in number only from the 1370s and the earliest extant such document to include mention of a porch is that written in 1371 by Roger de Northwold, rector of Flordon, which records his request that his body be buried in his church's porch.[15] His will does not, however, record a bequest to the porch or any instruction to build one, only a more general 100s to the 'emendation' of the church which was to be disbursed by his executors, presumably as they saw fit. Evidently either the porch already existed or perhaps Roger de Northwold left specific verbal instructions for its construction before, *'langues in extremis'*, he composed his will.

The end date of 1540 for medieval testaments is also relatively arbitrary. Although donations to the fabric of parish churches declined at the Reformation they had been doing so previously and similarly this form of giving did not cease immediately after England's break from Rome. The latest record of a bequest to an East Anglian porch in the medieval period is the 1540 will of Robert Lincoln who bequeathed 6 marks for leading the porch at Bunwell (equivalent to £4).[16] This is a not insignificant amount and considerably more than the average gift of £2 7s 0d. Fifteen other extant testaments record donations to the fabric of this church, commencing in 1458 (12d given for the painting of the font) and ending in 1542 (a gift of 20s to 'mend the church').[17] So what does one bequest within a wider documentary evidence relate about the porch? Was Bunwell porch built c.1540? The painting of the font in 1458 suggests that the nave was in use at that time and there is no indication that it (the nave) was rebuilt. The most numerous and informative collection of bequests for Bunwell relate to the tower, which was seemingly built up against the pre-existing nave. On the basis of nine documents dating from 1499 to 1508 the tower was constructed in the first decade of the sixteenth century as a discrete project,

---

[15] NRO NCC Heydon 16.
[16] NRO ANF Liber 10 (Dowsyng), 50.
[17] Cattermole and Cotton, 'Church Building in Norfolk', 241.

some thirty-two years before the porch. Taking a standard building rate of six feet of walling per single six-month construction season, a period of nine years (1499–1508) would leave a tower just 54ft high. A useful document is the 1505 will of William Taylor, which reads: 'toward the makyng up of the stepill of Bonewell every yere when the masons work on it 6s 8d until the sum of 33s 4d be paid'.[18] If the masons did work every year, the funding was therefore intended to last five years, perhaps indicating that another 30ft or so were, in 1505, yet to be built. The bequest takes the project through to 1510 and adds at least 12ft more to the tower's height, bringing it to around 66ft. Absent from the written record is any reference to the finishing of the tower or to the parapet. As the porch bequest is to the leading, presumably of the roof, it probably marks the end of the works. The period of time between the building of the tower and the leading of the porch would seem to indicate that the two projects were independent of each other. Other evidence which might support the porch being built c.1540 comes from the bequests made in 1541 and 1542 for the mending of the church side. This nave work might relate to the building of the porch, but it is also plausible that by 1541 the church side needed repair following the removal of the rood stair. Visual evidence which might be present in the fabric to support this suggestion is today lost beneath a thick coat of render. However, the way in which the building materials are used indicates a similarity between the tower parapet and the porch. Both elements have vertically-elongated, crocketed, flushwork ogees which are filled with carefully selected square white stones, although the selection appears to have been more carefully made for the porch than for the tower parapet. In the case of Bunwell neither the written record nor the building itself provides sufficient evidence to date the porch with confidence more accurately than between about 1510 (the last reference of a gift to the tower) and 1540 when money was given for the leading of the porch. Visual evidence does not support a phasing distinction between the tower being finished and the porch being constructed, but rather argues for a single, if protracted, campaign of works.

On a case-by-case basis, information that testaments convey about post-mortem contributions to the building or upkeep of porches, as Bunwell has demonstrated, is often imprecise or deficient as an aid to establishing construction dates. Taken in isolation, testamentary bequests to the fabric of East Anglian church porches are insecure as a means of dating the buildings. In most cases they provide little more than a touch-point indicative of a planned or ongoing building project, or simply the existence of a porch. Specific instances which provide more detail regarding the responsibility for the construction of porches are the focus of the next chapter.

[18] Ibid.

The 189 pieces of primary or antiquarian evidence relating to porches do, however, show that these buildings were very much part of the practice of giving to one's parish church throughout the later Middle Ages. The dating evidence for their construction and upkeep, taking into account the vagaries of document survival, shows that porches were a facility sought by East Anglian parishioners for at least two hundred years up to the end of the medieval period.

Architecture as Document – Scoping the Form of East Anglia's Church Porches

The flaws and limitations of written source materials stimulate alternative methods of exploration and in this section the fabric of the buildings is taken as a distinct form of historical documentation. As the writings of Richard of St Victor and William of Worcestre have already shown, church porches, like other architectural types, have long been interrogated by means of measurement and analysis of their physical form. The following pages are a continuation of that well-established tradition.

To inform the following architectural documentation, the floor plan, entrance arch and church door of the 119 extant East Anglian church porches have been measured. Considered in isolation, the size of porches does little more than establish the parameters, but taken in conjunction with the presence and design of four principal elements it is possible to analyse the relationship between the size and elaboration of church porches. The four most commonly encountered attributes of porches (entrance arches, windows, buttresses and base courses) have been analysed for each building and grouped into formal types. What follows is a distillation of this analysis and a simplified summary of porch form.

Four key components, all of which are commonly found in East Anglian church porches, comprise the architectural outline of each building. They are: (i) an open entrance arch (100% occurrence), (ii) window-like apertures in the side walls (94% occurrence), (iii) buttresses (89% occurrence) and (iv) a base course (72% occurrence). Other elements that might have been considered are parapets and gables, but in too many cases the uppermost elements of porches have been altered. To investigate the four key elements, each component is divided into the minimum number of valid formal types and each porch is assigned to the closest corresponding type. Classifications are numbered to begin with the simplest form (Type 0 or Type 1) and incrementally develop through stages of increasing complexity to reach the most sophisticated type for each component.

Open entrance arches can be divided into three types, two of which have further subdivisions thus creating six types:

Type 1: These archways are identified by the absence of either a capital or base, with the jambs being half-octagons leading to a moulded arch with the increased moulding detail (where present) commencing part way up the jamb or at the springing point of the arch. Example: Gooderstone (Norfolk).

Type 2: The jambs are single half-shafts with bases and capitals, above which there is a moulded arch. Example: Little Waldingfield (Suffolk).

Type 2a: As Type 2 with the addition of a vertical beading continuing upwards from the jamb which meets a horizontal string course and forms spandrels above the shoulders of the arch. Example: Swannington (Norfolk).

Type 2b: As Type 2a with the addition of fleurons or other ornamentation of the moulded section. Example: Southwold (Suffolk).

Type 3: In the most complex examples the jambs are constructed of multiple half-shafts each having an independent base and capital. The capitals are often carved with foliate, animalistic or human motifs. Example: Great Cressingham (Norfolk).

Type 3a: As Type 3 with the addition of spandrels above the shoulders of the arch. Example: Yaxley (Suffolk).

Window-like apertures in the side walls have been classified by the number of main lights. This classification is designed to avoid subjective ranking of stylistic tracery designs:

Type 0: devoid of apertures. Example: Castle Acre (Norfolk).
Type 1: a single main light. Example: Alderford (Norfolk).
Type 2: a double main light. Example: Combs (Suffolk).
Type 3: a triple main light. Example: Little Waldingfield (Suffolk).

Buttresses of porches can be divided into four basic types. In East Anglia, diagonal buttresses (denoted 'D') are predominant compared with the few instances of angle buttresses (denoted 'A').

Type 0: Unbuttressed. Example: Castle Acre (Norfolk).

Type D1: These buttresses appear to be primarily for structural support. They are unadorned and consistently of the same fabric as the main body of the porch. Example: Deopham (Norfolk).

Type D2/A2: These are stepped buttresses with a horizontal division marking each stage. The treatment of the front face presents coherent use of materials, either being entirely of ashlar or a frame of ashlar quoins infilled with flint. The lower stage acts as a base course, either continuing that around the rest of the porch or solely skirting the buttress. Example: Stoke by Nayland (Suffolk).

Type D3/A3: These buttresses are also stepped and have horizontal divisions at each stage. It is the decorative use of the front face that specifically sets this group apart. Examples display flint flushwork patterns, motifs or imagery carved in ashlar and/or image niches, all of which visually create multiple planes increasing the apparent sophistication of the buttress. Example: Southwold (Suffolk).

Base courses, where present, can be divided into three categories, according to the ways in which they are architecturally articulated:

Type 0: No base course or thickening of the wall at ground level. Example: Brisley (Norfolk).

Type 1: The lower courses of the walling are thickened but without architectural accent and use the same material as the main body of the porch. Example: Aslacton (Norfolk).

Type 2: A horizontal division between the lower courses of the wall and the upper section is created by a moulded ledge which acts as a coping for the underlying masonry which protrudes from the vertical line of the wall above. Example: Wymondham (Norfolk).

Type 3: The base course is ornamented with panels of carved stone or flint flushwork which create a horizontal frieze of decorative, iconographic or heraldic motifs, often raised above the lowest level of the walling and covered by a drip-mould. It is notable that this type rarely protrudes very much beyond the line of the main body of walling and can therefore be considered as decorative rather than functional in emphasis. Example: Beccles (Suffolk).

Analysis of the Data – Shades of Difference

In summary an overall correlation does exist between the degrees of complexity in the four elements present above – for example, there is a high likelihood of the more sophisticated types of each element coinciding. Consistency in the occurrence of elements is not, however, guaranteed, with many porches featuring combinations of simplicity and complexity. For example, the south porch at South Walsham, built c.1454 (fig. 41) and north porch at Acle, c.1497 (fig. 43) both have a deep, elaborate base course on the façade, which continues around the buttresses. This is accompanied by a horizontal frieze, image niches and spandrels, but the masonry of the side elevations is consistently plain with no emphasis at the lowest level. In these and many other instances, the façades of fifteenth-century church porches are treated very differently from the side walls and elaborated to a much greater degree. A slight variation on this is the design of New Buckenham porch which has an elaborately carved, panelled base course present all the way around the porch, including the side walls and across the buttresses. This degree of decoration does not, however, appear on the flanks of the buttresses which are plain ashlar. The tall, crenellated parapet takes the base course motifs to the top of the porch, but the section between is relatively plain. For example there are no spandrels flanking the entrance arch and minimal flushwork decoration low down to either side. Taken case by case, church porches are varied and distinctive but this simple classification effectively shows the correlation between the levels of complexity of the four basic components.

Entrances and Apertures

The design of porch entrance arches is divided into six categories and as they are ubiquitous to the building type they serve as good evidence for the correlation between dimensions and elaboration. Type 3a entrance arches are the most elaborate and collectively have the greatest width, but they are not the tallest, that attribute belongs to the Type 2b arches. The average width of Types 3, 2a and 2 are all equal at approximately 65in and perhaps unsurprisingly at the lower end of the scale the simplest form (Type 1) are the smallest entrances in both width and height. In general terms therefore the dimensions and elaboration of porch entrance arches do correlate. There is however a sense that in some cases greater elaboration of the façade was desired even though the porch was not particularly large.

An entrance arch is of course a necessity, so its ubiquity is unsurprising. Window-like apertures are the next most common feature of East Anglian porches, with approximately 94 per cent having them in the ground storey. The small number without side apertures is significant as it shows that visual access between the porch and churchyard (other than through the entrance) was not always provided. Side openings create sightlines to the events taking place inside. Published studies have analysed sightlines within churches as a means of recognising relationships between different locations, furnishings and monuments.[19] Similar motivations can be applied to visual connections between the churchyard and the church (exterior and interior). Providing sightlines from without to within was a specific response to the way in which porches functioned, as is borne out by the height of the sills from existing floor level; the mean being slightly less than 50in. In many instances the porch windows are noticeably lower than the sills of the adjacent aisle or nave windows. As well as providing illumination for events taking place within the porch, side apertures start

---

[19] See Simon Roffey, 'Constructing a Vision of Salvation: Chantries and the Social Dimension of Religious Experience in the Medieval Parish Church', *Archaeological Journal* 163 (2006), 122–46.

at a height appropriate for looking through. This facility is not, however, achieved at the expense of architectural propriety. The low sills are not discordant or contrived but rather scaled according to the elevation in which they are set, in general terms the amount of walling above and below is of equal depth, for example. This observation really only applies to single-storey porches. The lowness of porch windows becomes more apparent in instances where the building is scaled differently, where externally it extends to a height of two storeys but internally is a single space. A prominent and already discussed example, North Walsham, illustrates how, even where the height of the building extends through more than one stage, the side openings remained at a low level, communicating with the area of the porch which people occupied.

54 Exterior view, south porch, Alderford

55 Exterior view, south porch, Swaffham

There is considerable diversity in the formal characteristics of the window-like apertures which pierce the side walls of so many porches, the stand-out example being the sculpturally ambitious, pale clunch south porch at Boxford (Suffolk) which is pierced by two pairs of four-light openings. Porch aperture designs range from narrow, single lights as at Alderford (fig. 54) to three-light traceried windows as at Swaffham (fig. 55). These two porches are very different in size and design, and the form of the windows in each case is perhaps to be expected; put simply, they are appropriate to the building. The floor area of the Alderford porch is 72 sq ft whilst that of the Swaffham porch is 225 sq ft. The Alderford porch is unbuttressed, with the entranceway moulded from the springing point of the arch, constructed of brick and flint with decorative features being limited to the use of moulded or shaped brick detailing. By contrast, at Swaffham the diagonal buttresses are precisely faced with ashlar, the archway is moulded and surmounted by an intricate frieze, and the gable surmounted by crocketed pinnacles. Yet although the designers of these two porches worked to very different briefs, in both circumstances windows were evidently deemed necessary, whether to provide light, visual access, for aesthetic appeal or some other reason. If a tight typological classification could be applied to the sample porches, it might be expected that small, simple windows would be found in small, simple porches, and large, elaborate porches would have correspondingly elaborate windows. Whilst the examples of Alderford and Swaffham support this premise, it cannot be consistently upheld across of wider corpus. The simple, unbuttressed and undecorated south porch at Foulden (fig. 56) has a large window (leaving little walling above or below it) with beautifully reticulated tracery. Conversely, the porch at East Tuddenham (fig. 42) is elaborate in its form and decoration but the two-light windows are small and without top-lights.

Architectural openings and apertures, including windows, have an impact on the experiential nature of buildings, what it feels like to be

56 Exterior view, south porch, Foulden

outside or inside. The connection between the internal porch space and the surrounding churchyard is dependent to a considerable degree on the presence (or not) of different forms of opening. Whilst windows range in terms of design complexity and size, they all permit some sort of visual access, unlike those porches without side apertures of any kind. Perhaps therefore the most interesting examples are the small, simple porches which, like Alderford, indicate that windows were a desirable and appropriate element even when funds and architectural detailing were constrained. It is perhaps worth recalling the specification of windows in the biblical account of Solomon's porch: 'And slanting windows in the little chambers, and in their fronts, which were within the gate on every side round about: and in like manner there were also in the porches windows round about within, and before the fronts the representation of palm trees.' (Ezekiel 40.16).

Buttresses and Base Courses

Buttresses and base courses are considered in tandem as both can enhance the perceived strength and solidity of the building. Buttresses on the porches in the survey sample are most commonly diagonal, however, Boxford, Mildenhall, Cley-next-the-Sea, Walpole St Peter and North Walsham are notable examples of porches with angle buttresses. The group with diagonal buttresses can be sub-divided into those which display no decorative motifs, those whose front elevation is materially elaborated to enhance their impact and status, and those which display decorative motifs either on the surface plane or have multiple surfaces by means of niches and carved details. The off-sets of buttresses tend not to align with other elements of the porch; they do not serve to establish the registration of the building. In the majority of cases there are two off-sets which create three vertical planes, and this happens regardless of whether the porch is single or double storey.

Considering the presence and elaboration of base courses also ascertains whether there is a link between their development and articulation. Base courses fall into three main groups: those which are simply a thickening of the walling, those which are architecturally differentiated by a coping made in a contrasting material and which protrude at an even depth beyond the wall plane, and those where the base course is used for decorative purposes. In extreme cases the base course is raised from the ground and a blank section of plain walling is set beneath it. As buttresses not only broaden the perceived width of the building but suggest solidity and rigidity, base courses serve to ground the porch on firm foundations. Both elements are principally architectural modes of conveying a sense of permanence rather than being structural necessities.

The extent to which buttresses and base courses are elaborated correlates reasonably well and indicates some consistency in the external treatment of porches. Those which have Type D3 buttresses in the main also have Type 3 base courses, both of which display a high degree of architectural or ornamental elaboration. Many examples in this group feature flint flushwork, which enhances the porch exterior. In some instances, it is used only on the buttresses and base course, whilst other examples have elevations almost entirely covered in flushwork. Its use on base courses and buttresses, the design of which can provide drip moulds to protect the often-intricate patterns from weathering, is not reserved for porches but is commonly found on towers and clerestories and other elevations of churches.[20] At the other end of the spectrum are the porches which have simple (D1) buttresses, examples of which are noticeably more prevalent in Norfolk than Suffolk. It is noteworthy that porches with D1 type buttresses very rarely have a base course. The high frequency of buttressed porches in the survey sample, coupled with the wide variation in their architectural sophistication, suggests that, by the late fifteenth century, buttresses were a convention of porch design.

Fabric and Form

An advantage of the sample of porches analysed here is that it is non-selective; there is no bias in terms of size, decoration or location of the porches. For the period from which textual evidence survives (see above), it therefore enables recognition of the full scope of porch form from plain, simple examples to the most architecturally sophisticated. It is within these parameters that porches can be expected to reside decorously. After this discussion of the treatment of the four basic architectural components, some broader conclusions can be drawn regarding the size and shape of porches and the materials used in their construction and decoration.

Most medieval church porches in East Anglia are relatively consistent in their fundamental form but diverse in architectural and decorative detail. A hypothetical description of the extremes anticipates the range within which actual examples will fall. A simple porch is a single-storey rectangular building, constructed under a pitched roof and the front wall is punctured with an open arch. The fabric of the walls is uniform, most commonly flint rubble, with no decorative detail, whilst the entrance is likely to be constructed of a contrasting material, either stone or brick. Internally the porch is again unadorned, with the only detail being the mouldings of the church door. At the opposite end of the spectrum is a

---

[20] Hart, *Flint Flushwork*, 106–8.

porch both compositionally and decoratively complex. The basic rectangular form covered by a pitched roof remains, as does the entrance archway in the front elevation but the structure is now of two storeys (actual or notional), with angle buttresses supporting the additional height, elaborated by flushwork and canopied niches. On the façade further image niches, flushwork and carved stonework surround the entrance. A well-defined base course underpins the porch and this is also ornamented with mouldings and emblems. Large, traceried three-light windows pierce the east and west walls, and where there is an upper chamber all three elevations have windows, though of a smaller and simpler form than those below. A horizontal frieze above the apex of the entrance is filled with decorative or 'patronal' motifs and spandrels flanking the shoulders of the entrance are filled with carved imagery. The side elevations, if not faced in ashlar, are decorated with combinations of materials set in geometric patterns. Internally, the most elaborate porches have vaulted ceilings with

57 Exterior view, north porch, Langham

carved bosses at each junction of ribs. Other features include a holy water stoup positioned to the east of the church door and stone benches along either side; both features are integrated into the architectural structure of the porch, indicating that the scheme has been planned in its entirety. These extremes of the form an East Anglian church porch could take occur in actuality at, for example, Langham, built c.1508 (fig. 57), which is plain and simple, and the south porch at Walpole St Peter, built c.1435 (fig. 35), which is large and elaborate. The dating and architectural form of these two examples show that simple porches continued to be built long after the possibilities in scale and design had expanded considerably.

Size and Shape

Buildings which make an immediate visual impact tend to have elaborated external elevations, otherwise they do so by their sheer size. To what extent does this apply to porches? It is perhaps not surprising that a tendency for larger porches to display a greater degree of architectural complexity is observable. However, the most elaborate porches are not necessarily the largest. The average floor area of those surveyed is approximately 118 sq ft and those which are considerably larger than this tend to be characterised by highly sophisticated characteristics in all four key components, whilst such detailing is almost absent in the smallest of porches. This is not, however, consistently the case. For example, two of the smallest porches display contrasting levels of ornamentation. The decoration of Aslacton (with a floor area of 80 sq ft) is limited to simple flushwork panels and geometrically carved spandrels (fig. 58), but Dickleburgh (with a floor area of 82 sq ft), with its considerable use of flint flushwork, intricately canopied image niches and the carved quasi-heraldic devices in the spandrels, is one of the most elaborate porches in the county (fig. 59). At the other end of the spectrum, two of the larger porches display the same diversity. Swaffham has a floor area of 225 sq ft yet displays restraint in its elaboration (figs 55, 60), whilst Walpole St Peter, measuring 226 sq ft, combines a considerable quantity of carved stone displaying heraldic devices as well as geometrical designs, intricately carved pinnacles and large image niches (fig. 35). The extent of external decoration is not necessarily related to the size of floor plan. As Dickleburgh clearly shows, small porches can be highly elaborated. Conversely, the porch at Wighton is remarkably straightforward considering the floor plan measures 174 sq ft, which is considerably larger than the average (fig. 61).

The range in north-south dimensions of the East Anglian porches surveyed for this study is considerable, the shallowest being approximately 8ft 3in and the deepest 22ft. The collective average comes in at around

58 Exterior view, south porch, Aslacton

59 Exterior view, south porch, Dickleburgh

11ft 6in. By comparison, east-west dimensions lie in a much narrower range, between approximately 7ft and 14ft 9in, with an average of 9ft 7½in. Neither the shortest north-south and east-west measurements, nor the longest, are found in the same porch. Converting these measurements into ratios shows that porch ground plans are consistently rectangular, with the longer length almost always being on the north-south line. Rectangular floor plans create a sense of direction or progression from the entrance to the church door and this effect is enhanced by the relationship in size and width of their two arches. In the vast majority of cases the church door

60 Exterior view, south porch, Swaffham

is smaller in both height and width than the porch entrance. Thus, the church door is framed by the porch entrance. A similar effect is created at Norwich Cathedral where, as noted by Roberta Gilchrist, the design of the Erpingham Gate 'allows the west front of the cathedral to be seen from Tombland. The arch frames the view towards the principal entrance to the cathedral church, perhaps indicating that the gate may have been intended as a grander "west front" to the relatively plain western façade'.[21]

Around 30 per cent of East Anglian parish church porches are two-storey structures. Chambers above ground level are rare in parish churches, and a room above the porch is, in most churches, the only such space, apart from the tower ringing chamber. In towers, however, each floor has a different yet established purpose: the first-floor stage generally being the ringing chamber and the second-floor stage being the belfry. The potential function of chambers above porches is much more varied, and in most cases simply unknown, as has been discussed in an earlier chapter. In similar manner to the relationship between porch size and design complexity,

[21] Gilchrist, *Norwich Cathedral Close*, 51.

61 Exterior view, south porch, Wighton

two-storey porches do not necessarily have the largest ground plans. Two examples of two-storey porches which are considerably smaller in plan than the average are Loddon, built c.1492 (fig. 62), and St Peter Hungate in Norwich, built c.1497 (fig. 63). Conversely, there are single-storey porches with overt architectural ambition, for example, at North Walsham, c.1382–1406 (fig. 25), and East Dereham, c.1482 (fig. 64). These two porches were built a century apart and therefore indicate that an upper storey was not considered a prerequisite for an architecturally sophisticated porch at either date.

62 Exterior view, south porch, Loddon

63 Exterior view, south porch, Norwich St Peter Hungate

64 Exterior view, south porch, East Dereham

By implication therefore upper storeys were primarily practical, providing additional, separated spaces where needed. In the majority of cases the stair doorway is located within the church, not the porch. Even where the upper storey of a porch is a later addition, access to the stair is set within the church, as seen at Catfield, for example. Porch stair doorways average 6ft x 2ft and are therefore only very slightly larger than rood stair doorways which average 5ft 6in x 1ft 9in. Whilst a stone vice provides necessary and reasonably convenient access, their relatively narrow, steep and winding form suggests that ascent to and descent from the chambers above porches was not in the majority of cases a grand or ceremonial event.

Use of Building Materials

As already noted, East Anglia's medieval buildings are constructed predominantly of indigenous flint, imported ashlar, manufactured brick or hardwood timber and all of these materials were used in the construction of porches. Around one-fifth of East Anglia's medieval church porches include brick in their construction, used either as the main building material or for details such as entrance archways or side apertures. Brick was already being used in the construction of porches in the 1370s, with early examples including the fourteenth-century parish porch at the Great Hospital in Norwich, and continued in use at least through to 1521.[22] This period saw a renewal in the architectural application of brick and the development of the necessary skills to employ the material in a manner which made it comparable with stone.[23] Variously shaped bricks were used to make moulded windows and archways and as a result brick porches stand comparison with their stone and flint counterparts. A notably ambitious pairing of East Anglian brick porches are at Needham (Norfolk) and Shadingfield (Suffolk) (figs 65 and 66), and entirely brick porches are indeed more common further south in Suffolk and into Essex, than in Norfolk.[24] The porches at Needham and Shadingfield show the formal similarities between brick and stone porches: a rectangular floor plan, windows in the east and west walls, an open entrance which is larger than the church doorway and diagonal buttresses, although in both cases these are polygo-

---

[22] 'Alderford: 1374 make a porch and window on the south side, Robert Mayn (NRO NCC Heydon 39)' in Cattermole and Cotton, 'Church Building in Norfolk', 236. 'Frenze: 1521 a cow to the reparation of porch, Margaret James, NCC Herman 23'. Ibid., 248.
[23] R.W. Brunskill, *Brick Building in Britain* (London, 1990), 115.
[24] 'Examples in moulded brick are of fairly common occurrence, particularly in East Anglia, as at Feering and Sandon in Essex, and Winston in Suffolk.' Cox and Ford, *Parish Churches*, 111.

65 Exterior view, south porch, Needham

66 Exterior view, south porch, Shadingfield

nal rather than square. The limitations of working in brick on small-scale buildings are apparent in the detailing of these porches. Whilst high status brick structures were being commissioned in late-fifteenth-century East Anglia, such as Oxburgh Hall, or slightly further afield the entrance gate to Corpus Christi College in Cambridge, the impact and grandeur that brick architecture could achieve was not easily maintained when translated for use in parish church porches. Putting to one side the architectural success or otherwise of brick examples, porches were a building type which adopted the material at an early date. The porches at Alderford, built c.1374, and Swardeston, documented as existing by 1443, are two examples which stand in contradiction to Pevsner's suggestion that 'brick was then [in 1485] still a comparatively new material in England and one more readily accepted, at least in Norfolk, for domestic than for ecclesiastical building.'[25] In fact the porch at Alderford is coeval with the undercroft at the Museum of Norwich at the Bridewell and the Cow Tower, both in Norwich, which Pevsner offers as 'the earliest datable use of brick in the county'.[26] The brick porch at Needham, built c.1469–70, bears no relationship with the rest of the church; it is conceived as a miniaturised gatehouse, a resonance which is made apparent in the polygonal buttresses as well as the choice of material.

In addition to East Anglia's stone and brick porches a number of timber-framed examples exist, including the north porch at Shelfanger, datable to c.1506.[27] Unlike earlier or more ambitious timber porches, such as the north porch at Boxford (Suffolk), the example at Shelfanger essentially employs timber as a framework which is infilled with split black flints and ashlar, the wood serving a similar role to the ashlar which frames flint flushwork designs. The region's most celebrated timber example is the fourteenth-century north porch at Boxford (Suffolk). It is a vital document in the history of the late medieval East Anglian architectural carpentry. Boxford's timber porch has been convincingly contextualised in relation to Richard II's Westminster Hall carpenter, Hugh Herland.[28] It is a rare surviving example of miniaturised architectural conceptions expressed in timber, but it may not have been such a rare creation.

Flint and ashlar, used in combination, were by far the most commonly used building materials for medieval church porches in East Anglia. Like the region's buildings more broadly, ashlar is used for detailing – buttresses, quoins, window surrounds, archways and niches. Indigenous flint is used

---

[25] Nikolaus Pevsner, *Buildings of England: North-West and South Norfolk* (Harmondsworth, 1962), 41.
[26] Ibid.
[27] John Nolloth gave 40s in his will of 1506. NRO NCC Cooke 60.
[28] Beech, 'The Hammer-Beam Roof of Westminster Hall'.

as the main walling material, but it is treated in a range of different ways – from whole cobbles laid as though rubble to that which is precisely knapped and neatly coursed. The range of treatments used on porches is nothing out of the ordinary for the medieval architecture of the region. The manner in which the fabric relates to the church proper can, however, be more unusual. The porch at Loddon (fig. 62) was constructed as part of the major rebuilding of the church by Sir James Hobart, which was sufficiently complete in 1492 for his wife Margaret to be buried there. The side elevations of the porch and the design of the window tracery are remarkably like the body of the church. The main fabric of both parts of the building is apparently composed of almost equal amounts of ashlar and flint and each is of very similar block size. Yet the base course of the porch and the façade combine flint and ashlar in a manner not found on the aisle. The base course features trefoil-headed flushwork motifs which are also present on the tower, but not on the west wall of the south aisle which links these two elements of the building. The same is true of the parapet. Although both the aisle and the porch parapet are crenellated and use the same materials they are put to use in a very different manner. The porch is apparently given priority and emphasis.

The arrangement at Aylsham is rather different and less clear cut. The aisle wall is finished in pale-coloured, square-knapped flints, carefully chosen, worked and laid in perfect courses. The walling fabric of the porch is much less carefully selected. It appears that the ground stage of the porch is in fact a much earlier building, probably of the mid fourteenth century, and as such the small rubble-like flints contrast quite dramatically with the much more heavily worked fifteenth-century aisle wall. The upper storey of the porch is constructed of a different material again, although still flint. It is probable that this section of the porch was built at the same time as the aisle wall, but the specific material chosen for the latter was not used on the porch. The buttresses are fully faced in ashlar whereas those of the aisle are much more elaborate, having two tiers of thin white flint panels recessed beneath small ashlar canopies. A similar effect is used in flushwork on the porch frieze, but the design and execution are both different. Whereas at Loddon the basic fabric of the porch creates a sense of unity with the church, the treatment of the façade, base course and parapet set it apart from the aisle. The relationship between the porch at Aylsham and its accompanying church is much less straightforward even though, according to documentary evidence, the upper storey of the porch at least, although perhaps not the lower stage, was constructed along with the rest of the church. Such instances indicate that porches were treated differently to the body of the church, even when built together. Their architecture is thus of its own merit, not simply an extension of the larger building.

Three Ways to Build a Porch

The data gathered from surveying East Anglia's parish church porches have so far suggested that the architectural scope of these buildings tends towards variation rather than conformity. To underscore this conclusion, three chronologically proximate porches illustrate the variety of responses that could be made to the challenge of building a church porch and ultimately what sort of structure was created.

By around 1441 the church of the Assumption of the Blessed Virgin, Attleborough, was adorned with a north porch (fig. 67). Although now much eroded, the frieze above the entrance displays heraldic shields which formalise, and preserve, the relationship between the porch and the person or people who laid claim to it. The porch is traditionally attributed to Sir John Radcliffe (d.1441).[29] However, although the porch was probably built around this date its patron is unlikely to have been Sir John. Blomefield

67 Exterior view, north porch, Attleborough

[29] Including Pevsner, *North-West and South Norfolk*, 78.

recorded two of the four coats of arms cut in stone above the entrance; Radcliffe quartering Mortimer, and Radcliffe impaling chequy in chief fleury-de-lis. The presence of Mortimer arms has encouraged authors down to the present day to attribute the porch to Sir John Radcliffe, younger son of James Radcliffe of Radcliffe, Lancashire.[30] In c.1405 Sir John married Cecily Mortimer, coheir (with her sister Margery) of her grandfather Sir Robert Mortimer's estates following her father's death in 1387.[31] The heraldry shows Radcliffe quartered with Mortimer, not impaled, suggesting the person to whom the arms belong was either the offspring of that marriage or someone who wished to declare how the Attleborough estates had come into their possession. Sir John's heir, also named John, was his son by his second wife, Katherine Burnell, whom he had married in c.1425.[32] John II's wife, Elizabeth Fitzwalter, was sole heir to Baron Fitzwalter and the absence of Fitzwalter arms on the porch makes it implausible that it was constructed after this high status marriage, which took place at a date before 27 October 1444.[33] Therefore, although the single patron of the porch is unknown (and identification may rest on the unattributed coat of chequy in chief fleury-de-lis), it was seemingly constructed between c.1425 and 1444.

Whatever the nature of the Radcliffes' involvement in the building of the porch at Attleborough, the two-storey building enhanced the main entrance into the church, facing as it does both the principal area of settlement and 'Attleborough Hall'.[34] A large aisled nave was established by 1378, and the porch, although apparently also set out at that time, was built later as a separate project.[35] Externally the architecture of the porch conveys strength and permanence, created in part by the ashlar-faced diagonal buttresses, widening the base of the porch. The verticality and gradual narrowing of the stepped buttresses, which terminate in figurative pinnacles at the height of the apex of the gable, achieve two things. They balance the horizontal spread at the base of the porch by strengthening the

---

[30] Heslop, 'The Nave of Attleborough', 50.
[31] Biography of Sir John Radcliffe, available at: www.historyofparliamentonline.org/volume/1386–1421/member/radcliffe-sir-john-1441
[32] The Burnell coat is argent, a lion rampant, sable, crowned, or, in a bordure, azure.
[33] G.E. C[okayne], ed., *The Complete Peerage of England, Scotland, Ireland, Great Britain and the United Kingdom, extant, extinct or dormant, Volume 5* (London, 1926), 484.
[34] Blomefield provides details of the lineage of Sir John Radcliffe and his association with Mortimer's Manor which he indicates becomes known as 'Attleborough Hall', see Blomefield, *Topographical History*, vol. 1, 520. This hall is positioned to the north of the church, see *Faden's Map of Norfolk*, with an introduction by J. C. Barringer. Norfolk Record Society 42 (Norwich, 1973), 27.
[35] Fawcett, 'Sutton in the Isle', 81.

vertical and also mediate the boundary of the porch. Finishing the porch in consistently dark, knapped flint differentiates from the aisle elevations and suggests it was created as a façade, the choice of materials serving to focus attention on the porch as entrance. Also, the contrast of the dark knapped flint and pale ashlar detailing causes the buttresses, window traceries, open archway and pinnacle sculptures to appear to stand forward, enhancing their visual prominence.

Attleborough porch is 'crowned' with stone sculptures depicting the evangelist symbols, surrounding the figure of Christ blessing and holding a book and scroll (referencing Revelation 20.12–15) on the apex of the gable.[36] The figures oversee the entrance to the church and offer protection for those within. The iconography of this porch echoes that of the Erpingham Gate in Norwich, antiquarian drawings of which show that tetramorphic statues adorned the pinnacles of the gate.[37] As a response to the threat of Lollard heresy in eastern England, and specifically in the context of the 1428–31 Norwich heresy trials, it has been suggested that '[t]he imagery of Erpingham's gate is ... openly defiant of their [the Lollard] cause.'[38] Thus it can be interpreted as a statement of religious orthodoxy and social order. The apparent allusion to the Erpingham Gate in the design of the Attleborough porch suggests a patron who sought to promote similar political and religious sentiments. It also replicates and sustains the architectural conflation of porches and gates discussed in a previous chapter.

Inside the porch a tierceron star vault springs from angel corbels.[39] As Fawcett has noted 'several porches were provided with stone vaulting ... which emphasises the importance sometimes given to this adjunct of the church'.[40] This especially notable feature of porches is highlighted when contextualised by the rarity of stone vaulting in other parts of East Anglian parish churches – the chancel at Blakeney, the south transept chapel at Norwich St Helen's, and a small number of tower bases being so treated. The full implications and significance of vaults in porches were explored in chapter three.

In depicting the 'Five Joys of Mary' (Annunciation, Nativity, Resurrection, Ascension and Assumption/Coronation) the ceiling bosses display imagery appropriate to the dedication of the church. The central, and

---

[36] It should be noted that the apex of the gable has been altered, previously having a steeper pitch. There is no reason to suggest, however, that the position of the sculptures differs to any significant extent from their original placement.

[37] Thomas Brown, *Posthumous Works of the Learned Thomas Brown Kt, printed from his original manuscripts, viz. 1. Repertorium, or Antiquities of the Cathedral Church of Norwich* (London, 1712).

[38] Sekules, 'The Gothic Sculpture', 207.

[39] Nichols, *Early Art of Norfolk*, 323.

[40] Fawcett, *Architecture and Furnishings*, 17.

largest, boss shows the Coronation of the Virgin, aligned to be viewed when one stands facing south towards the church door. The image portrays the Virgin crowned as the bride of Christ, an iconography which (as previously noted) in England dates back to the early twelfth century.[41] The display of a marriage scene at the apex of the vault can be thought of as an aide to *memoria* – a reminiscence of the medieval weddings which occurred in the porch.[42] The coronation iconography, therefore, references much more than the dedication of the church, it is apposite for its setting, even an active element in the way in which the place was composed and received. It can be understood as a continuation of the Apocalyptic imagery on the façade by showing the 'marriage of the Bride and the Lamb', a subject also sourced from the concluding chapters of Revelation (Revelation 19.6–9).

Attleborough porch successfully references other architectural forms without compromising its status as a porch, and this careful balance of architectural mimesis and autonomy is central to the conception of church porches. A suitable case to contrast with Attleborough is the south porch at Great Cressingham, datable to c.1439 (fig. 37).[43] The comparison reveals something of the decisions made during the process of designing porches, and such choices were a response to the intended or perceived function of each example. Great Cressingham does not equal Attleborough in scale but displays an alternative, no less significant, series of components which convey the type of building it is. The elevations at Great Cressingham are not treated like each other. Those to the south and west are ashlar-faced, whereas the largely unseen eastern elevation is of unknapped flint. The use of ashlar also sets the porch apart from the rest of the church, differentiating it from the structure to which it is attached and of which it is a component. The absence of ashlar in any quantity elsewhere on the church implies that elevating the status of the porch by choosing a high quality, expensive material was deemed appropriate. Porches were not considered as a poor relation to other parts of a church; on the contrary they deserved and received special architectural treatment.

The only figurative element at Great Cressingham is a sculpture depicting St Michael standing in a canopied niche set centrally over the exterior arch (fig. 68). The church is dedicated to St Michael and so finding an image of the archangel here is not surprising – in the existing literature on

---

[41] T. A. Heslop, 'The English Origins of the Coronation of the Virgin', *Burlington Magazine* 147 (2005), 790–7.

[42] The association of Mary with marriage has been noted by scholars including Miri Rubin who comments that 'Mary served as a model for the church and, as importantly, as a model for Christian marriage and family life.' Rubin, *Mother of God*, 32.

[43] The sum of 10s to building the porch, 1439, John Blake, NRO NCC Doke 101. See Cattermole and Cotton, 'Church Building in Norfolk', 244.

68 Fragmentary sculpture depicting St Michael, south porch niche, Great Cressingham

porches it would even be considered conventional.⁴⁴ However, the invocation of St Michael by means of setting his image on or within a church porch also signifies something of its function. The sculpture, although severely damaged, depicts St Michael in battle against Satan, thus offering a visual rendering of Revelation 12.7: 'And there was a great battle in heaven: Michael and his angels fought with the dragon, and the dragon fought, and his angels.' The signification is one of salvation being attained through the conquest of evil. With porches being the setting for the opening scenes of the rite of baptism, and an accepted location for burial, the iconography is apt. Significantly, other East Anglian porches support this suggestion. Those at Hilborough and Colby in Norfolk and Palgrave in Suffolk display images of St Michael although none of the churches is dedicated to him. Just as imagery of the Coronation of the Virgin connects the architectural iconography with function at Attleborough, so too does the case of St Michael.

Internally, Great Cressingham porch is composed of wall arches springing from shafts which rest on integral stone benches and within each blind arch is a (now blocked) centrally placed window. These wall arches effectively form canopies over the bench seating, thus framing and protecting those in the porch. In providing a form of notional canopy the wall arches can be seen as an alternative to the vaulted ceiling at Attleborough, which serves as a canopy over the entire interior. As we have seen before, the articulation of porch walling to create protected seating is found in the twelfth-century porches at Malmesbury Abbey and Southwell Minster, and a variation of the same idea is seen in the early-fourteenth-century porch at Over in Cambridgeshire. Therefore the arrangement at Great Cressingham is a simplified version of an established idea. On a very basic level benches are an invitation to be seated, to stop and linger. Whatever the reason for taking that seat, respite, penance, conversation or debate, the effect is essentially the same. Internally porches were architecturally formulated as places, not simply passageways or extended thresholds.

Whilst the near contemporary porches at Attleborough and Great Cressingham present alternative versions of what may be considered a notable church porch in East Anglia, other examples demonstrate that simpler solutions were being adopted at the same time. Although by c.1440 some church porches had achieved a remarkable level of sophistication, others are relatively straightforward. A third case study illustrates this point. In 1438 William Martenet, vicar of Sporle, bequeathed 40s for the building of a porch at Little Fransham church. The details of this bequest are unusual; it is to the villagers that the porch is bequeathed (*Item lego villanis de*

---

⁴⁴ 'The principal decorative features of the porch usually consisted of an image of the Patron Saint and of a cross on the apex of the gable.' Wall, *Porches and Fonts*, 56.

Fransh[a]m parva uno porticu faciend' ante ost[iu]m australe ecc[les]ie p[ar] och'... xls).[45]

Martenet's porch was altered considerably by the addition of a brick upper storey built in 1743 to house the bells after the tower collapsed in 1700, but sufficient medieval fabric is extant to enable comparison between it and the porches at Attleborough and Great Cressingham. Fransham porch (fig. 69) demonstrates how similar architectural ideas can be realised in very different ways. Measuring 9ft 3in x 11ft 4in Fransham is similar in size to Cressingham, although the latter (at 10ft 7in x 9ft 1in) is one of the few late medieval porches of greater width than depth. Fransham porch is mainly constructed of flint rubble, with ashlar used at the usual key points: on the square-headed two-light windows, the front face of the diagonal buttresses and the two-centred entrance arch including the hood-mould. Notably the front elevation is composed almost entirely of black knapped flints, with the only exception being the trefoil-headed flushwork panels on the base course flanking the entrance. This selection and application of specific materials is not repeated on the east or west elevations of the building. Like Cressingham, this porch was designed to serve as a façade. Internally, Fransham porch is bare, without evidence for there ever having been stone benches, a holy water stoup or a vaulted ceiling. With a restricted budget, decisions had to be made and the choices taken evidently prioritised the exterior, particularly the façade.

A final point regarding Fransham is the treatment of the entrance arch. The decorative mouldings begin approximately half way between the ground and the springing point of the arch; below this level is a simple half octagon. Also, the arch is devoid of capitals, thus the mouldings run continuously up the respond and around the arch.[46] Whilst it is perhaps another instance of money being judiciously allocated, the result is that the porch entrance alludes to civic gateways where the lower part of the arch is often left plain as a response to possible damage by cart wheels and other passing traffic. This reference is not picked up in the other two porches, despite the apparent relationship between the Attleborough porch and the Erpingham Gate in Norwich, which carries this motif in the form of a deep two-stage ashlar plinth. Little Fransham certainly does not display the elaboration or sophistication of Attleborough or the refinement in detail of Cressingham, but despite the limitations of the elements from

---

[45] NRO NCC Doke 66.
[46] Several fourteenth-century East Anglian porches do not have capitals to mark the change from respond to arch, for example Besthorpe. But in such cases the moulding profile does not alter either. A third variation is where the moulding profile of the arch is more elaborate than that of the respond, for example, at Emneth.

69 Exterior view, south porch, Little Fransham

which it is composed it reflects the very specific decisions taken by those responsible for its construction. Whilst it is not possible to know how much Martenet's 40s paid for or the extent of his involvement in its design, his will provides evidence for its building c.1438 and that in some sense it was his gift to the parishioners he had served as rector.

Contrasting this porch with those at Attleborough and Great Cressingham makes apparent that coeval buildings differ considerably in their detail and architectural ambition. Taken together they suggest that for a building to serve as a porch (beyond giving protection to the church door) it did not rely on meeting any particular pattern although architectural allusion is regularly encountered. The social significance of a porch was to a considerable extent constructed by means of cultural tradition and association; even the simplest porch conjures with much more than its form might imply.

Conclusion

The surviving written evidence relating to East Anglian parish church porches is restricted in terms of its usefulness for dating the buildings. In many cases it amounts to no more than a single bequest of an insignificant amount of money, which is suggestive of little more than the existence of a porch. Very few porches have more than one piece of documentation relating to them, and therefore the weight of evidence needed to support secure conclusions is simply lacking. For the purposes of this chapter the written evidence has been used as the basis for constructing a non-selective sample of church porches in the region. It has been demonstrated that these buildings are varied in their form, size and architectural design. Whilst general relationships between complexity and size are observable it is only to a limited extent and dating evidence for the erection of the buildings available from textual sources shows that chronology is not a major contributing factor. Although the analysis and discussion has benefitted from the sample being non-selective, ensuring that all forms of porch have been recognised and considered, it is necessary to query what it conceals as much as what it reveals. Certainly the starting date of 1371 is contrived in the sense that it does not mark any significant point in the history of church porches, beyond the survival of their written record. Typological development in porch form or design is not evident in the analysis of these data, and this is in conflict with broader understandings of changes in medieval architecture over the same period. Although it has previously been argued that an essentially incremental development in the form and architectural detail of porches in East Anglia commenced at North Walsham,[47] such a progression is not evident in the large corpus of porches explored in this chapter.

---

[47] '[I]n the south porch of North Walsham, which can be dated to between 1362 and 1399 on the evidence of heraldry, we can see the seeds of a type of porch design which was to be developed through the remainder of the Middle Ages.' Fawcett, *Architecture and Furnishings*, 16.

The Patrons' Share

5

THIS FINAL CHAPTER EXPLORES the available evidence relating to the people who paid for church porches or are represented in the built fabric. What was the nature of their involvement and to what extent did they influence the building's form? The discussion is in two parts. In the opening section, geographical focus moves beyond East Anglia to nearby Essex and looks in detail at the fifteenth-century churchwardens' records for the large town church of St Mary in Saffron Walden. These accounts are a remarkable source of information for understanding the circumstances in which a church porch was planned and realised in eastern England. No comparable primary text survives for a porch in Norfolk or Suffolk. The Saffron Walden document informs where money to build the porch came from and between whom responsibility for the procurement of materials and labour was divided. The initiating benefaction appears to have come from Thomas Barker in the form of his testamentary bequest of 1466 but in what role should he be cast when the other players are recognised? Discussion subsequently turns to analyse the East Anglian testamentary material, specifically the textual sources which record bequests made to the building (rather than the repair or renewal) of a porch. From the most productive documents information is drawn concerning how, after the testator's death, the commission was realised.

In the second part of the chapter attention shifts from the documents and returns to the architectural evidence of the buildings themselves. Inscriptions and motifs bonded into the fabric of porches, such as inclusion of personal, often heraldic, motifs and inscriptions are evidence of direct patronal association, whether that be of an individual, family or other social network. One such example is the south porch at St Margaret's, Cley-next-the-Sea. As discussed earlier, the porch was built c.1414 and presents an elaborate display of heraldic and quasi-heraldic motifs framing the entrance, including the arms of England and Anne of Bohemia, several armigerous families connected to the parish and surrounding area, and saints' emblems presented in armorial fashion. The scheme is apparently a composition of the dynastic lineage, social connections and devotional allegiances of the likely patroness, Lady Beatrice Stafford. The exterior stone arch indicates her influence on the porch and registers her patronage of the project.

Heraldic devices are one form of imagery used to communicate the association of an individual with a porch, but other emblems, textual inscriptions and figural representations were also used. For example at Garboldisham (Norfolk) the now ill-restored inscription above the entrance arch requests prayers for the soul of chaplain William Pece (d.1500). A minimal version of the same idea is seen at Hartest (Suffolk). The north porch was added in the sixteenth century by John Phillipson who asked to be buried there with his wife Anne in 1546. The spandrel shields carry the couple's initials. Are such instances simply alternative forms of patronal display or does the invocation of parishioners' prayers alter the association of individual and object, emphasising the purpose of the donation? The range of different types of personal representation found on porches, as well as key examples, will help to define the circumstances in which intention, instruction and payment came to influence the end product. Where details such as names, dates and amounts of money are known, the individuals come into focus. Patrons, benefactors and donors will also be recognised through evidence in the built fabric. There was arguably no place more prominent in a medieval parish than the church porch, therefore claims of affiliation built into these edifices are powerfully communicative. Investigation of the manner in which decorative details were used to represent individuals reveals the extent to which this form of entrance architecture was appropriated for display by the patron, benefactor or donor.

St Mary's, Saffron Walden, Essex

Included in John Harvey's dictionary of medieval architects are masons William Glanforth (*fl.* 1466–68) and John Pollard (*fl.* 1466), both of whom Harvey describes as being 'contracted in 1466 to build the south porch at Saffron Walden Church, Essex'.[1] The basis for this statement is not a contract but rather the churchwardens' accounts of St Mary's, which survive for the period from 1439 to 1490.[2] During this time the parish undertook a major rebuilding campaign and accordingly the financial records include a wealth of detail concerning payments to craftsmen and for materials.

A porch was in existence in 1441/2 as the accounts record a payment for tiling the church porch – as the entry comes immediately after payments made for the repair of the south door it is plausible that the porch referred to was also on the south side. The expense accounts for 1451/2

---

[1] Harvey, *English Medieval Architects*, 117 and 233.
[2] Essex Record Office D/DBy Q18.

70 Exterior view, south porch, Saffron Walden

record the purchase of a considerable amount of timber and nails for the church porch and payments were made to John Houchat and Walter Carpenter – the former was certainly a carpenter and the latter is also likely to have been, on the evidence of his surname. Unfortunately, there is no indication in the document as to whether this work related to a porch on the north or south side, nor whether it was repair work or new building. However, in 1455/6 the north porch was tiled and the walls of the church porch were cleaned. It is therefore possible that by the mid 1450s Saffron Walden church had a porch on both the north and the south sides, as it does today. A decade later, however, the accounts provide clear evidence that, in accordance with the testamentary instructions of Thomas Barker, a new porch was built (fig. 70).

Thomas Barker, who died c.1466, had been a churchwarden in the years 1441/2, 1444/5 and 1446/7. This certainly would have given him an intimate knowledge of the fabric of the church, having administered the accounts for these three years. It appears that at some point he moved away from Saffron Walden, possibly going to London as he was there in 1464/5. Although Barker's profession is unclear, an entry in the accounts informs us that he went to Cambridge 'for stone cutting' for the king's works there. Barker is never described as a stone mason, but clearly he gained important first-hand knowledge of the building campaigns being undertaken at King's College whilst he was serving as warden of St Mary's. His likely connections in London and with the royal works in Cambridge provided complementary experience and a knowledge of buildings in the vanguard of design.

For the year 1466 the Saffron Walden accounts state that 'the cost of the porch' was given by the hands of Richard Eswell and Richard Barker, executors of Thomas Barker, and receipt of 26s 9d is noted. Prior to this date, although expenditure related to the porch (a total of 28s 1d) is accounted, there is no record of income for the same purpose. Whilst some of the payments are made for what seems to be repairs and upkeep of existing porches, payments to townspeople in return for supplies of timber suggest that materials were being collected in advance of a more considerable project. It was Thomas Barker's gift of 26s 9d which apparently enabled the masons to go to the quarry to procure stone, which, given the wording of the accounts, was intended for the beginning (the word used is 'foundation') of a new porch. The next entry in the accounts is the payment of 26s 8d 'by the hands of Sir Thomas Benygte and William Sweyn and John Pollard, executors of John Hegne to William Glarnforthe and John Pollard, masowyns'. Glanforth and Pollard had 'made a bargyn' for the porch, and the wardens' monies went to them for that project. The difference between Thomas Barker's gift and that of John Hegne seems to be that the former specified that the money was to be spent on a new porch, whereas the latter did not make any such stipulation. However, as the expense accounts reveal, the cost of the porch was considerably more than both of these bequests combined. Based on the entries in the accounts, £7 10s is a conservative estimate for the amount spent on the building of Saffron Walden porch. Thomas Barker's monetary gift was considerably less than the actual 'cost of the porche'.

Patronage and Benefaction

The funding and building of the porch at Saffron Walden encourage questions around the notion of architectural patronage in the medieval period. Clearly the money left by Thomas Barker for the 'foundation' of the porch was spent to that end. It is also apparent that the amount given could not have been anticipated as payment for the whole structure. Despite his long-term involvement with St Mary's and his funding of the 'foundation' of a project which the town apparently supported, there is no evidence of him influencing the design of the porch. Decision-making and oversight of the project was the responsibility of the churchwardens and the masons with whom they contracted. In light of this evidence it is pertinent to ask what nature of relationship existed between the people who gave money for a porch to be built and the detail of the resulting structure.

Where the written record indicates that a person gave a reasonable sum of money, perhaps a pound or two, to a building project, or it features their personal monogram, rebus or coat of arms, scholarship tends to give primacy to this person and term them 'patron'. By contrast those giving less are more likely to be considered 'benefactor'. Where individuals are represented figuratively in or on the porch, generally in an attitude of prayer or supplication, 'donor' is likely to be epithet (and the representation of them termed a 'donor figure'). Constructing appropriate patterns of interchange between people and art in the setting of the medieval parish is fraught with dangers due to the paucity of material. The definition of these labels and roles came under some scrutiny in 2011 when the annual Harlaxton Medieval Studies Symposium was dedicated to the subject of 'Patrons and Professionals'.[3] In the Introduction to the resulting volume of papers, the editors Paul Binski and Elizabeth New characterised patronage as 'the active concept, clientage the passive'.[4] Etymologically, regarding a person as a 'patron' confers upon them a higher status and greater power than that which they patronise, and thereby influence over it. This hierarchy also gives the patron a responsibility to act as a provider and protector. Theoretically patronal acts (i.e., patronage) follow a course comprising two parallel tracks; rights are coupled with responsibilities, actions with reactions. All of this requires a period within which negotiations beyond monetary exchange can mature. Inherent in the term is a relationship forged over a period of time; the principle is applicable to patronage relationships between people, and between people and objects.

---

[3] Paul Binski and Elizabeth New, eds, *Patrons and Professionals in the Middle Ages*. Harlaxton Medieval Studies 22 (n.s.) (Donington, 2012).
[4] Ibid., 1.

Whereas diachronicity is central to the concept of patronage, benefaction can simply be a singular independent act. Literally meaning good work, or good doing, casting a person as a benefactor anticipates no more than the act was a good one, although by what measure goodness is judged is a more complicated matter. In that patronage is inherently beneficial, a patron may be considered a benefactor, but a benefactor is not necessarily a patron. Where evidence does not support the suggestion that a person had any greater involvement in the making of art or architecture than giving money or goods in kind it is more appropriate to term them benefactor as opposed to patron, and this is perhaps representative of Barker's role at Saffron Walden. On this basis, observing the terms of testamentary bequests makes possible a more detailed awareness of the relationship between those who gave money, the decision-making process, and the resulting building.

John Alvard and the Porch at Fritton

Of sixteen surviving wills written by the parishioners of Fritton St Catherine in Norfolk between 1461 and 1545, all but one records the testator's desire for their body to be buried in the churchyard.[5] The exception is the 1506 will of John Alvard which conveys his wish for interment in the porch.[6] From other wills of the same period it can be inferred that the parish church was being rebuilt in the opening years of the sixteenth century, with Roger Brome bequeathing in 1502 'to the heynyng of the walls of the seyde church xxvjs. viijd'.[7] In 1510 John Johnson gave 6s 8d to the 'rep[ar]acon' of the church roof.[8] The chancel screen includes images of the donor John Bacon (d.1511), his wife and children (eleven boys and three girls) and the now partially illegible accompanying inscription which begins '*orate pro animabus Johannis Bacon* ...'. The screen was later gilded in accordance with the bequest in 1528 by Stephen Browne.[9] It seems therefore that c.1502 the nave walls were heightened, by 1510 the nave was roofed and in the following year a chancel screen was erected. In the course of these renovations to the main vessel of the church the porch was also built. John Alvard's request for burial in the porch in 1506 is not accompanied by any gift to its fabric, only £7 to 'ye rep[ar]acon of ye churchroffe in freton'.[10] Also, after his wife's death, the lands which he passed to her were

---

[5] My thanks go to Simon Cotton for sharing his notes and thoughts on the circumstances of the rebuilding of Fritton St Catherine.
[6] NRO ANF Liber 3 (Davy) 96.
[7] NRO NCC Popy 309.
[8] NRO NCC Johnson 1.
[9] NRO NCC Attmere 7.
[10] NRO ANF Liber 3 (Davy) 96. Further details of this part of the will are unknown as the document is damaged, seemingly by fire.

to be put into the hands of twelve honest men of the town and used in 'reparation and use' of the church and for the singing of a placebo, dirige and mass on the anniversary of his death. If John Alvard had contributed significantly to the building of the porch in his lifetime he might possibly, but not necessarily, have referred to this when specifying his place of burial. He and his wife are however commemorated in the church. At the base of a St Christopher wall painting, rediscovered in 1850, two figures kneel before a cross and their inscribed scroll identifies them as John and Joan Alvard. Although the details of the porch at Fritton are lost under a layer of modern render the spatial arrangement of the porch burial and the wall painting opposite the church door can be construed as stations of commemoration. In light of his attention to detail and interest in the fabric of Fritton church it seems reasonable to suggest that John Alvard would have had some involvement in the planning of the porch, even if he had not considered it as his burial place at the time. Yet in the absence of any contracts for the building of church porches and with few relevant records such as churchwardens' accounts, lifetime actions are difficult to assess in detail. It is therefore necessary and valuable to investigate the contents of wills which record an intention to build a porch.

Testamentary Instructions – Post-Mortem Outcomes

The terms of testamentary bequests to porch fabric tend to give little away as to what testators envisaged. Late medieval wills often include vocabulary which today is vague and without clear meaning. Three words often used in the terms of bequests to church fabric are reparation, edification and emendation. Ascertaining their meaning with any accuracy is largely dependent on identification of the work to which they allude and its place within the broader history of the building. For example, three bequests of 6s 8d were given in relation to the porch at Swannington between 1452 and 1478. The earliest was the gift by John Bott for the 'reparation' of the porch on the south side. Five years later William Hase gave the same amount towards 'making' a south porch. Finally, Thomas Elyes left 6s 8d to the 'reparation' of the porch.[11] Unless the porch took an implausible twenty-six years to build, here 'reparation' relates either to new works or some sort of later renovation of an existing structure. Evidently the word did not carry the same meaning in all instances. Therefore, at such historical distance what John Bott and William Hase envisaged would happen when they gave 6s 8d to the 'reparation' of Swannington porch can only be a matter for speculation.

[11] Cattermole and Cotton, 'Church Building in Norfolk', 268.

Documentary evidence for porch construction indicates something of what porches are in terms of how they were funded, the nature of the opportunity they provided for people to meet their moral and social obligations of endowing their parish church, and the extent to which porches were constructed through individual benefaction or as community projects. By the mid fifteenth century, moral and social obligations were met through bequests of money or goods to the fabric of one's parish church; few late medieval wills do not include some such gift. It is therefore the larger amounts and the more specifically worded instructions which, although scarce, are most useful for understanding relationships between testators, their bequests and post-mortem outcomes. In 1457 Richard Befeld bequeathed £3 6s 8d for building a new north porch at Catfield in Norfolk, if work was begun in three years. This church has a south porch, but the fabric presents no indication of there ever having been one on the north side. It seems therefore that the parish failed to act within the stipulated three years, perhaps in the absence of other funding the bequest was redirected to a different project. The wording of Befeld's testament indicates that the proposed porch had not been started when he wrote his will ('*sub ista condicio[n]e quod opus p[re]dictum incipiat[ur] infra triennium post obitu[m] meu[m] alioqum pred[i]c[t]a*').[12] The south porch at Catfield was built as a single-storey structure, heightened at a later (unknown) date, as evidenced by the scar of the original gable roof line in the walling above the entrance arch. It is just possible that the churchwardens decided to build an upper storey on their existing south porch with Befeld's bequest rather than a new porch on the north side.

The apparent mismatch between the terms of Robert Befeld's will and the fabric of Catfield church is a demonstration that the responses of executors and churchwardens to the receipt of post-mortem bequests to the church fabric were not necessarily straighforward. A testator's request would not necessarily be honoured, as happened in the case of John Hobard, priest of the Trinity Guild in Bassingbourn, Cambridgeshire. His will, written 1 June 1518, records that he desired his body to be buried by that of his mother in the 'sowthe porche of the chirche ther of the blessid apostellis Petur and Paule; for the buriall and grownd ther breking and pavyment reysing and ageyne repayring, I bequeathe iii s. Item for a marble stone with owr namys gravid theruppon to be layd upon owr gravys, for all maner costes to it fynished, I will xl s'.[13] Later on in the will further instructions are given relating to his grave. Certain lands are to be sold and three 'milche bestes' purchased to provide money for the

---

[12] NRO NCC Brosyard 44.

[13] A transcription of the will is given in Dymond, *The Churchwardens' Book of Bassingbourn*, 174–5.

celebration of Hobard's obit. The residue from the sale of the lands is to go 'to the buylding of a new porche of lyme and ston' ovyr wher my body and my mother's is buryed'.[14]

The south porch at Bassingbourn, although heavily restored in the lower part, is predominantly of timber and stylistically pre-dates Hobard's will. That he wished the porch to be rebuilt in stone suggests his discontent with the timber one in which his mother's body had been interred. The residue from the sale of lands came to £2 0s 3d and was put towards an image of St George.[15] However, judging by other testamentary gifts, such as the £7 plus spent on the south porch at Saffron Walden (which paid for a large two-storey porch of exceptional quality and detail), if the parish had been willing Hobard's residue could probably have been made sufficient to pay for the construction of a straightforward stone porch. In this instance, however, the churchwardens made their own decisions regarding what the testamentary bequest was to be spent on. John Hobard was presumably buried at the church door, next to his mother and beneath the pre-existing porch, and perhaps the churchwardens felt they had done right by the spirit of Hobard's testament, if not by the letter. In cases such as those of Richard Befeld at Catfield and John Hobard at Bassingbourn, the arrangements made by the testator for a porch to be built were in some manner deficient and not respected by either their executors or the wardens. Therefore, casting a testator in the role of patron based solely on the evidence of a financial bequest mentioned in their testament is unsound. Evidently the decision to build a porch or not and the particularities of its form were not necessarily in the gift of the individual who left money for the purpose.

Whilst the wording of testamentary documents can be vague and misleading, it is possible to make some reasonable presumptions regarding what the written evidence suggests about a building's chronology; the use of the words 'building' or 'making' in bequests can surely be taken as evidence of the desire to construct new fabric. One such example which deserves clarification is the bequest by Richard Duplake in 1516 for a porch at Hilborough. The Hilborough church porch has been circumstantially but quite securely dated to the mid fifteenth century, on the basis of repeated design motifs and evidence for other works at nearby churches at this time. It has been concluded that 'the bequest of 1518 [*sic*] was for the completion of works which had been started much earlier but possibly abandoned incomplete ... work was in progress at Hilborough at about this time [c.1447–1458], and ... the exact re-use of details employed at Wiveton and Great Cressingham was not simply an extraordinary sixteenth-century

---

[14] Ibid.
[15] Ibid., 176, n.883.

anachronism.'[16] It is worth returning to the terms of the will itself, which read:

> Item I bequeath to the rep[ar]acon and making upp of the south ile of the church of Hilberworth a forsaid and to the making of a new porch ther xx[ti] marke starling w[i]t[h] such tymber as I have redy hewm if the town will go a bout it and cause it to be made and fynnysed w[i]t[h]in ii years next aft[r] my decease or the said xx[ti] marke to be bestowid on some jowell or orname[n]t to the said church as it may be fownd most necessary by the discret[i]on of my executors.[17]

It is difficult to imagine why Richard Duplake would want to replace the existing south porch, and more plausibly he intended a 'new porch' for the north side. What matters more than the intended location for present purposes is that his principal testamentary instruction was not followed through; the parish decided that either a second porch or a replacement of the existing one was not a priority and Richard Duplake's porch at Hilborough was never built.[18] It does not imply that work on the south porch stalled for over half a century and was completed at his request. Duplake's instruction is important in two respects. The stipulation that the money was to be spent on a porch 'within two years' implies that he wished his 20 marks to be converted into something tangible and identifiable. The money given was not the end but rather the means of facilitating an object with which he would be associated and thus be remembered. Yet Richard Duplake thought in practical terms about the building he proposed; the provision of specific timber is a reminder of the quantity of wood required for the scaffolding, burning of lime, and roofing of a stone building. Although the contribution of building materials indicates that he was thinking in real terms about the building of the porch, if the 20 marks were not spent on that then a jewel or ornament would suffice. Whilst the detail in the will gives a sense that Duplake has given some consideration to the outcome of his instructions, he passes responsibility for deciding whether or not to build a porch to 'the town' and it is they who will 'cause it to be made'. If the town decided against a porch (which evidently they did), then decision-making responsibility passed to Duplake's executors – he

---

[16] Fawcett, 'St Mary at Wiveton', 42.
[17] NRO NCC Briggs 67.
[18] In Cattermole and Cotton, 'Church Building in Norfolk', the entry for Hilborough also includes the 1490 bequest of '20d to reparation of parvise' by Margaret Est (NRO NCC Wolman 73). This suggests the porch once had an upper chamber, but there is no evidence for it in the fabric. See Appendix below, under Hilborough.

placed his trust in them to select a suitable 'jowell or ornament', something the parish needed and of which the benefactor would have approved.

The terms of Richard Duplake's will, the roles given to the parish and executors and, as far as building a porch is concerned, the negative outcome, are similar circumstances to those relating to Margaret Davy, widow of Spixworth. Her last testament is dated 2 August 1499 and the pertinent part reads:

> Item I be qweth to ye byldyng off a porche of ye sowythe syde of ye chyrche of Spyxwothe a for mentyn xxti so[lidos] if ye p[ar]iche wyll be willyng to helpe and contynew ye byldyng of ye seyd porche and if ye wyll not helpe to ye byldyng of ye porche fore seyde yt yan [that then] ye seid xxti [shillings] be disposyd be ye wyse of myn executars in a [... ....] to theme most nessessary to ye churche of Spyxworthe foreseyd.[19]

Again, the parish has to support the building campaign and if they are not willing, then the money will be spent at the discretion of the executors but on something that the parish needs. In the wills of both Richard Duplake and Margaret Davy any sense of the testator anticipating control over the decisions relating to a building project is explicitly renounced. To cast either of these individuals in the role of patron (that is, one who influenced the pattern) would be to misinterpret the evidence, although benefactors they certainly were. The issue at stake here is not one of semantics but rather our understanding of in whose hands rested responsibility for the building of church porches. Whilst these individuals provided the means by which construction could commence, the ultimate decision was taken by representatives of the parish and in both cases their authority is confirmed in the terms of the will.

The wording of John Drolle's testamentary instruction for the building of a porch at Norwich St Andrew cast the parishioners in a similar role, but the specification of the document implicates his executors in the negotiations to a much greater extent than the previous two examples. The relevant part of the will reads:

> Item I be[q]whethe to seynt andrew chyrch xx li to be spente by the advyse of myn executoris on a newe chyrche porche on the sowth syde of the chyrche if the p[ar]ysshoners will helpe to p[er]forme the same and also the sayd mony to be spente upon the poyntyng of the perke in the same chyrch by the advyes of my executoris.[20]

Approval for the project is sought from the parish, presumably represented by the churchwardens, and the importance of their help is clearly

---

[19] NRO ANW Fuller alias Roper 301.
[20] NRO NCC Betyns 135.

recognised. Yet John Drolle, an alderman of Norwich, did not give control of the project, nor the money, to the parish. He placed both in the hands of his executors, Agnes his wife and 'mayste' Henry Cossey, clerk.[21] The will makes a distinction between the executors and 'the parish', and whilst the help or support of the latter is a prerequisite, the decisive advisory role resides with the former: Agnes and Henry, charged with representing John's interests, were to take key decisions about the detail of the building. John Drolle not only provided the considerable sum of £20 for the porch, he essentially set up a committee to work on the project and collectively realise his desired building. Drolle's patronal involvement even after death is implicit in the way that, during life, he structured arrangements for the making of his porch on the south side at St Andrew's.

On the basis of the testamentary instructions discussed above it seems that porches were often built as communal parish projects, at least in the late fifteenth and early sixteenth centuries, the period from which a suitably large corpus of written evidence survives. It is unfortunate and frustrating that, in the majority of documented instances, the corresponding porch does not exist. Therefore attempts to align the circumstances in which they were commissioned and the attributes of the end product (i.e. the porch) are elusive.

The material discussed so far in this chapter makes it apparent that a patron needed not only to give money to a project but also effectively to wield a degree of power and influence. John Hobard apparently did not establish a strong enough set of circumstances and relationships to ensure that his instruction for a porch to be built was respected. Richard Duplake and Margaret Davy placed responsibility in the hands of the parish, which suggests a recognition of their not being in a position to take on a fully 'patronal' role. By contrast John Drolle recognised the need to manage the situation much more closely; relying on 'goodwill' was a risky business and likely to lead to failure. Power and influence, however, perhaps need to be nuanced. Whilst some patrons may have 'bullied' others to achieve their objective, these examples demonstrate a desire to invite negotiation and thus correspond with the role of patron as provider and protector. An ability to speak and be listened to (a 'call and response' effect) was an important trait shared by many whose involvement appears to have been a decisive impetus for commencement of the project, rather than the guiding force throughout.

---

[21] Henry Cossey was rector of Rushworth College and at the same time of Gonville Hall, Cambridge, from 1475 to 1481. He was an associate of John Drolle and another Norwich alderman, Richard Brown, from whom he extracted donations to Gonville Hall (as it was then). My thanks go to Dr Claire Daunton for this information.

5. THE PATRONS' SHARE

The porches at Saffron Walden and Norwich St Andrew evidently resulted, in no small part, from the initiating acts of Thomas Barker and John Drolle, the former in the capacity of a benefactor and the latter as patron. Yet neither building appears ever to have held in its fabric any identifier of those by whose will it came to be. In form and content they are designed in accordance with the building they precede, and they do not feature any sign or emblem denoting their patron.[22] There are however many instances where porches do carry such markers and it is those which will now be investigated.

Donors

Showing individuals in a pose of supplication is a mode of representation widely understood to be representative of donors, those who make a gift or presentation. Where the donated object is a building or furnishing, visual renderings often show the donor holding or presenting a miniaturised model of their gift. Often the posture of supplication and an active gesture of presentation are also involved, see for example the depiction of Sir Simon Drayton in stained glass at Lowick, Northamptonshire.[23] The representation of donor figures in medieval art visually constructs a connection between person, object and receiver: the donor is foregrounded in a manner that patrons and benefactors are not and evidence of donors is held in the artefacts more so than in associated written material. This particular form of bond between people and architecture is evident in the stonework of church porches.

The principal boss of the porch vault at Worstead is carved with the Coronation of the Virgin (fig. 71), the Virgin seated in the centre foreground with God the Father and Son to either side slightly further back, and presumably the Holy Spirit hovered over the group, but this area of the carving has been damaged. The same basic composition is also shown on the central boss at Wymondham, but the Worstead Coronation features four additional figures, two on either flank. They wear early-fifteenth-century dress, their hands are placed in front of their bodies as in prayer and it has been plausibly suggested that these are donor figures.[24] Implicit in this identification is that these figures represent the people who paid for

---

[22] Both examples are urban parishes, and as seen in the city of Norwich at large, porches in urban settings are much less elaborately decorated and rarely feature personal motifs.
[23] Jonathan Alexander and Paul Binski, eds, *Age of Chivalry: Art in Plantagenet England, 1200–1400* (London, 1987), 139.
[24] Nichols, *The Early Art of Norfolk*, 106.

71 Coronation of the Virgin vault boss, south porch, Worstead

this boss and perhaps the porch in general. By means of the composition of the scene, a vivid association is drawn between the donor figure and the Virgin's coronation in heaven. The people effectively witness the Coronation of the Virgin; their bodies cross over the architectural frame and are not segregated from the Virgin and the Trinity. This composition of donor figures placed alongside, but differentiated from, potent religious events establishes porch imagery as part of a much larger corpus of art in which donors are represented in a position of devotion and supplication.

A second instance of donors placed in the midst of visual references to the Virgin is to be found flanking the entrance of the north porch at Acle (fig. 43). In the dexter spandrel a man and woman kneel in supplication (fig. 72), and across from them in the sinister spandrel is a carved rose, plausibly here being representative of the Virgin. Unlike at Worstead, documentary evidence records who paid for Acle porch and therefore who is represented in the spandrel. The testament of Robert Bataly records his wish that his 'body be beryd in the chircheyard of Seynt Edm[und] kyng and martir of Acle before the north dore' and bequeathed 'to the byldyng of a newe porche upon the north side of Acle chirche xxti marke'.[25] The north porch at Acle is a notable case as it was built despite there being a pre-existing south porch, with the possible implication that the primary approach to

[25] NRO ANW Fuller alias Roper 258.

72 Spandrel detail showing kneeling donor figures, north porch, Acle

the church changed as a result. Robert Bataly's stated desire to be buried at the north door and for a porch to be built over his grave, supported by the provision of 20 marks for the purpose, is a set of circumstances similarly repeated in other testaments. The sum of money is notable because not only is it considerable, but it implies that Bataly knew what his porch was going to cost, and therefore what sort of building he wanted it to be.

The pictorial representation of Robert Bataly and (presumably) his wife in the fabric of the porch suggests Bataly's influence on the pattern of the porch. As such fine details are not expressed in his will, the boss is likely evidence of in-life arrangements made for his sepulchre. Although the church is dedicated to St Edmund, Bataly's devotion was evidently to the Virgin, and it is to her that he kneels in supplication. This is good, if rare, evidence of porch imagery being a reflection of a patron's devotional allegiance. In such cases donor-patrons constructed a worshipful relationship between themselves and the Virgin, and the vehicle for doing so was the porch itself. The Coronation scene at Worstead, and the Virgin's rose at Acle, are not devotional images in the sense of being objects of parishioners' devotion, habitually honoured with gifts of lights to burn before them and garments to adorn them.[26] However, the posture adopted by the donors makes necessary a receiver of their devotions, and in both cases that is the Virgin.

Patronal and Non-Patronal Saints

As well as being evidence of donor involvement, the examples discussed so far have indicated that the company of heaven presented in church porches goes well beyond the saint to whom the church is dedicated. It is often stated that medieval porches in England display, or at least have a niche to house, an image of the church's patron saint.[27] In northern Europe the tradition was developed at least by the second quarter of the twelfth century, taking the form of tympanum carving at the main entrance, for example at the church of St Peter in Hanborough in Oxfordshire.[28] Yet the extant late-twelfth-century sculpture of St Peter in a niche at the apex of the central gable of the western narthex at Peterborough Cathedral is one instance of the move away from carved tympana towards an actual or implied architectural niche. This tradition is apparent in East Anglian parish porches from the second half of the fourteenth century and is coincidental with the reduction in the height of entrance arches relative to the gable. The porch at Alderford (fig. 54), built following the testamentary instruction of Robert Mayn in 1374, is one of the earliest examples in the region of a porch with a niche placed centrally above the entrance.[29]

Porch statuary survives only rarely but the few *in situ* instances in East Anglia, for example, Barton Bendish, Great Cressingham, South Walsham and Loddon, support the traditional view that the patronal saint was presented on the outside of the porch above the apex of the portal. The façade of the porch at St Andrew's, Barton Bendish, displays a unique arrangement of ashlar patterns and panels, including saltires relating to the

---

[26] A rare case of a burial specifically located before an image in a porch is that of Thomas Hall, who requested interment 'before the image of Our Lady' which was in the north porch at Mildenhall. TNA PROB 11/22/339.

[27] Wall, *Porches and Fonts*, 56.

[28] Marks, *Image and Devotion*, 70 and n.23.

[29] The façade now has a sun dial inserted where a niche would have been. A central niche above the entrance is shown in an early-nineteenth-century depiction. See Ladbrooke, *Views of the Churches in Norfolk*, vol. 3, plate 70.

73 Low-relief sculpture depicting St Andrew, south porch, Barton Bendish

martyrdom of the church's dedicative saint and were adopted as his identifying attribute. Over the entrance arch is set a rectangular stone panel carved in low relief showing the standing figure of St Andrew with the saltire resting against his right leg (fig. 73).

The scheme at St Michael's, Great Cressingham, combines a figure of the Archangel (in the micro-architectural vaulted niche above the entrance) with flushwork panels around the base on which are shown crowned 'M's and crowned swords held erect. These are positioned quite purposefully to flank the entrance arch and face each buttress. The mutual suitability of location and subject matter at Great Cressingham was also considered at St Mary's, South Walsham. The Annunciation is depicted in

74 Coronation of the Virgin sculpture, south porch niche, South Walsham

the spandrels – the Virgin in the dexter and the angel in the sinister, and an elaborately detailed scene of the Coronation of the Virgin is mounted on a plinth within an astonishingly verdant trefoil-headed niche (fig. 74). Set higher in the façade, the Coronation is appropriately elevated above the Annunciation.

The fourth instance of extant niche statuary is that of Holy Trinity, Loddon (fig. 62). Here not only is the church's heavenly patron still represented on the porch but, within the same scheme, so too are symbols denoting the earthly patron. The image niche set centrally in the upper register of the porch is filled with a *Gnadenstuhl* Trinity. A carved ashlar panel depicting a crowned 'T' also probably refers to the Trinity. Whilst this heavenly activity takes place high on the porch façade, lower down the arms of Sir James Hobart (sable, a star of eight points or, between two flaunches ermine) impaling those of his wife Margaret (née Naunton – sable, three martlets, argent), fill the spandrels and his surname is set in roundels on the base-course panel closest to the entrance. Within the porch, Hobart's radiant device is also depicted on the central ceiling boss. Sir James Hobart and his family of Hales Hall in Loddon maintained a long association with the parish. He is recorded as having built the bridge over the river Waveney, as well as the church.[30] Their service to the parish included a remarkable showpiece porch which memorialises in stone their roles as patrons; the extent to which the Hobarts influenced the pattern of this porch remains powerfully evident.

The Architectural Application of Heraldry

J. C. Wall was remarkably brief on the issue of heraldry as porch decoration, simply saying that shields 'figured largely in the decorative art of the porch, in the spandrels of the doorway or the bosses of the vault. They were generally the coat armour of the munificent donor of the structure or of a benefactor.' He gives the arms of Archbishop Chichele at Croydon as one such instance before closing by noting that 'shields charged with sacred emblems frequently take the place of family escutcheons'.[31] Wall's rather cryptic consideration of the application of heraldry not only fails to convey the frequency with which it occurs, it also fails to state what it reveals about the architectural allusions a commissioning patron could make through its use. The architectural application of heraldic devices promotes positive associations, either between people or between a person

---

[30] Blomefield, *Topographical History*, vol. 8, 18–19; vol. 10, 160–1.
[31] Wall, *Porches and Fonts*, 62.

and a building. Heraldic devices appear to have been used on both lifetime architectural commissions and on post-mortem works.

The architectural application of heraldry in England was initiated under royal patronage during the reign of Henry III. In 1240 the king instructed that window shutters of the great chamber in the Tower of London be painted with the royal arms.[32] A few years later, the idea of heraldic furnishings was taken a stage further and a 'series of shields carved in the stonework of the choir aisles in Westminster Abbey between 1245 and 1269 is the first known instance of heraldry used in an architectural context, and naturally included Henry [III]'s own arms'.[33] The association with royal artistic patronage makes the subsequent popularity of architectural heraldic display unsurprising. At Westminster the placing of different coats of arms was hierarchically planned and, as argued by John Cherry, '[t]he intention appears to have been to display the arms of those royal houses to which the king was connected by marriage, the most important shields being placed nearest the crossing ... The others were the barons who were his principal vassals in England. Amongst these were the three great officers of state – the earl marshal (Bigod), the constable (Bohun), and the steward (Montfort).'[34] From the earliest examples it is apparent, therefore, that heraldry conveys much about the social agency of a building project. Similarly, protection is a key constitutive in the formulation of porches as places. The hanging of shields, even blank ones, on the outside of a building is a mode of arming that place. Whilst heraldic devices feature elsewhere in churches, the permanent placing of someone's arms at the entrance to God's house on earth is a powerful statement.

Amongst the earliest examples of heraldry being displayed architecturally on a parish porch in East Anglia are the small ashlar shields which flank the shoulders of the entrance arch to the south porch at Little Massingham. Blomefield identified Thorp heraldry, but attributed it to 'Sir Robert [de Thorp] [who] bore azure, three crescents, argent, impaling Hengrave, argent, a chief indented, gules'.[35] The shields are still in sufficiently good order to see the heraldic device and there is no suggestion of an impaled shield. The arms are simply those of Thorp (azure, three crescents argent). It is more plausible that the porch was built by Sir Edmund Thorp (d.1417) who left 20s to the church in his will but was actively funding the renewal

---

[32] John Cherry, 'Heraldry as Decoration in the Thirteenth Century', in *England in the Thirteenth Century*, ed. W. M. Ormrod. Harlaxton Medieval Studies 1 (n.s.) (Donington, 1991), 128.

[33] Ann Payne, 'Medieval Heraldry', in *The Age of Chivalry: Art in Plantagenet England, 1200–1400*, ed. Jonathan Alexander and Paul Binski (London, 1987), 57.

[34] Cherry, 'Heraldry as Decoration', 129.

[35] Blomefield, *Topographical History*, vol. 9, 14.

of the churches of which he was patron from the 1390s. The shields at Little Massingham are minimal and discreet, small and simply set within the flint façade and in so being are characteristic of Edmund Thorp's mode of patronal expression. It is probable that Sir Edmund personally specified his arms be placed on the porch as he is known to have taken responsibility for such decisions in the context of the ornamented bosses on the nave roof at Ashwellthorpe.[36]

From the turn of the fifteenth century, East Anglian porches were employed much more overtly as vehicles for the display of heraldry and its associated patronal statement. The most straightforward reading of this tradition is to infer a relationship between people and places, as did Blomefield on several occasions. For example: 'It seems as if the church of Diss was built by this man [Robert Fitzwalter], his arms cut in stone still remaining on the south porch.'[37] Similarly at Bardwell in Suffolk shields carved in the spandrels reference the patronal association of the Bardwell and Pakenham families. However, heraldic devices on porches can evoke a more nuanced set of associations between a patron and the building patronised. One such example which demonstrates the communicative potential of porch heraldry is the south porch of Cley-next-the-Sea (fig. 48). As already noted, this entrance arch is one of the most heavily elaborated in East Anglia and it was designed to display heraldic and quasi-heraldic motifs in a scheme which suggests the dynastic lineage, social connections and devotional allegiances of Lady Beatrice Stafford.

Although no documentation exists for Lady Stafford directly overseeing the design of Cley porch, the stone entrance arch expresses a strong sense of her patronal input. The full frame of the arch is decorated with shields interspersed with a repeated floral motif. The headstops of the arch depict a king and a queen; the spandrels display the arms of the Passion and the symbol of the Trinity; set further out still are shields showing (on the sinister side) the arms of Anne of Bohemia impaled with the arms of England and (on the dexter side) those of Stafford impaling Roos. Through the mode of architecturally applied heraldic devices the south porch at Cley brings together religious and saintly motifs, for example, the Agnus Dei, a chalice and the crossed swords of St Paul, plus the contemporary signifiers already mentioned. The two groups are divided either side of the arch. The two highest shields, those at the apex of the arch, are the crossed keys (sinister) referencing St Peter, the principal apostle as the gatekeeper of heaven, and the arms of England (dexter). As at Westminster the specific arrangement and spatial proximity of the shields at Cley can be

---

[36] Paul Cattermole, 'A 14th-Century Contract for Carpenter's Work at Ashwellthorpe Church', *Norfolk Archaeology* 40 (1989), 297–302.

[37] Blomefield, *Topographical History*, vol. 1, 1–2.

understood as arranged to convey marital relationships and social bonds. The input that any of these people may have had into the actual building of the porch is not known, but clearly the architecture is here used as a means of public display, formalising in stone the associations of Beatrice Stafford and her church at Cley to the national, even royal, elite. In that armorial shields require recognition to be useful, it follows that they would have been familiar to those viewing them (in this case the parishioners entering the church porch), otherwise it is difficult to explain why they would have been displayed. As evidence it permits us to glimpse a sphere which combines the familiar and the revered – Christ, the Blessed Virgin, the apostles, the king and the most important Norfolk families, and all of the latter had a connection to the parish through their estates. Porch façades such as that at Cley were important vehicles for the creation and reflection of aristocratic display, community pride, strength and constancy, examples of architectural patronage facilitating social patronage.

Architectural Fanfares for the Common Man

The image-rich culture of medieval England was replete with modes of expression in addition to the written word. Emblems and motifs were also displayed in the medium of flint flushwork, both purely decorative and significant or representative. The Maria monogram repetitiously stamped across the porch frieze at Great Witchingham is a representative example. Instances of personal representation do also exist and the gazetteer of flint flushwork designs in Norfolk and Suffolk by Blatchley and Northeast includes a considerable number of porches. This is perhaps somewhat inevitable given the correspondence between the popularity of flushwork in fifteenth-century East Anglia and the high level of investment in church fabric, including the building or rebuilding of church porches.[38] In my view, however, the architecture facilitated development of the art of flushwork rather than simply providing a canvas for its display. Masons with the technical skills needed to produce elaborate and intricate designs were encouraged by those deciding how their parish church should look, and these two factors successfully harmonised with the predilection for ambitiously ostentatious church façades.

From the thirteenth century, indigenous East Anglian flint was colour-selected and carefully worked so that it resembled cut glass or onyx. It could be used to create sheer reflective wall surfaces, and in imitating glass it was used in games of architectural mimicry and sleights-of-hand.

---

[38] John Blatchly and Peter Northeast, *Decoding Flint Flushwork on Suffolk and Norfolk Churches* (Ipswich, 2005), 2.

For example, blind windows filled with highly-worked flint could be made to appear glazed. By the fifteenth century the craft was widespread and much sought after. As its popularity and affordability increased, so too did its range of applications. However, despite its popularity flushwork was a regionally defined art form, and limited to religious settings (although the status of gatehouses inevitably blurs such a distinction).[39] The incorporation of flushwork designs into the repertoire of porch decoration is highly significant. The earliest known cases of fully developed flushwork in East Anglia are both gatehouses; even if they were not the first instances, the maturity with which the technique was applied on the Norwich and Butley Priory gates demonstrates how it was in the context of entrance architecture that the art form was formalised. Experimentation inevitably occurred earlier than either of these examples, and the tower-porch of St Stephen's, Norwich, and the porch at North Creake should be recognised as formative precedents. The close relationship between decorative flintwork and church porches is, like the hanging of heraldic shields, evidence of the architectural interplay between different types of entrance structure.

Flushwork was also used for the creation of patterns and motifs which appear to allude to individuals and thus represent them in a manner akin to heraldry or text. The porch at Badwell Ash is a well-known occupational example, where two panels are decorated with a blacksmith's tools, arranged to evoke the Instruments of the Passion, and another a husbandman's plough and sieve. Accompanying these motifs are the initials R and B, framed in different sorts of roundel, and potentially these are the initials of the blacksmith and husbandman alluded to in picture form.[40] Other instances of flushwork panels which have been identified as portraying trade-tools are at St Lawrence, Ipswich (draper), Thetford (forester), Bacton (shearman), Rougham (weaver) and the lost church of All Saints, Garboldisham (shearman and woolcomber).[41]

Where supporting evidence permits, initials in flushwork can be construed as reference to those who, to a greater or lesser extent, contributed to the fabric fund, or were memorialised for other services to the parish. One such instance is the entwined JB (denoting John Bacon) on the porch buttresses at Hessett in Suffolk. Bacon is reputed to have been responsible for the building of this porch (and much else besides) and lies buried beneath a coped tomb close by in the churchyard.[42] Yet despite the widely recognised prevalence of flushwork on the late medieval porches of Norfolk and Suffolk, the display of personal motifs is an unusual but sig-

---

[39] Luxford, 'Symbolism in East Anglian Flushwork', 120.
[40] Blatchly and Northeast, *Decoding Flint Flushwork*, 14–15.
[41] Ibid., 11.
[42] Ibid., 47.

nificant form. In the main panels either denote saints or they are abstract, decorative shapes and patterns, not representational at all.

From Memory to Written Record

Personal textual inscriptions on porches also contribute to the other modes of representation discussed in this chapter, the much abused flushwork at St John the Baptist, Garboldisham, being a well-known example. Above the portal a now defaced inscription once read '*Orate pro Anima Willi. Pece, Capellani*'. Inscriptions eliciting prayers for the souls of named people strongly suggest that a building was constructed soon after their death, the project functioning as an act of remembrance and the resulting building their memorial. Although common in other media, and of course on tomb slabs, such phraseology rarely occurs on porches; it is even absent from those porches known to have been built as a form of sepulchre over a grave.

The beautifully calligraphic, low-relief inscribed panels on the porch at East Dereham simply state 'Rogeris Boton' and 'Margaret uxor', each name given above an image niche. This inscription is not a request for prayers for their souls, although these may have resulted, but rather an aid to memory which permanently related the porch and the couple. Roger Boton's will does not survive, but that of Margaret is extant. She requested burial in the churchyard and left money for a window in the porch. By the time of her death she had seemingly changed her name, presumably having remarried.[43] The building of the porch and therefore the writing of the inscription were probably realised either during Roger's lifetime or as a result of a testamentary bequest by him. Margaret's will is also, incidentally, rare medieval written evidence for the glazing of porch windows.

Although not prevalent, architectural inscriptions which reference parishioners individually illustrate the carefully composed relationships between people and objects. Although very different in their artistic and literary composition, the inscriptions at Garboldisham (c.1500), and East Dereham (pre-1481), and similarly Hobart's roundels at Loddon (c.1480–92), denote individuals in the stones of a church porch façade. Perhaps the most dramatic collection of exterior inscriptions is that at Long Melford, including the legend commencing on the porch which stands as an enduring surrogate for John Clopton's presence in the parish.[44] A much

---

[43] NRO NCC Caston 111.

[44] Nigel Saul, *Lordship and Faith: The English Gentry and the Parish Church in the Middle Ages* (Oxford, 2017), 318–20; David Dymond and Clive Paine, *Five Centuries of an English Parish Church: the State of Melford Church, Suffolk* (Cambridge, 2012), 177.

75 Exterior flushwork inscription, south porch, Swannington

humbler example of a personal inscription is carved into the fabric of the mid-fourteenth-century church porch at Whittlesford, Cambridgeshire. It offers a progenitor for these later East Anglian examples. Carved along the purlins of this small timber-framed building is: 'h e r r i / c u s c i p / e r n m e / f e c i t' ('Herricus Cipern me fecit').[45] This form of words epitomises a tradition in which the gift-act of making an object (in this case a building) held greater importance than the intercessory function of publicly displayed inscriptions.

In fifteenth-century East Anglia, however, lettering bonded into the architecture of church porches tends to make devotional declarations. Formed as banners across the church façade, they can be read as statements of belief held aloft by the church militant. The carved ashlar lettering at Winterton reads: 'In honour of the Holy Trinity and All Saints' – an unconventional declaration of the church existing in honour of its heavenly patrons. Composed in flushwork and spanning the façade at Swannington (fig. 75), individually delineated letters compose 'ihc nazarenus' (Jesus the Nazarene); this is not a statement honouring the dedicative saint (that is to be found on the base course) but rather an invocation of Christ. Also the flushwork frieze on the church of All Saints, East Tuddenham (fig. 42) reads: 'Gloria tibi Tr[initas]' (Glory to thee O Trinity) – the opening words of the antiphon to the first psalm sung at vespers on the feast of the Trinity – set immediately above spandrels which present the Annunciation. These texts are very specific expressions of devotion which would have held particular resonance on important feast days as parishioners entered the church. Unlike motifs and inscriptions which foreground the individual, these examples emphasise cohesion and devotion. Perhaps the implication is, therefore, that the parish was the corporate patron of the porch.

A final pertinent instance of an inscription written across a porch façade is the previously mentioned Forncett St Peter. The inscription reads: 'St. Peter and Paul Patronys of this Place Pray to I.H.S. [sic] in Heven yt I may see his face' (fig. 15). The person who commissioned the inscription or the porch in general is not known but the words form a relationship between people and object. The 'patrons' of the place are clearly stated as the dedicative saints, Peter and Paul; it is they who are patrons of the church and intercessors between the devotee and Christ. Unlike William Pece's inscription at Garboldisham, the appeal is directed to the saintly intercessors, not to the parishioners entering the church. It is an example of the textual mode formulating a relationship between earthly donor and heavenly intercessor, a companion to the figurative representations at Acle and Worstead.

---

[45] Henry Cyprian left money for a chantry in 1351 and, on the inscription's evidence, paid to build the porch. A. P. M. Wright, ed., *A History of the County of Cambridge and the Isle of Ely*, volume 6 (London, 1978), 270.

Conclusion

This chapter has investigated the manner in which relationships were forged between people and the artefacts which they were involved in facilitating. The questioning has had two strands: What is knowable of the circumstances in which porches were constructed? And how was the fabric of these buildings employed in the service of their patrons, benefactors or donors? Although limited in number, textual sources provide some evidence of the differences between these three modes of involvement. Even where testamentary instructions and the bequest of money and goods initially indicate the testator to be the patron of the porch, in several cases responsibility for the choices made, including whether or not the project would go ahead, was placed in the care of the parish and its corporate representatives. Records of financial contribution do not necessarily equate to patronage if a prerequisite of the role is to have influence over the design (pattern) of the object. Accepting that in many cases porches were built on the approval of the parish it can be inferred that their form and content was also corporately sanctioned. Evidently, in fifteenth-century East Anglia, the decision was taken on more than one occasion not to build a porch and the testator's money was put to an alternative cause. In such circumstances the benefaction was maintained although the specifics were changed.

In general, East Anglia's church porches do not display direct references to their patrons and benefactors, although there are exceptions, as have been discussed. One category which does represent a close connection between person and object is that of architectural donation. Donors have a very particular impact on the fabric of the building of which they might otherwise be considered the patron. The evidence for this is in the details of the buildings themselves. Not only do donors provide for the fabric but also use it to convey aspects of their own belief system, as was seen in the case of Robert Bataly at Acle. In the same way that architectural features such as buttresses and parapets construct the form and content of a porch, so too do personal motifs, whether figural or symbolic, and other modes of decoration. A wide range of options were available in terms of the architectural design choices which could constitute a porch and as an inevitable result the circumstances in which they were built could be equally diverse. The identifiable types of relationship forged between people and porches are further evidence of how the architectural characterisation of these buildings responded to vital decision making. The exploration of relationships between people and porches has been a recurring theme of this book, and this chapter has extended those considerations to include the status of medieval patrons and displays of architectural appropriation. Augmenting the documentary evidence, the inscriptions, heraldic devices and flushwork motifs are cogent primary evidence of human desires publicly to claim title to the point of entry to a parish church. If contextualised with reference to the historical practice of placing representations of Christ as judge at liminal points of entry, these architectural interventions continue to astound in their audacious confidence.

Conclusion

THE AIM OF THIS BOOK has been to address one question – what sort of building was a church porch during the English Middle Ages? To do so the investigation has used methodologies which promote investigation of what a building can be phenomenologically as well as functionally and architecturally. Porches are particularly well suited to such an approach, because of the ubiquitous characteristic of a permanently open entrance. As a result, porches are architectural definers of space which can combine exteriority and interiority to an equal extent. The natural environment, climate and landscape influence one's experience of being within a porch more than in almost any other building.[1] The involvement of natural phenomena implies some similarity between porches and less permanent structures that might be termed shelters rather than buildings. The notion and function of providing shelter is one of the most frequently rehearsed justifications for why church porches were built; that they provided protection for the church door. Conceiving of church porches in that mode necessitates questions of permanence and transience. Are they to be understood as the grounded, settled manifestation of less formal structures? And is the provision of shelter at the core of what sort of buildings porches were in the late medieval period? The architecture goes some way to answering those questions.

Historically porch architecture has been a celebration of variation, as is evident in the twelfth-century porches at Malmesbury Abbey and Southwell Minster, to name just two early examples. Malmesbury porch is replete with religious imagery and heavily articulated surfaces including the rib-vaulted ceiling. In contrast, at Southwell the large entrance leads into a simple barrel-vaulted space with the intersecting wall arcade and geometric mouldings of the seven-ordered door into the church being the only decorative elements. Neither porch has side apertures, but the interior design causes the former to feel close and intense; the latter expansive and airy. In the architecture of church porches constructed in East Anglia

---

[1] Helen E. Lunnon, 'A Phenomenological Study of the English Parish-Church Porch, 1200–1399', in *Towards an Art History of the Parish Church*, ed. Meg Bernstein and James Alexander Cameron (London, forthcoming).

between the mid thirteenth century and the early sixteenth century, however, there is evidence of a particular tension. Whilst this tradition of variation in terms of form is maintained, a sense of typological development has also been identified. It has become apparent through direct engagement with their architecture that East Anglian parish church porches underwent a change of status around the mid fourteenth century. This change had consequences for how they were designed, particularly in terms of balancing the transition between the open external environment and the space within. East Anglia is rich in extant late medieval church porches, and a few important earlier examples. Those constructed before the mid fourteenth century lack evidence of being conceived of as sacred places, but rather as having been considered beyond the bounds of the church. In the mid-century tentative moves were made towards external elaboration and by the turn of the fifteenth century considerably greater emphasis was placed on the outer skin of the porch. From this date, façades projected religious imagery, with the notable early examples being at North Walsham and Lynn St Nicholas. As porch exteriors came to be employed in the service of the sacred, implicitly the space inside became less peripheral than previously and porch interiors were notionally integrated with the church body. Convincing evidence of the sanctification of porch space in East Anglia is the prevalence of vaulted ceilings and the accompanying representational bosses often showing Marian image cycles.

Elsewhere in England notable earlier instances of architecturally applied religious sculpture adorning porch interiors (as opposed to a tympanum above the church door), include Malmesbury Abbey and the early vaulted interiors at Tewkesbury Abbey, the inner north porch at St Mary Redcliffe in Bristol and Barnack (Northamptonshire). Understanding an architectural vault as a form of honorific canopy comparable with a ciborium over an altar makes implicit that porches could be places of elevated status well before their apparent inclusion within the sacred confines of East Anglian parish churches. For this issue to be more fully understood regional studies elsewhere in England will be needed.

Bound up in questions of inclusion and exclusion, the quasi-sacred status of porch space, is the evidence for porches being the outward expression of the church, the point from which the building communicates its purpose and engages with the world beyond its walls. The external elaboration of porches implies that the place within is reserved to the elect. It also serves a related but distinct purpose. The design of porch interiors can convey the sanctity of the place, often in conjunction with external display. However, porch exteriors also function independently from the interior; an elaborate exterior does not necessitate comparable treatment within. In fifteenth-century East Anglia, porches functioned as the principal church façade, regardless of their interior form or detail.

CONCLUSION

The treatment of materials, architectural and decorative elements, imagery, inscriptions and motifs are all evidence of the decisions made by the people responsible for a porch's design. Highlighting the variation which is ever present in their form, two examples serve as explanatory evidence. At Attleborough the roof pinnacles represent Christ displaying his wounds and the four beasts of the Apocalypse, whilst lower down over the entrance to the porch was an armorial display by the lord of the manor and probable patron of the architecture (fig. 67). Conversely, at Pulham St Mary the central pinnacle represents a wildman seated cross-legged, as though in mockery of traditional judgement, whilst surrounding the entrance is displayed the Annunciation, an angelic orchestra and devices alluding to Christ's Passion and the Trinity (fig. 49). Both porches are realisations of the decisions that people made when considering appropriate content; both were designed to communicate visually something of the sensitivities of the patron and the convictions held by the parish congregation as ritualised within the church.

The composition of porches as façades and their architectural function of providing shelter are not, however, mutually exclusive. Prominent in the iconographic repertoire of church porches are motifs associated with protection and salvation. Whether through the inclusion of carved shields, crenellated parapets, warrior saints or more subtly through Christ in judgement or the Annunciation to the Virgin, porches embody the Christian creed of eternal salvation for the elect. Imagining porches in this mode extends beyond representations of broad Christian doctrine and specifically relates to what these buildings were used for and how they functioned in that capacity.

The recurring spatial designation of 'at the church door' in the rites of baptism and marriage could be interpreted in practical terms as either within the porch or outside it. Location actively formulates the nature of events. In late medieval England significant events in individual and community life-cycles took place at the entrance to the church, facilitating the participation of one's earthly peers and placing the real-life drama symbolically before Christ the door. The nature and social value of these Christian sacraments can be equated with the anthropological notion of 'territorial passage', a concept fundamental to how the rites were composed and experientially enforcing the societal significance of the event. Transition is both notional and actual, with actual transition ('territorial passage') being made apparent by means of differentiated places distinguished at a threshold. As the significant limen of the church was relocated from the church door to the porch entrance, the treatment of the outer surface of porches changed to serve this end, a marker of a point of ritualised transition.

The enhanced sense of the porch entrance marking the limit of the church from the mid fourteenth century onwards is evidenced not only in the architectural iconography but also in the scale and form of the various apertures. Whereas before the mid fourteenth century large open entrances dominated the front elevation, the lateral windows were small and reminiscent of those in peripheral locations such as clerestories, from the later fourteenth century the size of the entrance decreased in relative terms and side windows not only increased in size but were styled in keeping with those of the body of the church. The elaborated façades of fifteenth-century porches could provide backdrops for extra-mural celebrations but, as the porch remained open and accessible, it continued to provide shelter whenever and for whatever purpose it was needed.

Porches that were cast in the role of shelters not only provided protection for the church door or people caught in a moment of transition standing immediately before it, they were also places to protect the vulnerable: the poor seeking alms; the penitent expelled from the church or the deceased seeking prayers for their soul's passage through purgatory. Paupers and penitents reside outside the church door, and therefore the presence of a porch is a form of physical succour to their cause almost regardless of the form the building takes. The use of church porches as burial locations and their architectural response to this function is, however, more instructive of the sort of building they were. Testamentary evidence demonstrates that the ground immediately before the church door was culturally recognised as an appropriate place for interment. When burial instruction is accompanied by provision for a porch to be built over the grave a strong memorial association is constructed between the burial and the building which gave it shelter. The longevity of porches as appropriate sites for Christian burial evokes the functional meaning of *porticus*, and the practice was more widespread than the documented instances of porches constructed in conjunction with a burial suggest. Recognition of porches as monumental grave covers reveals the connections between their architectural form and that of other memorial structures. At St Mary's church in Nottingham, for instance, it is not possible to state with confidence which edifice, the tomb of John Samon or the south porch, replicates the other; despite their close similarities neither deviates from early-fifteenth-century expected norms for each object type – tomb or porch.[2]

Porches were at least three different sorts of building: entrances which introduce the larger building beyond, façades to communicate social and doctrinal sensitivities, and protective canopies which shelter and edify those who reside within. The variety of architectural forms results from negotiation between these different functional demands. If a building is to be well suited to its practical and social function it must be conceived in an appropriate architectural manner. It is evident that church porches

---

[2] Lunnon, "'I will have one porch of stone …'".

could be used for a broad range of activities, some unchanging and some fleeting. As a result, tension exists between a clear developmental trajectory and deviation from it. In counterbalance, however, are the specific references observable in individual examples. Through the course of this book the range of influences on late medieval church porches has been scoped, and it is now possible to recognise their place within the wider study of medieval architectural forms and cultural resonances.

Options for those taking design decisions were evidently numerous and consequently the pattern of the building is evidence of the patron's interests, although not all are easy to construe. The north porch at Yaxley in Suffolk is known from testamentary evidence to have been built prior to the death of John Herberd in 1458.[3] According to his will, Herberd was buried in the porch, a stone was placed over his grave and the whole of the rest of the porch was paved at his expense. The porch includes motifs representing the Virgin, the church's patron saint, but there is much else besides. In addition to the frieze of crowned 'M's in flushwork is a row of 'IC' panels around the base, and the (now damaged) parapet pinnacles depict Christ in Majesty and the four beasts of the Apocalypse, as at Attleborough. At Yaxley, this imagery is repeated internally on the vault bosses – Christ displaying his wounds is surrounded by the evangelists' symbols. This visual scheme is appropriate for a burial porch, in this instance built as the canopy over John Herberd's grave. It is plausible, in light of other known tomb porches, that his choice of burial location influenced the design of the porch considerably. There is, however, a less conventional element. In the spandrels are carved two large figures of 'men', each differently rendered. The figure on the sinister side is covered in hair and holds a form of club whilst the other is dressed in contemporary apparel, with a short tunic and forked beard, but also holding some form of weapon. Each man appears to face an unidentifiable animal and another creature runs down the frame of each spandrel. Although basic interpretations of good versus evil, or tamed against untamed, are possible, the particular purpose or resonance of this imagery has no ready explanation. What it does convey is how even a location as potently significant as the shoulders of the porch entrance arch did not necessarily conform to a model, pattern or a restricted visual vocabulary.

A wide array of architectural choice was open to patrons and designers. Little of the pattern was predetermined and each building is, to a large extent, evidence of negotiations between people, money and materials. Commissioning a porch was a very particular benefaction, a provision for the parish, a gift to the church, and an overt public statement. However, in several documented instances control of decisions concerning the form

[3] TNA PROB 11/4/287.

of a porch was placed in the hands of the parish corporate or its representatives. Even where considerable sums of money were given for building a porch, the benefactor's influence over the design did not necessarily follow and some potential 'patrons' simply chose not to adopt that role. This formulation of the relationship between those who provided funds for church-building projects and the actual structure is not widely recognised in the existing literature on medieval patronage and benefaction. It offers a workable middle ground between those of high status, who can be evidenced as influencing all or part of the building, and those whose small gifts formed part of a general fabric fund.

Whilst the focus of this book has been the parish church porches built in late medieval East Anglia, wider implications have been observed, including allusions to porches built by King Solomon in entrance buildings of late medieval England. There are two ways in which Solomon's influence can be recognised in English medieval church porches: their architectural form in relation to the Old Testament accounts of the buildings and their subsequent function as known from the New Testament accounts of healing miracles. Solomon's wisdom and his role as judge make him an attractive model for a medieval architectural patron, and imitation of his buildings plausibly follows.[4] There is scope in the evidence, however, for a more detailed interpretation. The case of St Mary Redcliffe is most apposite, but the south porch at Cley-next-the-Sea also presents tantalising evidence of the possible influence.

Although the church is dedicated to St Margaret, the porch is essentially built in honour of the Virgin as it is her imagery which predominates. The porch features the heraldic arms of Richard II and Anne of Bohemia and, therefore, the crowned male and female headstops of the external hoodmould may plausibly be interpreted as representing their joint monarchy. However, crowned figures, notionally kings and queens, flanking church entrances are relatively common in East Anglia and rarely can they be said to have a direct royal connection. There ought, therefore, to be another explanation for the popularity of this imagery, and Solomon and Sheba are one good option.

Flanking each side of the church door at Cley is the head of a lion which, again, recurs elsewhere in East Anglia, although more often encountered at the porch entrance, as at Palgrave for example. These lions currently do not have a recognised resonance. The pairs of lions which flanked Solomon's throne offer one possible justification for the imagery. The porch at Cley is unusual in having steps leading into the porch, and further steps into the church. Today there are, in total, seven steps but the original arrangement is likely to have had fewer. The steps and other particularities of this porch

---

[4] Lunnon, '*Inventio Porticus*'.

can be interpreted as allusions to King Solomon. For example, it is essentially a double square (ratio of 2:1) divided into two, not only by wall shafts connecting the vault to the benches but the two spaces are differentiated by the presence of windows in the front section and their absence in the part closest to the church door (even though this is where lateral light would be most beneficial). Is this to be construed as a porch before a porch? The conflation of Solomon's throne and the womb of the Virgin presents a tentative means of interpreting the predilection for Marian imagery in porches. The bosses at Cley include the Joys of the Virgin (her Assumption being at the centre of the vault), the winged beasts of the Apocalypse, and six angels holding scrolls. If the architectural attributes of this building are accepted as references to Solomonic porches, then it is plausible to interpret the expanded narrative of the life of the Virgin as representing the New Testament realisation of the Old Testament prefiguration.

The ambitious architectural and representational iconography of the porch at Cley contrasts with many other late medieval examples, some of which are plain although not necessarily inconsequential structures. Evidently a straightforward developmental trajectory or typology is not a fitting description of, or explanation for, the architecture of church porches. However, distinctiveness is only recognisable when compared with a fuller range of examples, the majority of which are less particular. Interpretation of architectural iconography can be developed on the basis of models provided by biblical accounts as the ultimate textual source, not purely on historical written evidence such as wills. Where the contemporary written record is lacking, buildings offer an alternative and equally fruitful source of primary evidence. Particular architectural programmes, combining form and decoration, as seen at Cley, strongly imply the direct involvement of patrons (identified on heraldic evidence), who had a clear sense of what sort of building they wanted and helped to direct the design decisions. Discovering rewarding ways to think through the circumstances and implications of parish church architecture requires a methodology that brings all of these different approaches together, one that enables buildings not simply to become better known but to be understood. In return this knowledge will shape our understanding of the relationships between people and things.

A little over one hundred years after J. C. Wall published on church porches, this book has celebrated the medieval history of these overlooked and little-understood buildings. If it stimulates greater recognition and further contemplation of their contribution to European architectural history, it will have served its purpose.

Appendix

Written evidence relating to medieval parish church porches in East Anglia.[1]

Castle Rising (Norfolk), St Lawrence (porch rebuilt)

'In the porch was a gravestone, with part of an inscription, viz Isabelle Regina, in memory no doubt of some of that queen's servants, or retinue, which induced some persons to fancy that she herself was here buried.' (Blomefield 9.57).

Bedingfield (Suffolk), St Mary

1371, Peter de Bedingfield left 6s 8d to the making of a new porch (NRO NCC Heydon 18).

Flordon (Norfolk), St Michael

1371, Roger Northwold, rector, requested burial in the church porch (NRO NCC Heydon 16).

Alderford (Norfolk), St John the Baptist

1374, Robert Mayn left instruction for the making of a porch and window on the south side (NRO NCC Heydon 39).

---

[1] Data are taken from: Francis Blomefield and Charles Parkin, *An Essay Towards a Topographical History of the County of Norfolk*, 11 vols (London, 1805–1810); Paul Cattermole and Simon Cotton, 'Medieval Parish Church Building in Norfolk', *Norfolk Archaeology* 40 (1983), 235–79; Peter Northeast, ed., *Wills of the Archdeaconry of Sudbury 1439–1474: Wills from the Register 'Baldwyne' Part 1: 1439–1461* (Woodbridge, 2001); Peter Northeast and Heather Falvey, eds, *Wills of the Archdeaconry of Sudbury 1439–1474: Wills from the Register 'Baldwyne' Part 2: 1461–74* (Woodbridge, 2010) unless otherwise stated. Where extant wills support the secondary statements only details of the primary source are given. Where only secondary evidence is available this source is cited. When a primary source is cited the sums of money given are as stated per the original document; for information taken from secondary sources the published format has been retained. Note that one mark is equivalent to 13s 4d.

Barsham (Suffolk), Holy Trinity

1375, Dionysia de Ty wished 'that a porch be made over my buried place [if my goods allow]' (NRO NCC Heydon 94).

Great Hockham (Norfolk), Holy Trinity

1385, Thomas Caus requested burial in the church porch (*corpus meu' ad sepeliend' in porticu eccl[es]ie de Hokham*) and left 20s to its emendation (NRO NCC Harsyk 60).

Carleton Forehoe (Norfolk), St Mary

1397, Agnes Fulbone left 5s to the emendation of the porch (NRO NCC Harsyk 242).

North Walsham (Norfolk), St Nicholas

'On the porch of the church were the arms of France, semi of de luces, and of England quarterly, also the arms of St Benet's Abbey, - sable, crozier in pale, between two ducal coronets, or.' (Blomefield 11.79).

Stowlangtoft (Suffolk), St George

1401, Robert Davey de Ashfield bequeathed £20 to finishing the porch. (Norman Scarfe, *Suffolk in the Middle Ages* (Woodbridge, 1986), 161).

Holme-next-the-Sea (Norfolk), St Mary

1405, Henry Notyngham's memorial brass reads: 'Henry Notyngham and hys wyffe lye here Yat maden this chirche stepull and quere' (Cattermole and Cotton, 252). The ground stage of the tower (or steeple) at Holme serves as the porch.

Cley-next-the-Sea (Norfolk), St Margaret

'At the west end stands a four square tower, and was built, as I take it, (by the arms) in the reign of Henry VI. About the arch of the south porch are many arms carved in stone; France and England, quarterly; Lord Ross; Mortimer earl of March; and Burgh quarterly; de la Pole Duke of Suffolk; and Wingfield, quarterly; Narford; Vaux; Erpingham; a plain cross, St George's shield; St Peter's two keys in saltire; a cup with a serpent issuing out of it, St John; a saltire, St Andrew; the emblem or arms of the Trinity; three escallops, St James; two swords saltire, St Paul, etc.' (Blomefield 9.379).

Mildenhall (Suffolk), St Mary the Virgin

1415, Thomas Heth requested burial in the [north] porch and bequeathed 4 marks of silver to the body [*corpus*] of the church (TNA PROB 11/2B/11).

1527, Thomas Hall [Hull], requested to be buried within the north porch of Mildenhall church, before the image of our Lady (TNA PROB 11/22/339).

Little Massingham (Norfolk), St Andrew

Arms of Sir Edmund Thorp (d.1417) on porch façade. Blomefield incorrectly observed, 'Sir Robert [de Thorp] bore azure, three crescents, argent, impaling Hengrave, argent, a chief indented, gules, as carved on the porch of this church.' (Blomefield 9.14).

Mendham (Suffolk), All Saints

1417, Thomas Preed left 2 marks to the fabric of the church, viz. to the porch (NRO NCC Hirning 40).

Seething (Norfolk), St Margaret and St Remigius (porch rebuilt)

1417, John Lyon bequeathed two bushels of wheat to the porch (NRO NCC Hirning 39).

Salle (Norfolk), SS Peter and Paul

South porch: 'On the south porch, and on the battlements of the south cross isle, are the arms of Brigg.' (Blomefield 8.274).

North porch: The inscription on an incomplete (now lost) brass once known to be in the north porch read: 'Pray for the souls of Geoffrey Melman and Agatha his wife at whose expense, for both timber and carpentry, this whole porch ...'.[2] Geoffrey died in 1404; the year of Agatha's death is not known. The fabric of the north porch indicates that it was laid out with the aisle which, based on the heraldry on the west tower was built between c.1405 and 1420 (Cattermole and Cotton, 263).

Ashwellthorpe (Norfolk), All Saints

1420, John Quetyll requested burial in the porch (NRO NCC Hirning 73).

Great Finborough (Suffolk), St Andrew

1422, John Parmenter of Great Finborough ('*Fymburugh Magna*') bequeathed 26s 8d 'to the fabric of the porch of the said church' (Northeast, 2.2).

1445, John Ladyesman left a quarter of malt to the emendation of the porch of St Andrew of Great Finborough (IW 1/12).

1446, John Ive the elder requested burial 'in the churchyard of the aforesaid Finborough, next to the porch ...' (Northeast, 1.131).

---

[2] W. E. Parsons, *Salle: The Story of a Norfolk Parish, its Church, Manors and People* (Norwich, 1937), 24–5.

Ludham (Norfolk), St Catherine

1422, Richard Rokelle bequeathed 40s to the reparation of the vestibule (*vestibuli*) (NRO NCC Hirning 105).

Oakley (Suffolk), St Nicholas

1430, John Hubert bequeathed 20 marks to building a porch (*lego fabricac[i]on' porticus xx marc'*) (and wished to be buried in the porch) (NCO NCC Surflete 65).

1453, Simon Cordeburgh left 20s for repair of the porch (*ad emendacione porticus xxs'*) (NRO NCC Aleyn 167).

1506, Philip Curson bequeathed money to paint porch (NRO NCC Ryxe 384).

Brisley (Norfolk), St Bartholomew

1435, Robert Ediman left instruction for the porch to be leaded (NRO NCC Surflete 182).

Walpole St Peter (Norfolk), St Peter

'The [south] porch bears the arms of Sir John Goddard (d. 1435)' (Cattermole and Cotton, 279 n.73).

Trimingham (Norfolk), St John the Baptist

1437, John Garleck left 40s to edification of porch (NRO NCC Doke 46).

Aslacton (Norfolk), St Michael

1438, Isabel Randolph left one combe of malt to the building (*fabricu'*) of the porch (NRO NCC Doke 58).

Little Fransham (Norfolk), St Mary

1438, William Martenet left 40s to the making of the south porch (NRO NCC Doke 66).

Athelington (Suffolk), St Peter

1439, Robert Sax left 6s 8d to the reparation of the porch (NRO NCC Betyns 50).

Great Cressingham (Norfolk), St Michael

1439, John Blake gave 10s to building the porch (NRO NCC Doke 101).

Woolpit (Suffolk), St Mary

1439/40, John Turnour of Woolpit, bequeathed 13s 4d 'to the fabric of the new porch there' (Northeast, 1.24–5).

1442, John Welde of Woolpit, bequeathed 2s 'to the fabric of "le porche" of the same church' (Northeast, 1.95).

1451, John Stevynesson of Woolpit, bequeathed 13s 4d 'to the fabric of the new porch of the same church ... If the fraternity of the gild of the Nativity of the Blessed Mary in any way trouble my executors, the bequests to the church porch of Woolpit, and the community of the same, to be null and void.' (Northeast, 1.180).

1451/2, Margery Koo of Woolpit, widow, gave 6s 8d 'to the fabric of the new porch of the church' (Northeast, 1.230).

Woodbastwick (Norfolk), SS Fabian and Sebastian (porch rebuilt)

1440, Adam Reeve gave 6s 8d to construct the porch (NRO NCC Doke 129).

Attleborough (Norfolk), Assumption of the Blessed Virgin Mary

'The north porch was completed by John Radcliffe (d.1441) to judge by the arms on it.' (Cattermole and Cotton, 276 n.4,).

Boxford (Suffolk), St Mary

1441, Roger Wygenale of Boxford, gave 6s 8d 'to the making of a new porch (*novi vestibuli*) of the church' (Northeast, 1.45).

1444/45, John Cowpere of Boxford, gave 5 marks 'to the porch of the same church' (Northeast, 1.118).

1447, John Facoun, the elder of Boxford, gave 26s 8d 'to the new porch of Boxford' (Northeast, 1.145).

1451, Thomas Cowpere of Boxford ('Boxforth'), gave 'to the building of the new porch' (Northeast, 1.176).

1452, John Coo of Boxford, 'barbour', gave 'to the building of the new porch ... of the church a bedcover with a 'le tester' of blue colour ...' (Northeast, 1.207).

1456, John Cowper at the Stone at Boxford requested 'To be buried in the new porch on the south side of Boxford church' and gave 20 marks 'To the building of the new porch in which I wish to be buried' (Northeast, 2.147).

1456/57, Margaret Reche of Boxford, widow, gave 6s 8d 'to the new porch of the same church' (Northeast, 1.376).

1465/66, Thomas Bockyng, the elder of Boxford, gave 20d 'to the fabric of the new porch of the said church' (Northeast, 2.194).

1468, William Mawdyon of Boxford, gave 6s 8d 'to the fabric of the new porch (*porticus*) of Boxford' (Northeast, 2.193).

1469, Robert Wasshscher of Boxford, gave 6s 8d 'to the new porch there' (Northeast, 2.262).

Nayland (Suffolk), St James

1441, John Wareyn of Nayland, barker, requested 'to be buried in the north porch of the church of St James of Nayland ... the making of a new porch (*vestibuli*)' (Northeast, 1.41).

Stowmarket (Suffolk), SS Peter and Paul

1443, Robert Kent requested to be buried in the porch newly built on the north side (*de lat' aquilon*) (Archdeaconry of Sudbury, Baldwyne 56).

Swardeston (Norfolk), St Mary

1443, Katharine Kensy bequeathed 20d to the emendation of the porch (NRO NCC Doke 97).

Mattishall (Norfolk), All Saints

1445, Richard Deen gave 6s 8d to the building (*fabrico*) of a new (*nove*) porch (NRO NCC Wylby 120).

1453, Thomas Deen gave 40d for 'le castyng and whityng le porche' (NRO NCC Aleyn 159).

Southolt (Suffolk), St Margaret

1449, William Bomelot asked to be buried in the porch, if the parishioners were willing. 'To the leading of the porch if my body be buried there 10s, but if not 6s 8d' (Archdeaconry of Suffolk, 1.161).

1452, Alice Bomelot left 10s to the leading of the porch (IW 1/166).

Sibton (Suffolk), St Peter

1450, William Chamber gave 6s 8d to the fabric of the porch (*vestibule*) to be built on the same church on condition that it be built on the north side, otherwise nothing (IW 1/28).

Tannington (Suffolk), St Ethelbert

1451, John Denys left 10s to the fabric of the new porch if the parishioners wished to make that porch in the place where the present one was built (IW 1/167).

Dickleburgh (Norfolk), All Saints

1452, Robert Gamyn made a bequest to pave the porch (NRO NCC Betyns 87).

Fordham (Cambridgeshire), St Peter

1452, William Hurt bequeathed 'To the porch on the south side, for which I have made an agreement with Thomas Mason of Littlebury ('Lytylbery'), [Essex], to be built and completed in the best manner with my goods. ... After the death of Joan my wife an acre of land to remain to the upkeep of the said porch in perpetuity.' (Northeast, 1.208).

Swannington (Norfolk), St Margaret

1452, John Bott gave 8d to the reparation of the porch on the south side (NRO NCC Aleyn 156).

1457, William Hase gave 8d to the building (*fabric*) of the church, that is (*viz*), 'le porche' (NRO NCC Brosyard 61).

1478, Thomas Elyse bequeathed 6s 8d to the reparation of the porch (NRO ANW Fuller alias Roper 4).

Gressenhall (Norfolk), St Mary

1453, John Sekker gave 10s to the building of the new porch (*Item lego fabricu' nov' porti[c]u' de ead[e]m xs*) (NRO NCC Aleyn 194).

Hopton (Suffolk), All Saints

1453, John Broun bequeathed 40d 'If they make a "porche" at the north door' (Northeast, 1.263).

Ipswich (Suffolk), St Margaret

1453, Geoffrey Shryd gave 10s to the fabric of a new porch (IW 1/128).

1454, William Silvester gave 20s to the fabric of a new porch (IW 1/106).

South Walsham (Norfolk), St Mary

1454, John Odgyf bequeathed one combe of malt to the building (*ad fabrica*) of the new porch (*novi portic*) (NRO NCC Aleyn 209).

Beccles (Suffolk), St Michael

1455, Emma Goodrich bequeathed 2s to the fabric of the new porch (IW, 1/128).

1455, Beatrix Silverton bequeathed 20s to the fabric of the new porch (IW, 1/131).

Great Melton (Norfolk), All Saints (porch rebuilt)

1455, Joan Hervey gave 12 marks of silver to the new south porch (*ad novum porticum ex parte australi*) (NRO NCC Brosyard 7).

Pulham Market (Norfolk), St Mary Magdalen

1456, John Intwood gave 26s 8d for a new porch (NRO NCC Brosyard 41).

Catfield (Norfolk), All Saints (porch not extant)

1457, Richard Befeld bequeathed £3 6s 8d towards the building of a new north porch if begun in three years (NRO NCC Brosyard 44).

Stoke by Nayland (Suffolk), St Mary the Virgin

1457, Thomas Wodesey bequeathed 5s to the repairing of 'le north porch' (Northeast, 1.331).

East Tuddenham (Norfolk), All Saints

1458, John Teny bequeathed 8d to building the porch (NRO NCC Brosyard 144).

1502, William Attewelle bequeathed 13s 4d to 'soleryng' the church porch (NRO NCC Popy 343).

Little Walsingham (Norfolk), St Mary

1458, Thomas Yong bequeathed 20d to the emendation of the porch (NRO NCC Brosyard 96).

Ousden (Suffolk), St Peter

1458, John Frost bequeathed 6s 8d 'to the fabric of a porch of the same church' (Northeast, 1.447).

Norwich (Norfolk), St Laurence

1459, Richard Playter gave 46s 8d to build a new porch and 40 stone of lead to cover it (Blomefield 4.269).

Wickham Skeith (Suffolk), St Andrew

1459, John Brakstret of Wickham Skeith ('Wykham') 'to the new porch on the south side of the said church 6s 8d ... but if no porch be built there, my executors to pay the 6s 8d to the fabric of the church; to the church of Norwich 6s.' (Northeast, 1.441).

Winterton (Norfolk), Holy Trinity

'The porch has arms of Fastolf. Sir John Fastolf (d. 1459) acquired St Benet's manor in Winterton' (Cattermole and Cotton 279 n.79; Blomefield 11.196).

Yaxley (Suffolk), St Mary

1459, Joan, widow of John Herberd [fn. Will pr. June 1459 (PCC Stokton); said he wished to be buried in the north porch of Yaxley church (Corder, *Visitation*, p. 13)...] (Northeast, 1.443).

Bardwell (Suffolk), SS Peter and Paul

1460, William Inglond bequeathed 2s 'to the repairing of the porch' (Northeast, 1.420).

Cowlinge (Suffolk), St Margaret

1460, John Wode bequeathed 4s to the repairing of the porch (Northeast, 1.479).

Caister St Edmund (Norfolk), St Edmund

1462, R. Mylls made a bequest to pave the porch (NRO NCC Grey 88).

Great Horringer (Suffolk), St Leonard

1462, Simon Custe of Great Horringer ('*Magna Horniygserthe*'), gave 6s 8d 'to "le porche" of the same church, to be newly made' (Northeast, 2.52).

1470, Walter Noble of Great Horringer ('*Magna Hornynghesherth*'), gave 20s 'to the reparation of the porch of the same church' (Northeast, 2.256).

1474, Adam Rodyng of Great Horringer ('*Mekyll Hornyngesherth*'), gave 6s 8d 'To the reparation of the porch' (Northeast, 2.387).

Walpole St Andrew (Norfolk), St Andrew

1463, William Wellys, capellanus, bequeathed 20d to the building (*fabrico*) of a porch (*unius portic*) (NRO NCC Brosyard 319).

Woodrising (Norfolk), St Nicholas (Porch rebuilt)

1463, Walter Shepherd gave 40s to building the porch and church (NRO ANF Liber 4 (Grey), f. 117).

Postwick (Norfolk), All Saints

1464, John Thurkeld requested executors to pave north porch (NRO NCC Brosyard 347).

Ufford (Suffolk), Assumption of Our Lady

1465/6, Robert Cuttyng of Eyke gave 6s 8d to the building of Ufford porch (IW 2/150).

1468, Robert Godhard bequeathed .... [illegible] bushels of malt for the making of Ufford porch (IW 2/177).

1468, Richard Crispyng gave 10s to Ufford porch (IW 2/176).

1473, Thomas Symonds gave 13s 4d to the fabric of the new porch (NRO NCC Hubert 44).

1475, Isabel Thoryld gave 13s 4d to the new porch (IW 2/312).

1475, Thomas Symonds gave 3s 4d to the fabric of the new porch (IW 2/312).

1475, Roger Mannyng gave 6s 8d to the making of a porch in the churchyard (IW 2/312)

1523, Robert Covelde requested to be buried in the church porch by Margery, his wife (IW 9/130).

Little Waldingfield (Suffolk), St Lawrence

1466, John Breon of Little Waldingfield ('Waldyngfeld Parva'), 'bocher', 'to the reparation of the porch (*vestibuli*) of the same church 6s 8d ... to the making of the new doors (*hostiorum*) of the said church 13s 4d.' (Northeast, 2.204).

Norwich (Norfolk), St Mary Coslany

1466, Joan Hall requested burial in the porch (NRO NCC Jekkys 31).

Norwich (Norfolk), St Andrew

1467, John Drolle bequeathed £20 to build a new south porch ('Item I bewhethe to seynt andrew chyrch xxli to be spente by the advyse of myn executoris on a newe chyrche porche on the sowthsyde of the chyrche') (NRO NCC Drolle 135).

1474, Nicholas Plumstead requested burial in or next to the porch (NRO NCC Gelour 67).

1525, Thomas Clerk requested burial in the south porch (NRO NCC Palgrave 39, 40).

Walcott (Norfolk), All Saints

1467, John Coke gave 6s 8d to the reparation of the porch (NRO ANF Liber 4 (Grey) 212).

Wiggenhall (Norfolk), St Mary the Virgin

1467, Edward Romney, vicar of the church of 'S Mary the mother of Christ', Wiggenhall, wished for burial in the porch (*sepeliend' in porticu*) (NRO NCC Jekkys 80).

Cockfield (Suffolk), St Peter

1468, Thomas Forthe of Cockfield ('Cokefeld'), 'I wish the porch (*vestibulu*) of the said church to be built at my own cost, out of my goods, for the stone and "menys", on condition that the parishioners of the town will provide "le tymber" for the work.' (Northeast, 2.205).

Needham (Norfolk), St Peter

1469, Edmund Feld gave 8d to the building of the porch (NRO NCC Jekkys 168).

1469, John Cottrell gave 40d to the making of the porch (NRO NCC ANF Liber 4 (Grey) 271).

1470, Hugh Lost gave 6s 8d to the building of the porch (NRO NCC Jekkys 203).

Felsham (Suffolk), St Peter

1470, Rose Goddrych of Felsham, widow, 'I wish to pay for an offering to (*p' oblacoe' de*) "ley porche" of the same church [no sum]; I wish to pay for the glass and work of a window of the same "ley porche" [no sum]' (Northeast, 2.315–16).

1471, Isabel Machon of Felsham, 'I wish to pay for the glass of a window of "ly porche" of the same church' (Northeast, 2.328).

Rougham (Norfolk), St Mary

1471, Edmund Fincham requested burial in the south porch (NRO NCC Jekkys 228).

Frettenham (Norfolk), St Swithin

1473, Clement Fyssh gave a bequest to the porch (NRO NCC Paynot 10).

Stoke Ash (Suffolk), All Saints

1473, Henry Dawe gave 20s to the new fabric of the porch (BW Hervye 7).

Gissing (Norfolk), St Mary

1474, Robert Scole gave 40d to construct the porch (NRO NCC Gelour 62).

Waxham (Norfolk), St John

1477, Michael Salle gave 20s to the making of a porch on the south side (NRO NCC Gelour 172).

1485, Thomas Franceys gave 20s to the making of the porch (NRO NFK Liber 1 58).

Foulden (Norfolk), All Saints

1479, Richard Powle requested burial in the new porch (NRO NCC Gelour 228).

Kirby Bedon (Norfolk), St Andrew (Porch rebuilt)

1479, John Osberne requested his executors to make a new porch (NRO NCC Aubrey 38).

New Buckenham (Norfolk), St Martin

'The present church was built at diverse times ... the north isle was built around 1479, by the contribution of several great men, some of whose arms still remain in the windows ... the south isle, porch and tower, were begun soon after, by that Sir John Knevet who married Clifton's heiress, and finished by his grandson, Sir William Knevet, as the arms in the windows and on the tower plainly demonstrate.' (Blomefield 1.397).

Norwich (Norfolk), St Michael Coslany (porch not extant)

1479, Gregory Clerk, citizen and alderman of Norwich, had built the south porch and aisle. Clerk died in 1479 and was buried in the aisle. (Blomefield 4.494).

Norwich (Norfolk), St Stephen (porch not extant)

1479, David Payn, citizen and locksmith, requested burial in the south porch (NRO NCC Caston 27).

1483, Joan Payn (wife of David Payn) requested burial in the south porch (NRO NCC Caston 167).

1503, Joan Aylemer (alias Moor) requested burial in the south porch (NRO NCC Popy 445).

Potter Heigham (Norfolk), St Nicholas

1479, James Smith bequeathed 20s to the new porch (NRO NCC Aubrey 24).

Stibbard (Norfolk), All Saints (porch rebuilt)

1479, John Capell gave 6s 8d for the making of the porch (NRO NCC Aubrey 28).

Cockthorpe (Norfolk), All Saints

1480, Thomas de Ringstede, by his will orders his body to be buried at the door of the church porch (Blomefield 9.218).

Weston Longville (Norfolk), All Saints

1481, Thomas Curmyng gave 12d for making of the porch (NRO NCC A Caston 88).

Badingham (Suffolk), St John the Baptist

1482, John Smyth bequeathed 3s 4d 'unto makyng of a newe porche' (IW 3/7).

East Dereham (Norfolk), St Nicholas

The porch bears the names of the donors, Roger and Margaret Boton (will dated 1482, NRO NCC A Caston 111) (Cattermole and Cotton 277 n.23).

Ipswich (Suffolk), St Mary le Tower

1485, William Wymbyll gave 40s to the making of a new porch to the church of 'Seynt Mary of the Towre' (TNA PROB 11/8/106).

Barking (Suffolk), St Mary

1486, Robert Flegge of Needham Market (at that time a chapel-of-ease to Barking, with no churchyard) requested '... my body to be buried in the porche of the churche at Berkyng' (TNA PROB 11/10/120)

1500, John Flegge of Needham Market, wished to be buried in the porch of the parish of Barking by my mother (NRO NCC Cage 131).

Aylsham (Norfolk), St Michael

'This Richard Howard was Sheriff of Norwich in 1488, he built the church-porch here and R.H. remains carved on the roof and this over the door – *Orate pro animabus Ricardi Howard, Alicie, Margarete, et Cecelie uxorum eius, qui obit &c.* [he died 1505] On the front of the porch are the arms of England and France, quartered, St George's cross, and a cross flore, and there are also two shields with a saltier on each.' (Blomefield 6.277).

Stradbroke (Suffolk), All Saints

1489, John Pype bequeathed £20 to the building of a new north porch (IW 3/101).

Fersfield (Norfolk), St Andrew

1493, Galfrid Ellingham gave 4 marks to edifying the new south porch (NRO NCC Aubrey 141).

Stradishall (Suffolk), St Margaret

1493, Thomas Screvener requested burial in the porch at Stradishall church and gave chalices, a pyx and censers to the church (Northeast, 1.494).

Wighton (Norfolk), All Saints

1494, Robert Fysher left 6s 8d to the building of the south porch (NRO ANW Fuller alias Roper 248).

1497, William Ryngsted requested burial in the porch and gave 6s 8d for its building (NRO ANW Fuller alias Roper 294).

Rollesby (Norfolk), St George

1496, Edmunde Churche gave 10 marks to make the new north porch (NRO ANW Fuller alias Roper 271).

Acle (Norfolk), St Edmund

1497, Robert Bataly bequeathed 20 marks to the new north porch ('my body to be buried in the churchyard of Saint Edmund King and Martyr of Acle before the north door ... also I bequethe to the byldyng of a newe porche upon the north syde of Acle chirche xxti marke') (NRO ANW Fuller alias Roper 258).

Fakenham (Norfolk), SS Peter and Paul

1497, date on porch noted by Blomefield (Cattermole and Cotton, 246; Blomefield 7.96).

Filby (Norfolk), All Saints (porch rebuilt)

1498, William Botolph bequeathed £13 6s 8d to make the south porch (NRO ANW Fuller alias Roper 304).

1538, John Buttell gave 6s 8d for the making of the south porch, mentioned in the will of William Mariett (NRO ANW Athowe 85).

Cromer (Norfolk), SS Peter and Paul

1498/9, Robert Strong(e) gave 6s 8d for the reparation of the south porch (Morton Register II 12).

Norwich (Norfolk), St Peter Hungate

1499, Nicholas Ingham requested burial in the new porch (NRO NCC Wight 2).

Spixworth (Norfolk), St Peter (porch not extant)

1499, Margaret Davy bequeathed 10s to build south porch (NRO ANW Fuller alias Roper 301).

Garboldisham (Norfolk), St John the Baptist

1500, William Pece, chaplain, is remembered in an inscription on the porch asking for prayers for his soul (Cattermole and Cotton, 277 n.30; Blomefield 1.267).

Norwich (Norfolk), St Peter Mancroft

North porch: 1501, Margaret Bacon requested to be buried in the north porch (NRO NCC Popy 44).[3]

Transept porch: 1523, Robert Boys, grocer, requested burial in the church yard and for the porch to be built over his grave (NRO NCC Alblaster 148).

Snetterton (Norfolk), All Saints

1501, Alice Secker made bequest to making the new porch (NRO NFK Davey 4).

Stoke Holy Cross (Norfolk), Holy Cross (Porch rebuilt)

1501, Robert Snell gave 6s 8d for the making of the porch (NRO NCC Popy 73).

Tuttington (Norfolk), SS Peter and Paul

1502, Edmund Richeman of Aylsham left 20s for the building of the north porch (NRO NCC Popy 256).

Bawburgh (Norfolk), SS Mary and Walstan

1503, Robert Clerke gave 6s 8d to lead porch (NRO NCC Popy 427).

Hockwold (Norfolk), St Peter

1503, John Fynch gave 6s 8d for 'mendyng porch' (NRO NCC Bemond 28).

Beeston St Andrew (Norfolk), St Andrew (porch not extant)

1504, John Wegge requested 'My body to be buried in the church porche of Beeston aforesaid. I bequeath to the reparation of the said porche 13s 4d' (NRO ANW Fuller alias Roper 360).

---

[3] Notably the 1500 will of Thomas Wortys (NRO NCC Cage 175) requested burial in the alley coming to the north door, suggesting there was no porch at that time. Both documents are cited in David King, *The Medieval Stained Glass of St Peter Mancroft*, Norwich (Oxford, 2006), 150–1.

Crostwick (Norfolk), St Peter

1504, Richard Davey left 5 marks for making the porch (NRO ANW Fuller alias Roper 357).

Elmswell (Suffolk), St John

1504, inscription '*Orate pro animab' Jo Hedge et Agnet ux*' noted c.1750 by Thomas Martin. The will of John Hedge of Bury, made in 1504, mentions his wife Agnes (Archdeaconry of Sudbury, Pye 146).

Necton (Norfolk), All Saints

'In the porch of this church, which is leaded, about 1504, was buried Sir Jeffrey Norman, parson of Dunham.' (Blomefield 6.49).

1506, Robert Bird of Sparham in Necton requested burial by the holy water stoup (NRO NCC Ryxe 369).

Norwich (Norfolk), St Peter Parmentergate

1504, John Gyllyng requested burial in the porch 'and the same porch to be honestly paved at his cost' (NRO NCC Ryxe 131).

Hitcham (Suffolk), All Saints

1504, Thomas Fyssher, parson of the church of Our Lady of the Arches in London requested burial in the porch and instructed 'my executors do buy a little marble stone to be set in the wall at my sepulture and therein to be set a piece of laton and therein written in letters my name and the day of my sepulture so as my good friends may have remembrance to pray for my soul and the letters therein to be gilt.' (TNA PROB 11/14/548).

Thrandeston (Suffolk), St Margaret

1505, Robert Wodehill requested burial in the porch (IW 6/1).

Shelfanger (Norfolk), All Saints

1506, John Nolloth gave 40s towards the building of the porch (NRO NCC Cooke 60).

Langham (Norfolk), St Andrew

1508, Nicholas Marshall bequeathed 3s 4d to the making of the new porch (NRO NCH Cooke 84).

Cranworth (Norfolk), St Mary

1509, Thomas Sherrington made a new window in the north isle at the east end, also a new porch (Blomefield 10.203).

1519, Margaret Bernewell gave 6s 8d for reparation of the porch (NRO NCC Gedney 69).

1524, William Barnwell requested a 'webb' of lead to lay over the porch door (NRO ANF Liber 8 (Brokehole), 110).

Hoe (Norfolk), St Andrew (Porch rebuilt)

1509, Robert Catermole bequeathed 6s 8d towards 'covering of the south porche with lede' (NRO ANW Fuller alias Roper 417).

Feltwell St Nicholas (Norfolk), St Nicholas

1516, Isabella Denton bequeathed 20s for the reparation and amending of the porch (NRO ANF Liber 6 (Batman), 196).

Hilborough[4] (Norfolk), All Saints

1516, Richard Duplake bequeathed 20 marks to 'reparacion and makyng upp' of the south aisle and making the porch (NRO NCC Briggs 67).

Newton Flotman (Norfolk), St Mary

1516, John Thurrold left 6s 8s to 'making of a new porche' (NRO ANF Liber 6 (Batman) 62).

Loddon (Norfolk), Holy Trinity

'The rebuilding of the church has long been ascribed to Sir James Hobart (d. 1517) and his wife Margaret (d. 1492)' (Blomefield 10.161). The porch has a panel bearing the name HOBART (Cattermole and Cotton, 278 n.43).

Swaffham (Norfolk), SS Peter and Paul

South porch: 1518, William Coo (d.1518) gave porch roof and rowell (NRO ANF Liber 6, 261).

North porch: 1529, Robert Batman gave £20 for battlement of steeple or a north porch. The will reads 'my body to lie where it shall please God to dispose it to be buried in the churche yard of saint Peter and Paul of Swaffham before the church porche in the pathe before St Peters. Item I bequeath to the batylment of the steple of Swaffham or to the church porche to be made on the northe side of the church after the discretion of the …' (NRO NCC Palgrave 58).

---

[4] NRO NCC Wolman 73 (Margaret Est, 1490) was mistranslated by Cattermole and Cotton. Rather than recording a gift of '20d to reparation of parvise', the will reads, '*Item lego rep[ar]ac' pariet' ecclie' de hylberworth p[re]dict' xxd.*'. Thus the bequest was to the repair of the church wall, not a parvise, and is therefore excluded here.

Geldeston (Norfolk), St Michael

1519, John Bande makes bequests to hallow bells and threshold of porch (NRO ANF Liber 6 (Batman) 351).

Frenze (Norfolk), St Andrew

1521, Margaret James bequeathed a cow for the reparation of the porch. The will reads 'my body to be buried afore the porche dore in the churchyard of Frenys. Item my mortuary to be paid after the custom of the church. Item to the light before the sacrament a cowe, to our ladys light a cowe, to the reparation of the porche, a cowe.' (NRO Herman 23).

Aldham (Suffolk), St Mary

1525, Robert Clifford of Aldham willed to be buried in the churchyard of Aldham 'afore the churche porche' (TNA PROB 11/22/384).

Bracon Ash (Norfolk), St Nicholas (porch rebuilt)

1528, 'Roger Appleyard requested to be buried in the Greyfriars church in Norwich; he gave to this church, his vestment of blue sarcenet, and his gilt image that belonged to his chapel, and a legacy to build a church porch.' (Blomefield 5.84).

Mundford (Norfolk), St Leonard

1528, Sir John Lyster, hermit, requested burial in porch (NRO NCC Attmere 19).

1529, Thomas Bolymer gave 20d for the reparation of the porch (NRO ANF Liber 8 (Brokehole) 170).

Hindringham (Norfolk), St Martin

1529, Thomas Taverner bequeathed 6s 8d to the reparation of the porch (NRO DCN 69/2 f. 54a).

Combs (Suffolk), St Mary

1531, Thomas Tastard requested burial 'within the new porch of the south part of the church' (*Proceedings of the Suffolk Institute of Archaeology*, vol. 38 Part II, 1994, 233).

Saxtead (Suffolk), All Saints

1534, Thomas Norman gave 6s 8d to the making of the church porch of Saxtede (IW 12/91).

Aldeburgh (Suffolk), SS Peter and Paul

1536, John Lunnys requested the residue of the money of the sale of 'the said howses', his debts paid and legacies fulfilled, to go to the building of the porch, 'so that I will have a trental of masses said for my soul and my friends. I will have bread, drink and cheese at my burial or else when it may be convenient to the poor people' (IW 12/75).

1537, Agnes Sperks gave 20s towards the making up of the new porch (IW 12/233).

Bunwell (Norfolk), St Michael

1540, Robert Lincoln bequeathed 6 marks for leading the porch (NRO ANF Liber 10 (Dowsyng) 50).

Glossary of Architectural Terms

Aisle:	a subsidiary lateral interior space divided from the main vessel by an arcade
Arcade:	a series of arches supported on freestanding piers
Ashlar:	squared block(s) of stone
Base course:	continuous horizontal layer constituting the lowest part of a building
Blind arcade:	a series of arches supported on shafts connected to a solid wall
Boss:	a single piece of convex stone (or wood) placed at the intersection of vault ribs
Buttress:	a thickening mass of masonry or brickwork abutting the lower sections of a building or wall to provide strength and stability, or to visually suggest the same
Buttress, angle:	two buttresses meeting at right angles at the corner of a building
Buttress, diagonal:	a single buttress attached to the external corner of a building
Chancel:	the eastern vessel of a church containing the principal altar
Clerestory:	the uppermost storey of a nave or chancel pierced with a series of windows
Crenellated:	a form of battlement, frieze or parapet comprising alternating crenels (indents) and merlons (raised parts)
Cruck frame:	a structure comprising two large, timbers placed vertically and curving inward to form an arch, the apex of which supports a horizontal ridge beam. Each cruck timber is called a blade

Cusp:	in Gothic arch or tracery design, a point formed where two arcs or foils meet
Decorated:	Gothic architectural style that flourished in England c.1250–1350, the earlier period was dominated by Geometric design, the later by curvilinear or florid
Dexter:	the right-hand part (of an object, image or device)
Elevation:	vertical plane of a building
En délit:	the setting of a (monolithic) stone where the grain runs vertically
Façade:	the front or face of a building, the principal front
Fenestration:	the design of arrangement of windows in a building
Flushwork:	exterior surface patterning made by combining often dark-coloured knapped or split flints with paler dressed or carved stone
Four-centred arch:	a flattened form of Gothic arch made from two pairs of compass-drawn arcs – the lower, more tightly angled lower parts of the arch are drawn from two points located in line with the springing line, the more gently curved upper section is made of two arcs which originate from points below the springing line
Gable:	triangular-shaped upper section of walling beneath the roof ridge
Hood-mould:	projecting moulding framing a window or door, originally designed to shed water away from the building, but also used ornamentally
Jamb:	the vertical sides of a doorway, window or arch set at right angles to the wall plane or glazing
Label:	a square or rectangular form of hood-mould
Lancet:	a tall, narrow, two-centred pointed window or arch
Mouchette:	a curved motif used in curvilinear Decorated tracery, often referred to as dagger-shaped and arranged in threes to form a circle (mouchette wheel)
Nave:	the central part of a church, occupied by the congregation

GLOSSARY

Niche:	a recess in a wall, often designed to contain a statue or painted image (image niche)
Parapet:	a low wall framing and protecting the edge of a roof, bridge or gallery
Pier:	a square, circular or polygonal vertical support for an arch, beam or lintel
Pinnacle:	thin, conical vertical termination of a buttress, often decorated with crockets or carved figuratively
Plan / ground plan:	the horizontal layout of a building and its constituent parts
Plinth:	a base or skirting which projects from the lowest part of a building or structure
Reticulated:	'net-like' tracery pattern formed of multiple circles stretched into ogee shapes and arranged in rows
Rib:	a projecting band of stone, brick or timber which ornaments a vault
Sinister:	the left-hand part (of an object, image or device)
Spandrel:	an area of walling beyond the shoulder of an arch, window or doorway and is often contained by the right angles of an ornamental moulded frame
Stop:	a projection which terminates a hood-mould or label, sometimes ornamentally or figuratively carved
String course:	a horizontal projecting moulding running across the face of a wall
Tracery:	the ornamental design work in the upper section of a Gothic window; similar designs imitatively applied in other contexts, including church furnishings (e.g. screens)
Transept:	the transverse part of a church, set at right angles to and extending beyond the main vessel to the north and/or south
Two-centred arch:	a pointed arch made from a pair of compass-drawn arcs which both originate on the springing line of the arch (e.g. lancet)

Vault: a concave-arched roof or ceiling, often ornamented by a system of ribs and bosses

Voussoir: a wedge-shaped stone used to form an arch

Wall shaft: a vertical, projecting half-round column of stone attached to a wall or pier

Bibliography

Manuscript Sources

British Library, London
MS Add. 49598
MS Cotton Nero E ii
MSS Harley 4380, 4418
MS Royal 18 D X
MS Sloane 361
Essex Record Office
D/DBy Q18
Lambeth Palace, London
Morton Register II
Norfolk Record Office (NRO), Norwich
ANF Liber 3 (Davy) 96
ANF Liber 4 (Grey) 212
ANF Liber 6 (Batman) 196
ANF Liber 8 (Brokehole) 110, 170
ANF Liber 10 (Dowsyng) 50
ANW Athowe 85
ANW Fuller alias Roper 4, 248, 258, 271, 294, 301, 304, 357, 360, 417
DCN 69/2
NCC Alblaster 148
NCC Aleyn 156, 159, 167, 194, 209
NCC Attmere 19
NCC Aubrey 24, 28, 38, 141
NCC Bemond 28
NCC Betyns 50, 87, 135
NCC Briggs 67
NCC Brosyard 1, 7, 41, 44, 61, 96, 144, 319, 347
NCC Cage 131, 175
NCC Caston 27, 88, 111, 167
NCC Cooke 60, 84
NCC Doke 46, 58, 66, 97, 101, 129
NCC Drolle 135

NCC Gedney 69
NCC Gelour 62, 67, 172, 228
NCC Harsyk 60, 242
NCC Heydon 16, 94, 95, 182
NCC Hirning 39, 40, 73, 105
NCC Hubert 44
NCC Jekkys 31, 80, 168, 203, 228
NCC Johnson 1
NCC Palgrave 39, 58
NCC Paynot 10
NCC Popy 44, 73, 256, 309, 343, 427, 445
NCC Ryxe 131, 369, 384
NCC Surflete 65, 182
NCC Wolman 73
Suffolk Archives, Bury St Edmunds
BW Hervye 7
Suffolk Archives, Ipswich
IW 1/12, 1/28, 1/106, 1/128, 1/131, 1/166, 1/167, 2/150, 2/176, 2/177, 2/312, 3/7, 3/101, 6/1, 9/130, 12/75, 12/91, 12/233
The National Archives (TNA), Kew
PROB 11/2B/11, 11/4/287, 11/8/106, 11/10/120, 11/14/548, 11/22/339, 11/22/384
C 139/36/71 mm.1–2
Trinity Hall, Cambridge
MS 12, Boethius, *De consolatione philosophiae*

Published Sources

Alexander, Jonathan and Paul Binski, eds, *Age of Chivalry: Art in Plantagenet England 1200–1400* (London, 1987).

Archer, Rowena E., 'War Widows', in *The Battle of Agincourt*, ed. Anne Curry and Malcolm Mercer (New Haven and London, 2015), 216–25.

Batcock, Neil, 'Medieval Churches in Use and in Ruins', in *An Historical Atlas of Norfolk*, ed. Peter Wade-Martins (Norwich, 1993).

Beech, Robert, 'The Hammer-beam Roof of Westminster Hall and the Structural Rationale of Hugh Herland', *Architectural History* 59 (2016), 25–61.

Bell, Patricia L., ed., *Bedfordshire Wills 1484–1533*. The Bedfordshire Historical Society (Bedford, 1997).

Bennett, Josephine Waters, 'The Medieval Loveday', *Speculum* 33.3 (1958), 351–70.

Bernheimer, Richard, *Wild Men in the Middle Ages* (New York, 1970).

Binski, Paul, *Becket's Crown, Art and Imagination in Gothic England, 1170–1300* (New Haven and London, 2004).

Binski, Paul, *Gothic Wonder: Art, Artifice, and the Decorated Style, 1290–1350* (New Haven and London, 2014).

Binski, Paul and Elizabeth New, eds, *Patrons and Professionals in the Middle Ages. Proceedings of the 2010 Harlaxton Symposium.* Harlaxton Medieval Studies 22 (n.s.) (Donington, 2012).

Blatchly, John and Peter Northeast, *Decoding Flint Flushwork on Suffolk and Norfolk Churches* (Ipswich, 2005).

Blomefield, Francis and Charles Parkin, *An Essay Towards a Topographical History of the County of Norfolk*, 11 volumes (London, 1805–1810).

Blundell-Jones, Peter, *Architecture and Ritual – How Buildings Shape Society* (London and New York, 2016).

Boivin, Katherine M., 'The Chancel Passageways of Norwich', in *Norwich: Medieval and Early Modern Art, Architecture and Archaeology: Transactions of the British Archaeological Association Annual Conference 2012*, ed. T. A. Heslop and Helen E. Lunnon (Leeds, 2015), 307–23.

Bond, Francis, *Fonts and Font Covers* (London, 1908).

Branner, Robert, *The Cathedral of Bourges and its Place in Gothic Architecture* (Cambridge MA. and London, 1989).

Braswell, Mary Flowers, *The Medieval Sinner: Characterization and Confession in the Literature of the English Middle Ages* (London, 1982).

Braun, Roddy L., 'Solomonic Apologetic in Chronicles', *Journal of Biblical Literature* 92.4 (1973), 503–16.

Braun, Roddy, 'Solomon, the Chosen Temple Builder: The Significance of 1 Chronicles 22, 28, and 29 for the Theology of Chronicles', *Journal of Biblical Literature* 95.4 (1976), 581–90.

Brett, Gerard, 'King Solomon in the Middle Ages' in *The Collected Prestonian Lectures, volume 2 1961–1974*, ed. Harry Carr (London, 1983).

Brooke, Christopher N. L., *The Medieval Idea of Marriage* (Oxford, 1989).

Brown, J. E. and F. A. Page-Turner, eds, *Chantry Certificates for Bedfordshire with Institutions of Chantry Priests in Bedfordshire.* Bedford Arts Club (Bedford, 1908).

Brown, Thomas, *Posthumous Works of the Learned Thomas Brown Kt, Printed from his Original Manuscripts, viz. 1. Repertorium, or Antiquities of the Cathedral Church of Norwich* (London, 1712).

Brown, Vera, with Jocelyn Wogan-Browne, trans., *Guidance for Women in Twelfth-Century Convents* (Cambridge, 2003).

Brunskill, R. W., *Brick Building in Britain* (London, 1990).

Burgess, Clive, 'A Service for the Dead: the Form and Function of the Anniversary in Late Medieval Bristol', *Transactions of the Bristol and Gloucestershire Archaeological Society* 105 (1987), 183–211.

Byng, Gabriel, 'The Dynamic of Design: "Source" Buildings and Contract Making in England in the Later Middle Ages', *Architectural History* 59 (2016), 123–48.

Cahn, Walter, 'Architectural Draftsmanship in Twelfth-Century Paris: The Illustrations of Richard of Saint-Victor's Commentary on Ezekiel's Temple Vision', *Gesta* 15.1–2 (1976), *Essays in Honor of Sumner McKnight Crosby*, 247–54.

Camille, Michael, *Image on the Edge: The Margins of Medieval Art* (London, 1992).

Campbell, Bruce M. S., 'Medieval Land Use and Values', in *An Historical Atlas of Norfolk*, ed. Peter Wade-Martins (Norwich, 1993).

Carruthers, Mary, 'The Concept of *ductus*, or Journeying Through a Work of Art', in *Rhetoric Beyond Words*, ed. Mary Carruthers (Cambridge, 2010), 190–213.

Cassidy-Welch, M., *Monastic Spaces and their Meanings – Thirteenth-Century English Cistercian Monasteries* (Turnhout, 2003).

Cattermole, Paul, 'A 14th-Century Contract for Carpenter's Work at Ashwellthorpe Church', *Norfolk Archaeology* 40 (1989), 297–302.

Cattermole, Paul, and Simon Cotton, 'Medieval Parish Church Building in Norfolk', *Norfolk Archaeology* 40 (1983), 235–79.

Cautley, H. Munro, *Norfolk Churches* (Ipswich, 1949).

Chaganti, Seeta, *The English Poetics of the Reliquary: Enshrinement, Inscription, Performance* (New York, 2008).

Chaucer, Geoffrey, *The Preamble and Tale of the Wife of Bath*, ed. Richard J. Beck (London, 1964).

Chaucer, Geoffrey, *The Canterbury Tales*, ed. Jill Mann (London, 2005).

Cherry, John, 'Heraldry as Decoration in the Thirteenth Century', in *England in the Thirteenth Century: Proceedings of the 1989 Harlaxton Symposium*, ed. W. M. Ormrod. Harlaxton Medieval Studies 1 (n.s.) (Donington, 1991), 123–34.

Church, Stephen, 'King John's Books, Master Richard Marsh and the Interdict Proclaimed in 1208 on England and Wales', in *Writing History in the Anglo-Norman World: Manuscripts, Makers and Readers, c.1066–c.1250*, ed. Laura Cleaver and Andrea Worm (York, 2018), 149–65.

Clapham, A. W., *English Romanesque Architecture Before the Conquest* (Oxford, 1930).

Clark, Cecily, ed., *The Peterborough Chronicle 1070–1154* (Oxford, 1958).

Cocke, Thomas, and Peter Kidson, *Salisbury Cathedral: Perspectives on the Architectural History* (London, 1996).

C[okayne], G. E., ed., *The Complete Peerage of England, Scotland, Ireland, Great Britain and the United Kingdom, Extant, Extinct or Dormant, Volume 5* (London, 1926).

Coldstream, Nicola, 'The Mark of Eternity, The Cistercians as Builders', in *The Cistercian Abbeys of Britain. Far from the Concourse of Men*, ed. David Robinson (London, 1999).

Colgrave, Bertram, and R. A. B. Mynors, eds, *Bede's Ecclesiastical History of the English People* (Oxford, 1969).

Conybeare, F. C., 'The Testament of Solomon', *The Jewish Quarterly Review* 11.1 (1898), 1–45.

Cook, G. H., *The English Medieval Church* (London, 1954).

Cotman, John Sell, *Specimens of Norman and Gothic Remains in the County of Norfolk, Second Series of Etchings* (London, 1838).

Cotton, Simon, *NARG News* 49 (s.l. Norfolk Archaeological Rescue Group, 1987).

Cox, J. C. and C. B. Ford, *Parish Churches* (London, 1961).

Courtney, William J., 'Token Coinage and the Administration of Poor Relief during the Late Middle Ages', *The Journal of Interdisciplinary History* 3.2 (1972), 275–95.

Crossley, Paul, 'Medieval Architecture and Meaning: The Limits of Iconography', *The Burlington Magazine* 130.1019 (1988), 116–21.

Crossley, Paul, '*Ductus* and *Memoria*: Chartres Cathedral and the Workings of Rhetoric', in *Rhetoric Beyond Words*, ed. Mary Carruthers (Cambridge, 2010), 214–49.

Daniell, Christopher, *Death and Burial in Medieval England, 1066–1550* (London, 1997).

Davies, J. G., *The Secular Use of Church Buildings* (London, 1968).

d'Avray, David, *Medieval Marriage Sermons, Mass Communication in a Culture without Print* (Oxford, 2000).

de Voragine, Jacobus, c.1229–98. *The Golden Legend: Readings on the Saints, Volume 1.* trans. W. G. Ryan (Princeton, 1993).

Douglas, Mary, *Collected Works II: Purity and Danger: An Analysis of Concepts of Pollution and Taboo* (London and New York, 1970).

Draper, Peter, *The Formation of English Gothic* (New Haven and London, 2006).

Duchesne, Mgr. L., *Christian Worship, its Origin and Evolution* (London, 1903).

Dudley, Martin R., 'Sacramental Liturgies in the Middle Ages', in *The Liturgy of the Medieval Church*, ed. Thomas J. Heffernan and E. Ann Metter (Kalamazoo, 2001).

Dudley, E., C. Jackson and Eric G. M. Fletcher, 'Porch and Porticus in Saxon Churches', *Journal of the British Archaeological Association* 19 (1956), 1–13.

Dymond, David, 'God's Disputed Acre', *Journal of Ecclesiastical History* 50.3 (1999), 464–97.

Dymond, David, ed., *The Churchwardens' Book of Bassingbourn 1496–c.1540* (Cambridge, 2004).

Dymond, David, and Clive Paine, *The Spoil of Melford Church: The Reformation in a Suffolk Parish* (Ipswich, 1992).

Dymond, David, and Clive Paine, *Five Centuries of an English Parish Church: the State of Melford Church, Suffolk* (Cambridge, 2012).

Eastwood, Antony, ed., *Viewing Inscriptions in the Late Antique and Medieval World* (Cambridge, 2015).

Edwards, Dorothy, et al., eds, *Early Northampton Wills*, Northamptonshire Record Society, 42 ([Northampton], 2005).

Faden's Map of Norfolk, with an introduction by J. C. Barringer. Norfolk Record Society 42 (Norwich, 1973).

Fairweather, Janet, trans., *Liber Eliensis, A History of the Isle of Ely from the Seventh Century to the Twelfth* (Woodbridge, 2005).

Faraday, Michael, *Ludlow, 1085–1660: A Social, Economic and Political History* (Chichester, 1991).

Fawcett, Richard, *The Architecture and Furnishings of Norfolk Churches* (Fakenham, 1974).

Fawcett, Richard, 'Sutton in the Isle of Ely and its Architectural Context', in *Medieval Art and Architecture at Ely Cathedral*, ed. Nicola Coldstream, and Peter Draper (Leeds, 1979), 78–96.

Fawcett, Richard, 'A Group of Churches by the Architect of Great Walsingham', *Norfolk Archaeology* 37 (1980), 277–94.

Fawcett, Richard, 'St Mary at Wiveton in Norfolk, and a Group of Churches Attributed to its Mason', *Antiquaries Journal* 62 (1982), 35–56.

Fawcett, Richard, 'The Influence of the Gothic Parts of the Cathedral on Church Building in Norfolk', in *Norwich Cathedral: Church, City and Diocese, 1096–1996*, ed. Ian Atherton, Eric Fernie, Christopher Harper-Bill and Hassell Smith (London, 1996), 210–27.

Fawcett, Richard, 'Snettisham Church', in *King's Lynn and the Fens: Medieval Art, Architecture and Archaeology, The British Archaeological Association Conference Transactions 31*, ed. John McNeill. (Leeds, 2008), 134–47.

Fergusson, Peter, 'Modernization and Mnemonics at Christ Church, Canterbury: The Treasury Building', *Journal of the Society of Architectural Historians* 65.1 (2006), 50–67.

Fergusson, Peter, *Canterbury Cathedral Priory in the Age of Becket* (New Haven and London, 2011).

Fergusson, Peter, Glynn Coppack and Stuart Harrison, *Rievaulx Abbey* (London, 2006).

Fernie, Eric, *The Architecture of the Anglo-Saxons* (London, 1983).

Fernie, E. C., and A. B. Whittingham (eds), *The Early Communar and Pitancer Rolls of Norwich Cathedral Priory with an Account of the Building of the Cloister* (Norwich, 1972).

Fisher, J. D. C., *Christian Initiation: Baptism in the Medieval West: A Study of the Primitive Right of Initiation* (London, 1965).

Frere, Walter Howard, ed., *The Use of Sarum: The Sarum Customs as set forth in the Consuetudinary and Customary* (Cambridge, 1898).

Frere, Walter Howard, *Pontifical Services: Illustrated from Miniatures of the XVth and XVIth Centuries*, 2 volumes (London, 1901).

Frost, George L., 'Chaucer's Man of Law at the Parvis', *Modern Language Notes* 44.8 (1929), 496–501.

Garton, C., ed. and trans., *Metrical Life of St Hugh* (Lincoln, 1986).

Geddes, Jane, *Medieval Decorative Ironwork in England: English Ironwork from 1050–1550* (London, 1999).

Gem, Richard, 'Tenth-Century Architecture in England', in *Settimane di Studio del Centro Italiano di Studi sull'alto Medioevo, 38. Il Secolo di Ferro: Mito e Realta del Secolo X*. 2 vols (Spoleto, 1991), vol. 2, 822–36.

Gilchrist, Roberta, *Norwich Cathedral Close* (Woodbridge, 2005).

Goodall, John A. A., 'The Aerary Porch and its Influence on Late Medieval English Vaulting', in *St George's Chapel, Windsor, in the Fourteenth Century*, ed. Nigel Saul (Woodbridge, 2005), 165–202.

Goodall, John, *The English Castle* (New Haven and London, 2011).

Goodall, John, 'The English Gatehouse', *Architectural History* 55 (2012), 1–23.

Graves, C. Pamela, *The Form and Fabric of Belief: An Archaeology of the Lay Experience of Religion in Medieval Norfolk and Devon*, BAR British Series 311 (Oxford, 2001).

Greenwood, Roger, and Malcolm Norris, *The Brasses of Norfolk Churches* (Holt, 1976).

Hart, Stephen, *Flint Flushwork: A Medieval Masonry Art* (Woodbridge, 2008).

Harvey, John H., ed., *Itineraries [of] William Worcestre Edited from the Unique MS. Corpus Christi College, Cambridge, 210* (Oxford, 1969).

Harvey, John, *English Medieval Architects: A Biographical Dictionary down to 1550* (Gloucester, 1987).

Heslop, T. A., 'Orford Castle, Nostalgia and Sophisticated Living', *Architectural History* 34 (1991), 36–58.

Heslop, T. A., 'Contemplating Chimera in Medieval Imagination: St Anselm's Crypt at Canterbury', in *Raising the Eyebrow: John Onians and World Art Studies*, ed. Lauren Golden, BAR International Series 996 (Oxford, 2001), 153–68.

Heslop, T. A., 'The English Origins of the Coronation of the Virgin', *Burlington Magazine* 147 (2005), 790–97.

Heslop, T. A., 'The Nave of Attleborough, Norfolk, and the Architecture of Unknowing', in *Architecture, Liturgy and Identity*, ed. Zoë Opačić and Achim Timmermann (Turnhout, 2011), 47–60.

Hewett, Cecil A., *Church Carpentry: A Study Based on Essex Examples* (London and Chichester 1982).

Hindle, Steve, 'Destitution, Liminality and Belonging: the Church Porch and the Politics of Settlement in English Rural Communities, c.1590–1660', in *The Self-Contained Village? A Social History of Rural Communities, 1250–1900*, ed. Christopher Dyer (Hatfield, 2007).

Hudson, John, ed. and trans., *Historia Ecclesie Abbendonensis: The History of the Church of Abingdon. Volume I* (Oxford, 2007).

Huitson, T., *Stairway to Heaven: The Functions of Medieval Upper Spaces* (Oxford, 2014).

Jamroziak, Emilia, 'Spaces of Lay-Religious Interaction in Cistercian Houses of Northern Europe', *Parergon* 27.2 (2010), 37–58.

Kidson, Peter, 'Architectural History', in *A History of Lincoln Minster*, ed. Dorothy Owen (Cambridge, 1994), 14–46.

King, David, The Medieval Stained Glass of St Peter Mancroft, Norwich (Oxford, 2006).

Krautheimer, Richard, 'Introduction to an "Iconography of Medieval Architecture"', *Journal of the Warburg and Courtauld Institutes* 5, no. 2 (1942), 1–33.

Kristensson, Gillis, ed., *John Mirk's Instructions for Parish Priests* (Lund, 1974).

Ladbrooke, Robert, *Views of the Churches in Norfolk: Printed in Lithography, Illustrative of Blomefield's History of that County* (Norwich, 1823).

Leedy, Walter C., *Fan Vaulting: A Study of Form, Technology, and Meaning* (London, 1980).

Lehmann-Brockhaus, Otto, *Lateinische Schriftquellen zur Kunst in England, Wales und Schottland vom Jahre 901 bis zum Jahre 1307, Band I.* (Munich, 1956).

Lehmann-Brockhaus, Otto, *Lateinische Schriftquellen zur Kunst in England, Wales und Schottland vom Jahre 901 bis zum Jahre 1307, Band II.* (Munich, 1956).

Lunnon, Helen E., '"I will have one porch of stone ... over my grave": Medieval Parish Church Porches and Their Function as Tomb Canopies' *Church Monuments* 27 (2012), 53–65.

Lunnon, Helen, 'Inventio Porticus – Imagining Solomon's Porches in Late Medieval England', *British Art Studies* 6 (2017): http://dx.doi.org/10.17658/issn.2058-5462/issue-06/hlunnon

Lunnon, Helen E., 'A Phenomenological Study of the English Parish-Church Porch, 1200–1399', in *Towards an Art History of the Parish Church*, ed. Meg Bernstein and James Alexander Cameron (London, forthcoming).

Luxford, Julian, 'Symbolism in East Anglian Flushwork', in *Signs and Symbols. Proceedings of the 2006 Harlaxton Symposium*, ed. John Cherry and Ann Payne. Harlaxton Medieval Studies 18 (n.s.) (Donington, 2009), 119–32.

Luxford, Julian, 'Architecture and Environment: St Benet's Holm and the Fashioning of the English Monastic Gatehouse', *Architectural History* 57 (2014), 31–72.

Marks, Richard, *Image and Devotion in Late Medieval England* (Stroud, 2004).

McGregor, Margaret, ed., *Bedfordshire Wills Proved in the Prerogative Court of Canterbury 1383–1548*. The Bedfordshire Historical Record Society (Bedford, 1979).

McKinnell, John, 'For the People/by the People. Public and Private Spaces in the Durham Sequence of the Sacrament', in *Ritual and Space in the Middle Ages. Proceedings of the 2009 Harlaxton Symposium*, ed. F. Andrews. Harlaxton Medieval Studies 21 (n.s.) (Donington, 2011), 213–31.

McNeill, John T., and Helena M. Gamer, eds, *Medieval Handbooks of Penance* (New York, 1990).

Michael, Michael, 'The Privilege of "Proximity": Towards a Re-definition of the Function of Armorials', *Journal of Medieval History* 23.1 (1997), 55–74.

Middleton-Stewart, Judith, *Inward Purity and Outward Splendour: Death and Remembrance in the Deanery of Dunwich, Suffolk 1370–1547* (Woodbridge, 2001).

Middleton-Stewart, Judith, ed., *Records of the Churchwardens of Mildenhall* (Woodbridge, 2011).

Mollat, Michel, *The Poor in the Middle Ages: An Essay in Social History*. Arthur Goldhammer, trans. (New Haven and London, 1986).

Monckton, Linda, 'St Michael's, the Architectural History of a Medieval Urban Parish Church', in *Coventry: Medieval Art, Architecture and Archaeology in the City and its Vicinity, British Archaeological Association Transactions 33*, ed. Linda Monckton and Richard K. Morris (Leeds, 2011), 135–63.

Morris, R., ed., *The Blickling Homilies, Together with the Blickling Glosses* (London 1874–76).

Morris, Richard K., 'Thomas Witney at Exeter, Winchester and Wells', in *Medieval Art and Architecture at Exeter Cathedral*, British Archaeological Conference Transactions for 1985, ed. Frances Kelly (Leeds, 1991), 57–84.

Murray, Stephen, 'The Architectural Envelope of the Sainte-Chapelle of Paris' in *Pierre, Lumiere, Couleur: Etudes de histoire de l'art du moyen age en l'honneur de Anne Prache: Cultures et Civilisations Medievale, 20*, ed. Fabienne Joubert and Dany Sandron (Paris, 1999), 223–30.

Needham, A., *How to Study an Old Church* (London, 1944).

Nicholas, N. Harris, *The Controversy between Richard Scrope and Sir Robert Grosvenor in the Court of Chivalry* (London, 1832).

Nichols, Ann E., *Seeable Signs: The Iconography of the Seven Sacraments, 1350–1544* (Woodbridge, 1994).

Nichols, Ann E., *The Early Art of Norfolk: A Subject List of Extant and Lost Art Including Items Relevant to Early Drama* (Kalamazoo, 2002).

Northeast, Peter, ed., *Wills of the Archdeaconry of Sudbury 1439–1474: Wills from the Register 'Baldwyne' Part 1: 1439–1461* (Woodbridge, 2001).

Northeast, Peter, 'Suffolk Churches in the Later Middle Ages: The Evidence of Wills', in *East Anglia's History: Studies in Honour of Norman Scarfe*, ed. Christopher Harper-Bill (Woodbridge, 2002).

Northeast, Peter and Heather Falvey, eds, *Wills of the Archdeaconry of Sudbury 1439–1474: Wills from the Register 'Baldwyne' Part 2: 1461–74* (Woodbridge, 2010).

Ó Carragáin, Éamonn, 'The Term *Porticus* and *Imitatio Romae*', in *Text and Gloss: Insular Learning and Literature Presented to Joseph Donovan Pheifer*, ed. Helen Conrad O'Briain, Anne Marie D'Arcy and John Scattergood (Dublin, 1999), 13–34.

Owen, Dorothy, 'Historical Summary', in *A History of Lincoln Minster*, ed. Dorothy Owen (Cambridge, 1994).

Page, Rolph Barlow, *The Letters of Alcuin* (New York, 1909).

Page, William, *A History of the County of Norfolk*, volume 2 (London, 1906).

Page, William, *The Victoria History of the County of Bedford: Volume 3* (London, 1972).

Pantin, W. A., 'Chantry Priests' Houses and other Medieval Lodgings', *Medieval Archaeology* 1 (1957), 216–58.

Park, David, 'Medieval Burials and Monuments', in *The Temple Church in London: History, Architecture, Art*, ed. Robin Griffith-Jones and David Park (Woodbridge, 2010), 67–92.

Parker, John Henry, *A Concise Glossary of Terms Used in Grecian, Roman, Italian and Gothic Architecture* (Oxford and London, 1866).

Parsons, W. E., *Salle: The Story of a Norfolk Parish, its Church, Manors and People* (Norwich, 1937).

Payne, Ann, 'Medieval Heraldry', in *The Age of Chivalry: Art in Plantagenet England*, ed. Jonathan Alexander and Paul Binski (London, 1987).

Pevsner, Nikolaus, *Buildings of England Series: Somerset and Bristol* (Harmondsworth, 1958).

Pevsner, Nikolaus, *The Buildings of England: North-East Norfolk and Norwich* (Harmondsworth, 1962).

Pevsner, Nikolaus, *Buildings of England: North-West and South Norfolk* (Harmondsworth, 1962).

Pevsner, Nikolaus, *Buildings of England Series: Wiltshire* (2nd edition, revised by Bridget Cherry, Harmondsworth, 1975).

Pevsner, Nikolaus, and Enid Radcliffe, *The Buildings of England: Suffolk* (Harmondsworth, 1975).

Pevsner, Nikolaus, and Elizabeth Williamson, *The Buildings of England: Buckinghamshire* (2nd edition, London, 1994).

Pierce, S. Rowland, ed. *John Adey Repton. Norwich Cathedral at the End of the Eighteenth Century, with Descriptive Notes by William Wilkins* (Farnborough, 1965).

Postles, Dave, 'Micro-Spaces: Church Porches in Pre-Modern England', *Journal of Historical Geography* 33.4 (2007), 749–69.

Pounds, N. J. G., *A History of The English Parish* (Cambridge, 2000).

Procter, Francis, and Walter Howard Frere, *A New History of the Book of Common Prayer* (London, 1901).

Quiney, Anthony, '*In Hoc Signo:* The West Front of Lincoln Cathedral', *Architectural History* 44 (2001), 162–71.

Ragusa, Isa, 'Terror Demonum and Terror Inimicorum: The Two Lions of the Throne of Solomon and the Open Door of Paradise', *Zeitschrift für Kunstgeschichte* 40.2 (1977), 93–114.

Rahtz, Philip, 'Grave Orientation', *Archaeological Journal* 135 (1978), 1–14.

Rasmussen, Steen Eiler, *Experiencing Architecture* (Cambridge, MA, 1962).

Rickman, Thomas, *An Attempt to Discriminate the Styles of Architecture in England: from the Conquest to the Reformation* (London, 1817).

Robinson, David, ed., *The Cistercian Abbeys of Britain. Far from the Concourse of Men* (London, 1999).

Rogers, Nicholas, 'The Location and Iconography of Confession in Late Medieval Europe', in *Ritual and Space in the Middle Ages. Proceedings of the 2009 Harlaxton Symposium*, ed. F. Andrews Harlaxton Medieval Studies 21 (n.s.) (Donington, 2011), 298–307.

Roffey, Simon, 'Constructing a Vision of Salvation: Chantries and the Social Dimension of Religious Experience in the Medieval Parish Church', *Archaeological Journal* 163 (2006), 122–46.

Rowe, Nina, *The Jew, the Cathedral and the Medieval City. Synagoga and Ecclesia in the Thirteenth Century* (Cambridge, 2011).

Rubin, Miri, *The Mother of God: A History of the Virgin Mary* (London, 2009).

Rudolf, Conrad, 'Inventing the Gothic Portal: Suger, Hugh of Saint Victor, and the Construction of a New Public Art at Saint-Denis', *Art History* 33 (2010), 568–95.

s.n., *The Sarum Missal in English* (London, 1868).

Saul, Nigel, *Lordship and Faith: The English Gentry and the Parish Church in the Middle Ages* (Oxford, 2017).

Scarfe, Norman, *Suffolk in the Middle Ages* (Woodbridge, 1986).

Schulenburg, Jane Tibbetts, *Forgetful of Their Sex: Female Sanctity and Society, ca. 500–1100* (Chicago, 1998).

Sekules, Veronica, 'The Gothic Sculpture', in *Norwich Cathedral: Church, City and Diocese, 1096–1996*, ed. Ian Atherton, Eric Fernie, Christopher Harper-Bill, and Hassell Smith (London, 1996), 199–202.

Shelby, Lon R., 'Medieval Mason's Templates', *The Journal of the Society of Architectural Historians* 30.2 (1971), 140–54.

Shinners, John, and William J. Dohar, eds, *Pastors and the Care of Souls in Medieval England.* (Notre Dame, IN, 1998).

Skolnik, Fred, ed. in chief, *Encyclopaedia Judaica. Second Edition*, vol. 13 (Detroit etc., 2007).

Smith, Terence P., 'Three Medieval Timber-Framed Church Porches in West Kent: Fawkham, Kemsing and Shoreham', *Archaeologia Cantiana* 101 (1984), 137–63.

Stubbs, William, ed., *Memorials of Saint Dunstan, Archbishop of Canterbury, Rolls Series 63* (London, 1874).
Summers, Dominic, 'Norfolk Church Towers of the Later Middle Ages', 2 volumes, unpublished Ph.D. thesis, University of East Anglia, Norwich, 2011.
Symons, Thomas, trans., *The Monastic Agreement of the Monks and Nuns of the English Nation* (London, 1953).
Sweet, Henry, *The Student's Dictionary of Anglo-Saxon* (Oxford, 1896).
Taubman, Andrew W., 'Clergy and Commoners: Interactions between Medieval Clergy and Laity in a Regional Context', unpublished Ph.D. thesis, University of York, 2009.
Taylor, H. M., 'The Anglo-Saxon Cathedral Church at Canterbury', *Archaeological Journal* 126 (1969), 101–30.
Taylor, H. M., and Joan Taylor, *Anglo-Saxon Architecture. Volume 1* (Cambridge, 1965).
Thibodeau, Timothy M., trans., *The Rationale Divinorum Officiorum of William Durand of Mende, A New Translation of the Prologue and Book One* (New York, 2010).
Thomson, David, *Renaissance Architecture: Critics, Patrons, Luxury* (Manchester and New York, 1993).
Tilley, Christopher, *A Phenomenology of Landscape – Places, Paths and Monuments* (Oxford, 1994), 7–34.
Tilley, Christopher, *The Materiality of Stone: Explorations in Landscape Phenomenology* (Oxford, 2004), 1–32.
Toulmin Smith, Lucy, ed., *The Itinerary of John Leland in or about the Years 1535–1543: Parts I–III* (London, 1907).
Turner, Jane, *Grove Dictionary of Art*, volume 32 (Basingstoke, 1996).
Turner, Victor, *Dramas, Fields and Metaphors: Symbolic Action in Human Society* (Ithaca, NY, and London, 1974).
van Gennep, Arnold, *The Rites of Passage*, trans. Monika B. Vizedom and Gabrielle L. Caffee (Chicago, 1960).
Wall, J. C., *Porches and Fonts* (London, 1912).
White, C. H. Evelyn, ed., *The Journal of William Dowsing* (Ipswich, 1885).
Whyte, William, 'How Do Buildings Mean? Some Issues of Interpretation in the History of Architecture', *History and Theory* 45.2 (2006), 153–77.
William of Malmesbury, *Gesta Regum Anglorum, The History of the English Kings*, volume II, ed. and trans. R. M. Thomson (Oxford 1999).
Wilmart, Andre, 'La Legende de Ste Edith in prose et vers par le moine Goscelin', *Analecta Bollandiana* 56 (1938), 5–101, 265–307.
Wilson, Christopher, 'St Mary Redcliffe, Bristol, Outer North Porch, North Side', in *Age of Chivalry: Art in Plantagenet England, 1200–1400*, ed. Jonathan Alexander and Paul Binski (London, 1987), 413, cat. no. 490.
Wilson, Christopher, 'Calling the Tune? The Involvement of King Henry III in the Design of the Abbey Church at Westminster', *Journal of the British Archaeological Association*, 161 (2008), 59–93.

Wilson, Christopher, 'Gothic Architecture Transplanted: the Nave of the Temple Church in London', in *The Temple Church in London: History, Architecture, Art*, ed. Robin Griffith-Jones and David Park (Woodbridge, 2010), 19–44.

Wilson, Christopher, 'Why Did Peter Parlour Come to England?', in *Architecture, Liturgy and Identity: liber amicorum Paul Crossley*, ed. Zoë Opačić and Achim Timmermann (Turnhout, 2011).

Woodcock, Alex, *Liminal Images: Aspects of Medieval Architectural Sculpture in the South of England from the Eleventh to the Sixteenth Centuries* (Oxford, 2005).

Woodman, Frank, 'The Gothic Campaigns', in *Norwich Cathedral – Church, City and Diocese, 1096–1996*, ed. Ian Atherton, Eric Fernie, Christopher Harper-Bill and Hassell Smith (London, 1996), 161–3.

Wormald, Francis, 'The Throne of Solomon and St Edward's Chair', in *De Artibus Opuscula, XL: Essays in Honor of Erwin Panofsky volume 1*, ed. Millard Meiss (New York, 1961), 532–9.

Wright, A. P. M., ed., *A History of the County of Cambridge and the Isle of Ely, Volume 6* (London, 1978).

Wulfstan of Winchester, *Life of St Aethelwold*, ed. and trans. Michael Lapidge and Michael Winterbottom (Oxford 1991).

Index

Abingdon Chronicle 23
Acle (Norfolk) 88, 149, 191, 234
Aethelflaed of Mercia 26
Aethelred, ealdorman of Mercia 26
Aethelwold, bishop of Winchester 27
Alcuin of York 69
Aldeford (Norfolk) 190, 194, 209, 236
Algerkirk (Lincs) 9
alms/almsgiving 47, 58, 94–6, 252
Alvard, John and Joan 226–7
Anglo-Saxon Chronicle 23
arcades/arcading 10, 13, 32, 52, 102, 104–5, 112, 114, 115, 130, 152, 249, 277
Ardleigh (Essex) 173
apertures 3, 8, 10, 13, 21, 105, 106–7, 111, 112, 114, 119, 132, 189, 190, 192–6, 207, 249, 252
Ash Wednesday 9–10, 71, 72
Aslacton (Norfolk) 191, 199
Attleborough (Norfolk) 211–4, 217, 233, 251, 253
Augustine of Canterbury 20, 68
Aylric, Bishop of York, Durham and Peterborough 23
Aylsham (Norfolk) 201

Bacon, John, of Fritton St Catherine 226
Bacon, John, of Hesset 171, 243
Badingham (Suffolk) 171
baptism *see* Seven Sacraments
Bardney (Lincs) 26
Bardwell (Suffolk) 241
Barker, Richard 224
Barker, Thomas 221, 224, 225, 226
Barnack (Cambs) 3, 8, 134, 250
Barsham (Suffolk) 89
Barton Bendish (Norfolk) 236–8
base courses 153, 156, 158, 160, 189–91, 196–7, 198, 210, 217, 239, 246, 277
Bassingbourn (Cambs) 93, 228–9
Bataly, Robert 234–6
Bateman, Alice 86
Beccles (Suffolk) 191
Befeld, Richard 228
Beautiful Gate 39, 43, 47, 94, 96
Bede, the Venerable 19–20, 24, 26
benches 13, 58, 83, 96, 104, 105, 128, 132, 199, 216, 217
Benygte, Sir Thomas 224
Bertha, Queen of Kent 20, 26
Berthwald of Canterbury 20
Besthorpe (Norfolk) 108, 119
Beton, Cicily 86
Bible,
    Old Testament
        1 Chronicles 28.2–7 30
        1 Chronicles 28.11 30
        2 Chronicles 3.4 31, 126
        2 Chronicles 3.15–17 31
        Deuteronomy 16.18 78
        Exodus 33.20 91
        Ezekiel 36.25 65
        Ezekiel 40 33–5, 196
        Genesis 28.17 13
        1 Kings 6.3 31, 40, 126

Bible, (*continued*)
　Old Testament (*continued*)
　　1 Kings 6.38　31
　　1 Kings 7.6–8　32, 42, 44, 45, 50
　　1 Kings 7.14　31
　　1 Kings 7.13–22　31
　　Leviticus 12.1–5　68
　　Leviticus 15　68
　　Psalms 123　68
　New Testament
　　Acts 3.1–11　39, 40, 43, 47, 94
　　Acts 5.1–11　97
　　James 5.9　78
　　John 5.2–3　94
　　John 5.8　94
　　John 10.9　11, 92, 163
　　John 12.12–19　60
　　Luke 19.28–44　60
　　Mark 11.1–11　60
　　Matthew 21.1–11　60
　　Revelation 12.7　216
　　Revelation 19.6–9　214
　　Revelation 20.12–15　213
Bishopstone (East Sussex)　21–2
Blomefield, Francis　81, 184, 212
Blyth (Northumberland)　9
Bois, Robert　92
Boton, Roger and Margaret　244
Bott, John　227
Bourges Cathedral　80, 94–5
Boxford (Suffolk)　112–4, 185, 194, 209
Bradford on Avon　21–2
brick　125, 135, 182, 194, 207–9
Brigge, Thomas　165
Briningham (Norfolk)　119, 120, 121
Brisley (Norfolk)　89–90, 191
Bristol
　St Augustine　6
　St Mary Redcliffe　2, 6, 8, 43–7, 250
　St Stephen　15
Brome, Roger　226
Brooke, Christopher　74
Brosyard, John　135–7
Browne, Stephen　226
Bunwell (Norfolk)　187–8
Burgess, Walter　94

Burgh (Suffolk)　120
burial　19–20, 23, 24, 25, 26, 27, 52, 76, 88–94, 100, 116, 134–9, 216, 226–7, 228, 235, 244, 252–3
Burnell, Katherine　212
Bury St Edmunds
　Court Gate　47–51
Butley Priory Gatehouse (Suffolk)　128, 243
business transactions　97

Cahn, Walter　34
Camille, Michael　169
canopies　8, 32, 43, 50, 60, 90, 104, 114, 125, 134, 135, 137–9, 142, 150, 164, 175, 198, 199, 210, 216, 250, 252, 253
Canterbury
　Christchurch Cathedral　25, 31, 36–7, 78
　St Augustine's Abbey　6, 19, 21
Carpenter, Walter　223
Carruthers, Mary　16
Castle Acre (Norfolk)　190
Catfield (Norfolk)　88, 228
Cattermole, Paul　184
Cavenham (Suffolk)　116
chapels　21–3, 24–7, 52, 85–7, 94, 115
chapter houses　37–9, 43, 104
Chartres Cathedral　16
Chaucer, Geoffrey　71, 74–5, 82
Cherry, John　240
Cley-next-the-Sea (Norfolk)　131–2, 134, 160–1, 221, 241–2, 254–5
Chilmark stone　42
Chipping Norton (Oxfordshire)　43
Chipping Wycombe (Buckinghamshire)　76
church consecration　9–10
church door　2, 9, 11, 13, 21, 56, 57, 58, 59, 60, 62, 65, 66, 71, 73, 74–6, 88, 89, 92, 96–7, 120, 158, 175, 201–2, 229, 251, 252
Church, Stephen　99
Cipern, Henry　246
Cirencester (Gloucs), St John the Baptist　2

Civitas Dei (The City of God) 52
Clapham, Sir Alfred (A. W.) 21
Clerk, Thomas 92
Clopton, John 244
Clopton (Suffolk) 120
Colby (Norfolk) 149, 150, 170, 216
Coldstream, Nicola 115
Combs (Suffolk) 190
Commentary on Ezekiel 30
Company of Heaven 169–73
confession *see* Seven Sacraments
Cotton, Simon 184
Cotton (Suffolk) 111, 120
Council of Nantes 20
Coventry, St Michael 97
Crosse, Benedict 15
Crossley, Paul 16, 35

Davy, Margaret 231
Debenham (Suffolk) 116
de la Pole, Katherine 132
de la Pole, Michael, 1st earl of
  Suffolk 132
de la Pole, Michael 2nd earl of
  Suffolk 132
de Northwold, Rofer 187
Deopham (Norfolk) 190
Despenser, Henry, bishop of
  Norwich 83
de Rocceto, Petrus 80
de Roos, Isabel 92
de Ty, Dionysia 89
Dickleburgh (Norfolk) 199
Diss (Norfolk) 241
doorways *see* entrance arches
Douglas, Mary 59
Drolle, John 231–2
ductus 16
Duplake, Richard 229–30
Durandus, William 47

Eadmer, of Canterbury 78
Eadred, King 28
East Dereham (Norfolk) 203, 244
East Tuddenham (Norfolk) 149, 246
Ely Cathedral 28–9
  Lady Chapel 8
  Octagon 114
  west porch 105
Easter 63, 98
East Lexham (Norfolk) 93
East Tuddenham (Norfolk) 195
Ediman, Robert 89–90
Edington (Wilts) 85
education 81–4
entrance arches 8–9, 11–3, 21, 25, 42,
  62, 77, 96, 106, 111, 120–1, 158,
  160, 163–5, 169, 170, 171, 175,
  178, 190,192, 201, 217, 222, 236,
  241, 251–2
Elyes, Thomas 227
Eswell, Richard 224
Ethelbert, King of Kent 20, 26
expulsion 71–2, 81 n.62, 252
  from the Temple 97

façades 3, 11, 44, 50, 51, 76–7, 98, 111,
  121, 128, 130, 131, 132, 156–9, 163,
  164, 169, 170, 178, 191, 213, 217,
  242, 250, 251–2
Fawcett, Richard 149, 183
Fergusson, Peter 36, 81
Fernie, Eric 22
Fitz, William 85
Fitzwalter, Elizabeth 212
Fitzwalter, Robert 241
flint
  flushwork 91, 121, 150, 197, 199,
    242–3, 246
  masonry 105, 106, 125, 132, 150,
    155–6, 182, 209–10, 213, 243
Flordon (Norfolk) 187
Forncett St Peter (Norfolk) 90, 246
Foulden (Norfolk) 195
Fountains Abbey (N. Yorks) 91, 115
Fourth Lateran Council 59, 72, 74, 98
Fressingfield (Suffolk) 132–3, 134
Fritton St Catherine (Norfolk) 226

galilee *see* west porches
Garboldisham (Norfolk) 222, 244
Gardener, John 86

gatehouses 5, 8, 47, 128–31, 171, 209, 243
Gissing (Norfolk) 156–8
Glanforth, William 222, 224
Glastonbury Abbey (Somerset) 23–4
　Lady Chapel 8
Goodall, John 5
Gooderstone (Norfolk) 109, 133, 190
Goscelin of St Bertin 26
Grandisson, John, bishop of
　Exeter 72
graves *see* burial
Great Blakenham (Suffolk) 112, 163
Great Cressingham (Norfolk) 149, 156, 163, 190, 214–6, 229, 238
Great Massingham (Norfolk) 13, 83, 101–6
Great Witchingham (Norfolk) 174, 242

Hardingham (Norfolk) 119
Harpley (Norfolk) 160
Hartest (Suffolk) 222
Hase, William 227
Hasilbyche, John 76
Heckington (Lincs) 10, 11
Hegne, John 224
Hemsby (Norfolk) 88
Henry of Avranches 37–9
Herberd, John 253
Herland, Hugh 209
Hessett (Suffolk) 171, 243
Hevingham (Norfolk) 83
hexagonal ground plans 2, 6–8, 38–9, 43–5,
hexagram 39, 44–5, 50–1
High Wycombe *see* Chipping Wycombe
Hilborough (Norfolk) 149, 216, 229
Hobard, John 93, 228–9
Hobart, Sir James and Margaret 210, 239, 244
Hockwold (Norfolk) 107
Holkham (Norfolk) 120
Holme-next-the-Sea (Norfolk) 119, 120, 121, 125, 185

holy water 9, 56, 62, 63–5, 67–8, 93, 94, 169
holy water stoups 56, 64, 93, 100, 199, 217, 272
Honingham (Norfolk) 107, 119
Honorius Augustodunensis 68–9
Horsham (Sussex) 94
Houchet, John 223
Hunstanton (Norfolk) 110

Ingham (Norfolk) 84
Innocent III, Pope *see* Fourth Lateran Council
Interdict, 1208 98–100

Jamroziak, Emilia 96
John of Gaunt, Duke of Lancaster 126
Johnson, John 226
Joys of the Virgin 175, 213–4, 255
judgement 32, 78–81, 98, 178, 251

King's Lynn (Norfolk)
　St Margaret 83
　St Nicholas 84, 130–1, 134, 164, 250
Kirkham Priory 128

lamp lockers 64
Langham (Norfolk) 199
ledger slabs *see* burial
Leeds Priory (Kent) 115
Leland, John 82
le Romeyn, John, archbishop of York 80
le Strange, Sir John 110
Liber Eliensis 28
Life of St Dunstan 23
Life of St Aethelwold 28
limen 11, 57, 76, 87, 134, 163–9, 175, 248, 251
liminality 9, 57, 92, 168- n.48, 169
Lincoln Cathedral 16, 37, 43, 79–80, 105
Lincoln, Robert 187
Little Chishill (Essex) 13
Little Cressingham (Norfolk) 120
Little Ellingham (Norfolk) 120, 121

Little Fransham (Norfolk) 216–19
Little Massingham (Norfolk) 240
Little Melton (Norfolk) 173
Little Waldingfield (Suffolk) 190
Loddon (Norfolk) 163, 203, 210, 239
London, Temple Church 91
Long Melford (Suffolk) 60–3, 164, 244
Ludham (Norfolk) 185
Ludlow (Shropshire) 43

Malmesbury Abbey (Wilts) 3, 134, 216, 249
Mandeville, Geoffrey 91
Marsham (Norfolk) 70
Martenet, William 216
Martin, Roger 60–2
Matilda, countess of Warwick 91
Mattishall (Norfolk) 164
Mayn, Robert 236
Melman, Agatha and Geoffrey 165–8
Merleau-Ponty, Maurice 58
Metrical Life of St Hugh 37–8
Middleton-Stewart, Judith 183
Mildenhall (Suffolk) 82, 86, 158–60
Mirk, John 75
Mortimer, Cecily 212
Murray, Stephen 29
Mutford (Suffolk) 116

Narratio Metrica de S. Swithuno 28
narthex 6, 114–5, 236
Nassington (Northants) 9
Needham (Norfolk) 207, 209
New Buckenham (Norfolk) 191–2
new fire 56, 63–4
niches 6, 13, 50, 64, 109, 131, 158, 164, 236
Nicholas of Clairvaux 177
Northeast, Peter 184
Northampton, All Hallows 76
North Creake (Norfolk) 106, 119, 243
North Elmham (Norfolk) 116
Northill (Beds) 85
North Walsham (Norfolk) 126–8, 134, 203, 250
Norwich

Ethelbert Gate 47–51, 121, 128, 139, 171, 243
Erpingham Gate 202, 213, 217
St Andrew 92, 231–2
St Giles 135–7, 156
St George Tombland 141
St Gregory 141, 156
St John Maddermarket 141
St John Sepulchre 156
St Laurence 137–9, 156
St Margaret 156
St Mary Coslany 149, 150
St Michael at Pleas 156
St Peter Hungate 203
St Peter Mancroft 92, 141–2
St Stephen 139–40, 243
Nottingham, St Mary 252
Notyngham, Henry 125, 185

O'Carragáin, Éamonn 24, 26
Oswald of Worcester, bishop of York 27
Over (Cambs) 11
Oxford, Divinity Schools 14

Palgrave (Suffolk) 171, 216
Palm Sunday 56, 60–3, 69, 94
Paris, Matthew 82
Paris, Sainte Chapelle 29
Park, David 91
Parler, Peter 6, 114
parvise 81–2
Pece, William 222, 244
penance 68, 69–73
penitential rituals 71, 72, 91, 92
penitents 9, 69, 71, 72, 252
pentagram *see* hexagram
Percell, William 85
phenomenology 10, 13, 58–9, 249
pillars 31–2, 33, 35, 42, 64, 105
Phillipson, John and Anne 222
Playford (Suffolk) 119, 120, 121
Playter, Richard 137
Polebrook (Northants) 9
Pollard, John 222, 224
Polestead (Suffolk) 107

porticus 1–53, 91, 126, 185, 252
Postles, David 57
Pounds, N. J. G. 59
Prague Cathedral 6, 114
proportional ratios 35, 39, 120
    1:2 31, 39, 40, 43, 51, 52, 126, 255
    3:5 32, 45, 52
protection 9, 134, 160, 165, 169, 170, 213, 240, 249, 251
Pulham St Mary (Norfolk) 160–1, 169, 174, 251
Purbeck marble 42
purification 65, 67, 68–9, 100

Radcliffe, Sir John 211–2
Ragusa, Isa 178
Ramsey Abbey (Cambs) 27
Ramsey, John 6, 114
Regularis Concordia 27
Reynolds, Walter, archbishop of Canterbury 69
Riccall (N. Yorks) 97
Richard of St Victor 30, 34, 51
Rickinghall Inferior (Suffolk) 152
Rickinghall Superior (Suffolk) 150, 152
Rickman, Thomas 14
Rievaulx Abbey (N. Yorks) 91, 115
Rokelle, Richard 185
Rome
    Old St Peter 25
    St John Lateran *see* Rome, St Saviour
    St Paul Outside the Walls 25–6
    St Peter on the Vatican 25, 26
    St Saviour 25
Roudham (Norfolk) 120
Rubin, Miri 174

Saffron Walden (Essex) 221, 222–5
saints
    Andrew 237
    Anslem, of Canterbury 36–7
    Augustine, of Hippo 52
    Christopher 56–7, 227
    Dunstan 23
    Edith, of Wilton 27
    Ethelburgha 164–5
    George 170, 171, 174, 229
    Margaret 170
    Mary, Virgin 170, 173–8, 235–6 *see also* Joys of the Virgin
        chapel of 86, 87
        depictions of 115, 116, 130 n.31, 132, 150, 153, 156, 163, 169, 173, 174, 175, 214, 233, 239, 253, 254–5
        womb 176–8
    Michael 45, 170, 174, 214–6
Salisbury Cathedral 39–43
Salle (Norfolk) 87, 165–9
Samon, John 252
Sarum missal 62, 63 n.15, 68 n.29, 69 n.31, 71 n.39
Sarum rite 60, 62, 64
school rooms *see* education
Selby (N. Yorks) 3
Seven Sacraments 70, 72, 74, 99–100, 251
    baptism 10, 56, 58, 65–8, 77, 82, 92, 99, 216
    confession 69–73, 77, 99
    eucharist 81 n.62, 98, 99
    marriage 74–7, 175, 212, 214
Shadingfield (Suffolk) 207
Shardelowe, Sir John and Sir Thomas 111
Shelfanger (Norfolk) 209
shelter 10, 20, 252
Shelton (Norfolk) 135
Shelton, Sir Ralph 135
shield of David *see* seal of Solomon
Sideman, Bishop of Crediton 23
Skelton (N. Yorks) 3
Snetterton (Norfolk) 93
Snettisham (Norfolk) 6, 114–6
Solomon, King 29–35, 36, 37, 39, 45, 50–1, 81, 105, 126, 134, 254–5
    seal of Solomon 44–5, 51
    throne of Solomon 176–8
Somersham (Suffolk) 101–2
South Walsham (Norfolk) 149, 150, 163, 176, 191, 238–9

INDEX

Southwell Minster 3, 216, 249
Southwold (Suffolk) 190, 191
Spalding (Lincs) 72
spandrels 170, 174, 190, 191–2
Spixworth (Norfolk) 231
Sporle, John 111
Stafford, lady Beatrice 131, 134, 221, 241–2
St Albans Abbey (Herts) 173
Stanhoe (Norfolk) 119
Stillingfleet (N. Yorks) 9
Stoke-by-Nayland (Suffolk) 190
Strasbourg Cathedral 72
Stutton (Suffolk) 119
Swaffham (Norfolk) 194, 199
Swannington (Norfolk) 190, 227, 249
Swardeston (Norfolk) 209
Sweyn, William 224

Taylor, William 188
Testament of Solomon 45
Tewkesbury Abbey (Gloucs) 3, 250
Theodorus of Canterbury 20
Theodore of Tarsus 68
Thirsk (N. Yorks) 86
Thompson (Norfolk) 111
Thorp, Sir Edmund 240–1
Tintern Abbey (Mon) 115
Trailley, Sir John 85
threshold *see* limen
Tilley, Christopher 58
timber porches 17, 102, 112–4, 163, 207, 209, 229, 246
Tomms, Thomas 86
tower-porches 117–26, 139, 141, 185

Uffington (Oxfordshire) 8, 9
Ufford (Suffolk) 171
upper chambers 81–8

van Gennep, Arnold 11, 58
vaulted spaces 5, 32, 38, 41, 51, 87, 96, 130, 131, 132, 134–42, 175–6, 198, 213, 214, 216, 250, 251, 255 *see also* canopies

Wace, Christopher 76
Wacton (Suffolk) 9
Wall, J. C. 1–2, 55–6, 63, 64, 88, 239, 255
Walpole St Peter (Norfolk) 149, 199
Wareham St Martin (Dorset) 21–2
Warter (E. Yorks) 80
Wells
  Cathedral, Penniless Porch 96
  St Andrew (Somerset) 15
Westminster Abbey 164, 240
west porches 91, 105, 112, 114–7, 141
west towers 63, 121, 183
West Walton (Norfolk) 101–6
Whinburgh (Suffolk) 120
Whittlesford (Cambs) 246
Wibert, prior of Canterbury 36
Wicklewood (Norfolk) 119, 120, 125
Wighton (Norfolk) 117, 199
wildmen 164, 168–9, 174, 251
William I, King of England 23
William of Malmesbury 23–4, 26, 29
Wilson, Christopher 10
Wilton Abbey (Wilts) 27
Winchester, Old Minster 28
windows 34, 109, 110–1, 120, 125–6, 128, 189, 190, 192–6, 243, 252 *see also* apertures
Windsor, St George's Chapel, Aerary Porch 5
Wingfield, Margaret 132
Winterton (Norfolk) 246
Witnesham (Suffolk) 119
Wiveton (Norfolk) 149, 229
Woodnewton (Northants) 9
Woolpit (Suffolk) 156
Worcestre, William 15
Worsted (Norfolk) 233–6
Wygenhale, Roger 185
Wymondham (Norfolk) 191

Yaxley (Suffolk) 190, 253

www.ingramcontent.com/pod-product-compliance
Lightning Source LLC
Chambersburg PA
CBHW081824230426
43668CB00017B/2373